T0366851

THE PRICE OF TRUTH

THE PRICE OF TRUTH

*The Journalist Who Defied Military
Censors to Report the Fall
of Nazi Germany*

RICHARD FINE

CORNELL UNIVERSITY PRESS
ITHACA AND LONDON

First published 2023 by Cornell University Press

Printed in the United States of America

Library of Congress Cataloging-in-Publication Data

Names: Fine, Richard, author.
Title: The price of truth : the journalist who defied military censors
    to report the fall of Nazi Germany / Richard Fine.
Description: Ithaca : Cornell University Press, 2023. | Includes
    bibliographical references and index.
Identifiers: LCCN 2022034161 (print) | LCCN 2022034162 (ebook) |
    ISBN 9781501765940 (hardcover) | ISBN 9781501765957 (pdf) |
    ISBN 9781501765964 (epub)
Subjects: LCSH: Kennedy, Ed, 1905–1963. | World War, 1939–1945—
    Journalists. | World War, 1939–1945—Press coverage. |
    World War, 1939–1945—Censorship. | War correspondents—
    History—20th century.
Classification: LCC D798 .F56 2023 (print) | LCC D798 (ebook) |
    DDC 070.4/4994053—dc23/eng/20220729
LC record available at https://lccn.loc.gov/2022034161
LC ebook record available at https://lccn.loc.gov/2022034162

For Robert Bennett and Frank Ferguson

I've learned the hard way it is much easier to start
a war than to stop one.
CAPTAIN HARRY C. BUTCHER

Fiasco is the word for it.
AUGUSTA CHRONICLE

CONTENTS

ACKNOWLEDGMENTS

Digital technology has revolutionized archival research. When in 2005 I began investigating media-military relations during the Second World War, notes and transcriptions had to be handwritten on site, and documents reproduced at great expense. Work proceeded at a snail's pace. Modern-day laptops, scanners, and smartphones allow such research to proceed at comparative warp speed. One can now request, skim, and scan for later use in a matter of days what previously would have taken months. Such has been a boon for researchers, though it must mean more work for archivists and records pullers.

My thanks to the staff of the following institutions are thus all the more heartfelt: Army Heritage and Education Center, Archives and Manuscripts Division of the New York Public Library, Associated Press Corporate Archives, BBC Written Archive Center, Dwight D. Eisenhower Presidential Library, George C. Marshall Research Library, Harry S. Truman Presidential Library, Manuscript Division of the Library of Congress, National Archives and Records Administration, Rare and Manuscript Collections at the Carl A Kroch Library of Cornell University, Reuters Corporate Archive, United Kingdom National Archives, and Wisconsin History Society.

I especially benefitted from the help of the archivists Eric Van Slander at the National Archives, Kevin Bailey at the Eisenhower Library, and Lee Grady at the Wisconsin Historical Society. I need to single out two individuals for special mention. Valerie Komor and Francesca Pitaro initially alerted me to Ed Kennedy and the Reims surrender controversy while I was working at the Associated Press (AP) Corporate Archives on another project. Valerie subsequently invited me in 2011 to participate in a symposium the AP organized to highlight its public apology for having fired Ed Kennedy in 1945. This book began with that invitation, and it would not have appeared without their interest and aid ever since. For one thing, they introduced me to Julia Kennedy Cochran, Ed Kennedy's daughter and herself a journalist, at the same symposium. She, too, has earned my thanks for her encouragement over the years.

I also want to acknowledge the Lee Miller Archives and AP Images for permission to reproduce photographs from their collections. This book grew out of an initial article about Ed Kennedy and the German surrender published in *American Journalism* in 2016. My thanks to that journal's editor at the time, Ford Risley, for his support. At Cornell University Press, Michael McGandy saw the promise in an earlier version of this project and provided much wise advice on how to reshape it into this book. Clare Jones at the press proved a lifesaver as I was submitting the final version of the manuscript, and Jennifer Savran Kelly shepherded it through the production process with skill and tact. Copyeditor Irina Burns did a fine job in catching errors and infelicities. I'd also like to thank Lisa DeBoer for her skilled indexing.

I benefitted from the support of Virginia Commonwealth University's Humanities Research Center, College of Humanities and Sciences Faculty Council, and especially its English department for travel grants. Ginny Schmitz, Margret Schluer and Kelsey Cappiello in the department helped make state and university travel regulations comprehensible with efficiency and good cheer. I have enjoyed many conversations about press coverage of the Second World War with my colleague and good friend David Latané, who has been a great sounding board seemingly forever. Catherine Ingrassia, another friend in the English department and more recently its chair, found many ways to encourage this project and to nudge it along. Above all, thanks to Sara Ferguson for making life worth living.

Abbreviations

Organizations

AACL	Association of American Correspondents in London
AEF	Allied Expeditionary Force (WWI)
AFHQ	Allied Force Headquarters
AP	Associated Press
BBC	British Broadcasting Company
BPR	Bureau of Public Relations (War Department)
CBC	Canadian Broadcasting Company
CBS	Columbia Broadcasting System
CPI	Committee on Public Information (WWI)
G-2	Intelligence Division
INC	Information and Censorship Branch (AFHQ)
INS	International News Service
MOI	Ministry of Information (British)
NBC	National Broadcasting Company
OKW	Oberkommando der Wehrmacht (High Command of the German Army)

OWI   Office of War Information (U.S.)
PRD   Public Relations Division (of SHAEF)
PRO   Public Relations Officer
SHAEF   Supreme Headquarters, Allied Expeditionary Force
SOS   Services of Supply (U.S. Army)
SPJ   Society of Professional Journalists
UP   United Press
WAC   Women's Army Corps

Archives and Collections Cited in Notes

AHS   Arthur Hays Sulzberger Papers
APCA   Associated Press Corporate Archives (New York, NY)
DDEPP   Dwight D. Eisenhower Pre-Presidential Papers
EKP   Edward Kennedy Papers
EL   Dwight D. Eisenhower Presidential Library (Abilene, KS)
NARA   National Archives and Records Administration (College
         Park, MD)
NYPL   New York Public Library (New York, NY)
TL   Harry S. Truman Presidential Library (Independence, MO)
TNA   The U.K. National Archives (Kew, England)
WHS   Wisconsin Historical Society (Madison, Wisconsin)

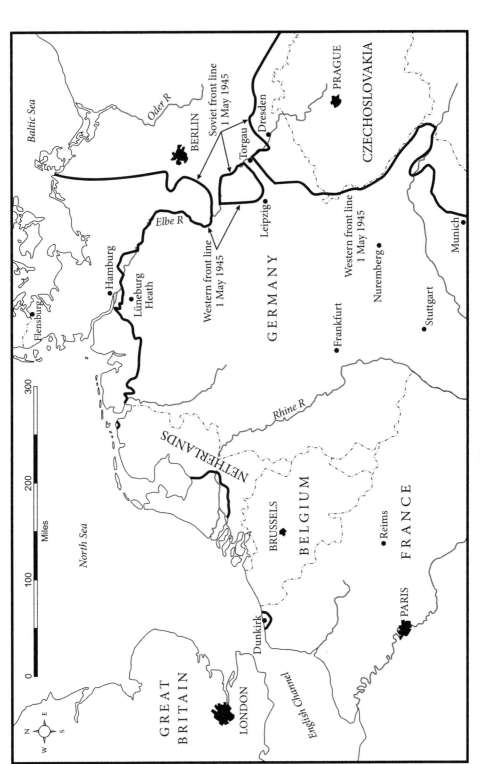

Figure 0.1. Map of Northwestern Europe, 1945. Mike Bechthold.

THE PRICE OF TRUTH

Introduction

The Messiest Media Story of World War II

A heated controversy, what Glaswegians would call a *stooshie*, erupted over the military's handling of the press during the Second World War just as that war was ending in Europe. Victory in Europe (V-E) Day is celebrated each year in the United States and the United Kingdom on May 8, commemorating the Allied victory over Germany in 1945. In Russia, Victory Day occurs on May 9. In actuality, Germany surrendered to the Allies in the early hours of May 7, 1945, and thereby hangs a tale. Seventeen journalists witnessed the event, crowded into one corner of the room chosen for the occasion at General Dwight D. Eisenhower's headquarters in Reims, France. Eager to break what was surely one of the biggest stories of the war, the correspondents dashed off eyewitness accounts only to be told that the Allied powers were withholding news of the surrender for at least thirty-six hours. Authorities offered the dismayed journalists in Reims no reason for the delay. In the hours that followed every reporter present at the surrender protested vehemently, but only one of them chose to act. The Associated Press correspondent and Paris bureau chief Edward

(Ed) Kennedy was so certain that the public was entitled to learn of the war's end that he risked both a court-martial and his career to do so. He knew of a means to circumvent military censorship and used it to break the story of the surrender he had witnessed.

The Associated Press in New York scrambled to place Kennedy's dispatch on its wire. Celebrations then broke out across the United States. New Yorkers flocked to Times Square in the thousands. In New Orleans revelers danced in the street as if it were Mardi Gras. Crowds gathered at the gates to the White House, anticipating an official announcement. The AP itself was initially jubilant, crowing that the story was "one of the greatest newsbeats in newspaper history."[1]

Kennedy's triumph, though, came at a high price. Angered military officials immediately suspended the reporter, citing him for a violation of military censorship and accusing him of recklessly endangering Allied soldiers in the field. Fifty-four members of the press corps in France also denounced Kennedy for what they memorably condemned as "the most deliberate, disgraceful and unethical double-cross" in the history of journalism.[2] The reporters were so unhinged by the scoop that they passed a resolution demanding that the army prevent the AP from any further reporting of the surrender, perhaps the only time in the war when the press sought to muzzle itself.[3]

Kennedy earned the immediate praise of his employer and the gratitude of millions of Americans desperate for word that the fighting in Europe had ended, but the AP's president, Robert McLean, faced mounting pressure to disavow its reporter. Within days, McLean pronounced his regret over the surrender story, a public statement that was taken as the agency's repudiation of its Paris bureau chief. Kennedy never wrote another story for the Associated Press. The AP severed ties with him and refused further comment on the matter. By the end of the year, Ed Kennedy's career was in shambles.

This, in a nutshell, is what some at the time referred to as the Kennedy affair and others more caustically as the surrender fiasco. No action by a US correspondent during the Second World War proved more contentious, leading to what one recent historian deemed "the most highly publicized and long-lasting journalistic controversy of the entire war."[4] The debate over Ed Kennedy's actions filled editorial pages and the airwaves for weeks. Some condemned the AP's bureau chief as unethical and overzealous, arguing that he had violated journalistic ethics in not honoring his pledge to the military to hold the story until the army released it. Others charged that he had placed his own judgment above that of the generals, particularly Eisenhower's. Still other critics claimed that Kennedy owed it to the press corps in Paris to alert them in advance that he was going to defy the news embargo. Conversely, his many defenders praised the correspondent for simply doing his job in reporting what he had witnessed, news that the US public had every right to know, and which officials had no sanction to suppress. They admired his courage in defying those authorities.

Although some accounts of US war reporting mention the surrender fiasco in passing, journalists recall it dimly, and the public has forgotten it altogether. The episode briefly resurfaced in 2012 when the Associated Press took the unprecedented step of apologizing for its treatment of Kennedy in 1945. Sixty-seven years after the event and nearly a half-century after Kennedy's death, the AP's then president Tom Curley reviewed the news agency's files and determined that Kennedy had acted precisely as the AP expected its reporters to act; his superiors at the time were the ones who merited censure. Kennedy "did everything just right," Curley concluded, calling the AP's dismissal of him "a great, great tragedy." A group of reporters and academics agreed and mounted a sustained if ultimately unsuccessful campaign to have Kennedy awarded a rare posthumous Pulitzer Prize. Even then, some journalists continued to maintain that Kennedy had violated a cardinal rule of journalism in breaking an agreement with a source of information.[5]

For all the debate over whether Kennedy was a principled and courageous defender of the public's right to know or a conniving competitor willing to sell out his colleagues and threaten soldiers' lives to achieve a scoop, crucial questions about the episode remained unanswered. How did Kennedy manage to get the story to New York, given the military's supposed control of all communications from France? Had the military released the surrender news even before his story broke, as Kennedy claimed? Did the Associated Press fire Kennedy, or did he resign? Why did the Allies want to delay the release of the news of the German surrender in the first place? Such questions lingered for years.

Kennedy wrote two separate but quite similar accounts of his actions. One was published in *The Atlantic Monthly* in 1948. The other, also written in the late 1940s, appeared (posthumously) in 2012 as a chapter in Kennedy's memoir of his days as a foreign correspondent.[6] Their general accuracy is often corroborated by records and by the recollections of others. Kennedy professed to have had few regrets. He claimed to harbor no ill will toward those who attacked him at the time. In both accounts he presents himself as a bemused and world-weary observer, in short, a typical reporter of his day.

Kennedy's accounts provide a starting point for understanding the episode, but the path to the complete story leads thereafter to various archives in both the United States and the United Kingdom. They contain unpublished memoirs of those involved, private letters of correspondents and military officers, documents from military and press organizations, and hundreds of editorials and articles written in the aftermath of the Reims surrender. When assembled with published sources that bear on the matter, they tell a story that forces us to reconsider much of what we think we know about how the military interacted with the press during the Second World War.

If Kennedy had been a novice or a known corner-cutter, then his actions on May 7 could be dismissed as unprofessional or unscrupulous. The record indicates otherwise. Ed Kennedy was an experienced and respected reporter who, in 1945, supervised from Paris the AP's coverage of the war throughout Northwestern Europe. After more than a decade's work domestically, Kennedy had jumped at the chance to join the AP's Paris bureau in 1935. He spent the rest of the 1930s reporting from France, from war-ravaged Spain, from Italy under Benito Mussolini, and then from the Balkans after war was declared in 1939. In 1940, Kennedy relocated to Cairo initially to cover the British army in Egypt but eventually to oversee the AP's coverage of North Africa and all of the Middle East. For the remainder of the war he served as bureau chief first in Algiers, then in Italy, and ultimately in Paris. Journalists admired Kennedy as an accomplished spot news reporter and for running effective bureaus. Although Kennedy professed to be a willing player in the hyper-competitive world of the news agencies where filing seconds ahead of rivals often defined success, the only harsh words against him before the Reims episode were spoken by those he had beaten on a story. His superiors at the AP and most others in the press corps expressed nothing but admiration for him as an aggressive but fair-minded journalist. By 1945, then, the résumés of only a handful of war correspondents could rival his.

The Kennedy affair is a compelling story on its own, but it also challenges accepted truths about the media's relationship with the military during World War II. "We were all on the same side," veteran CBS journalist Andy Rooney told an interviewer late in his life, referring to his work during the war as a reporter for *Stars and Stripes*. "It wasn't the usual confrontation between authority and the press."[7] Historians typically agree, one venturing that "the general consensus among military people, the press and academics is that the cooperative working relationship between the press and the military that had been established in World War II collapsed in the 1960s."[8] Some have argued that, if anything, the media was too close to the military during that conflict. Although nominally civilians, war correspondents were in several ways incorporated into the armed forces, placed in uniform, granted the equivalent rank of captain, and obligated to follow most military regulations.[9] They were totally dependent on the army for shelter, food, and transport while in the field. In Dwight Eisenhower's own famous formulation, they were "quasi-staff officers."[10]

The accepted history of US war reporting holds that this close and cooperative relationship between the military and the press established during the Second World War only ran off the rails in Vietnam, never to recover. Several historians, most notably Steven Casey, have presented a more nuanced view of the assumed amity between reporters and the military during World War II, emphasizing the service rivalries, institutional pressures, and political cross-currents that impinged on that relationship. This book follows that path.[11]

The controversy over Kennedy's surrender story challenges the very premise of this prevailing amity narrative. It reveals a relationship that was frequently testy and often quite confrontational and thus belies the reductionist portrait of that relationship as cooperative. During the course of the Second World War Kennedy routinely and other journalists with varying frequency clashed with military officials over matters small and large. Although those battles were often sparked by bureaucratic bungling or army snafus, they also involved more substantive opposition to the government's handling, or mishandling, of information. Kennedy constantly had to hold his ground with military officials—from junior censors to actual policy makers—over the limits of military security and prerogative. Kennedy's actions in May 1945 take on greater significance when seen not as an isolated event but rather as the culmination of career-long resistance when confronted with what he thought to be illegitimate political censorship. In this sense, the relationship of the media and the military in the Second World War, shorn of Good War nostalgia, looks more, not less, like that in future conflicts than existing accounts would have us believe.

Rife as the world is with widespread harassment of reporters abroad, with journalists branded as enemies of the people at home and charges of fake news everywhere, it might help to recall an earlier era when one reporter acted on his conviction that even in wartime the people's right to know transcended the government's desire to control information, and heartening to learn that many people supported him in doing so. The Kennedy affair is the story of government officials trying to bend the media to their own ends and of one journalist who risked much to do what he thought of as his duty—to inform a public sick of the fighting that the war in Europe had ended, finally.

REPORTING THE WAR IN EUROPE

The Hotel Scribe lies a short block from the opulent Palais Garnier, home of the Opèra de Paris, in one of the city's more fashionable quartiers. Built in the 1860s, the Scribe's stone facade, six-story height, and gabled mansard roof conformed to Baron Haussmann's specifications for his ambitious renovation of Paris. The Scribe claims a distinguished history: shortly after completion it became the home of Paris's famed Jockey Club; Louis Vuitton opened his first boutique in the Scribe; the Lumière Brothers unveiled the cinematograph there in 1895; and Josephine Baker lived in the Scribe when she was the toast of the city after World War I. For decades, Parisian high society favored its salons.

The hotel survived and even thrived in the early 1940s under German occupation, even as it remained a property of the Canadian National Railways. The German occupiers built an elaborate communications center in the Scribe while also using it as a plush hostel for Gestapo officers. The last of the Gestapo checked out on the morning of August 25, 1944, mere hours before Allied forces arrived in the city. The Scribe had been a preferred haunt of the foreign press before the war, so enterprising public relations officers (PROs) quickly commandeered the hotel for use as Allied press headquarters before rival units could claim it as their own. The horde of correspondents who had swarmed into the city with the Allied troops soon rushed to the Scribe to join the celebrations.[1]

"For the first time in my life and probably the last, I have lived for a week in a great city where everyone is happy," the *New Yorker*'s A. J. Liebling reported from the Scribe in early September. "Since this city is Paris," he could not resist adding, "everybody makes this euphoria manifest."[2] Nowhere was this truer than at the Scribe itself, which had quickly filled with public relations officers and an ever-growing crowd of carousing war correspondents. General Omar Bradley's 12th Army Group had sent Lieutenant Colonel John (Jack) Redding to oversee press arrangements in Paris. When he arrived at the hotel just hours after it had been liberated, he found that "everything was in an indescribable state of confusion" as "war correspondents, soldiers, FFI, and tramps jammed the lobby." Redding chose to overlook the fact that "everyone seemed to be carrying a heavy load of cognac or champagne." When Redding's deputy, Major James T. Quirk, arrived later that day, "the bar was open and the correspondents began to hammer out their stories and get drunk simultaneously." By midnight prostitutes had flocked to the Scribe and, according to Quirk, "were doing a thriving business." With the bacchanal still in full swing the next day, Redding ordered all women out of the hotel. When an air raid klaxon sounded that night, though, Quirk found that the corridors of the upper floors quickly filled with "men in pajamas and slippers and white-faced, scantily-clad women huddled together for protection."[3] For the remainder of the war the Scribe would serve as the workplace, home, and leisure center for the press corps assigned to Supreme Headquarters Allied Expeditionary Force (SHAEF), General Dwight D. Eisenhower's command. For the weary PROs of that command, the unruly goings-on at the Scribe marked the end of a very trying week.

The liberation of Paris had been something of a free-for-all for the press and an embarrassing debacle for army public relations. Once it had become clear that the Allies would try to capture Paris rather than circumvent it, just about every correspondent accredited to SHAEF had abandoned their assigned beat and stampeded toward the French capital. Communications channels, spotty throughout the campaign in Normandy, all but broke

Figure 1.1. Activity in front of the Hotel Scribe in late 1944. Lee Miller, who took this photograph, kept a room in the Scribe well past the German surrender. © Lee Miller Archives, England 2021. All rights reserved. leemiller.co.uk.

down. Reporters on the road to Paris were forced to hand over stories to dispatch riders who drove them to airfields as far away as Chartres to be flown back to First Army headquarters, weather permitting, for onward transmission to London. Many dispatches were lost along the way; most were delayed by hours if not days.

One story that did get through proved most embarrassing to CBS's Charles Collingwood and to censorship officials. On August 21 and four days before the actual liberation, Collingwood had written a story anticipating that event. Collingwood recorded his script ("Parisians had risen as one man to beat down the German troops . . .") and sent the recording and script to London. CBS then put Collingwood's story on the air two days before the Germans actually surrendered the city. Collingwood later claimed that he had been assured the story would not be released in London until Paris was indeed liberated; CBS and censors in London assumed it had been vetted in France.[4] Based on Collingwood's report, England's King George IV had also announced that Paris was now free, forcing SHAEF officials into the embarrassing position of having to contradict the monarch.[5]

At roughly the same time, the Allied advance paused at Rambouillet, some thirty miles southwest of Paris, where reporters and public relations officers alike were surprised to discover that Ernest Hemingway, on assignment for *Collier's*, was already there. Hemingway had taken it upon himself to play soldier and was commanding a scruffy band of French teenagers. Armed to the teeth in violation of the Geneva Convention, Hemingway strutted through Rambouillet, claiming that he and his irregulars had been spying on the German forces preparing to attack the town. "Since there was no conceivable reason for any Germans to try to take Rambouillet," remarked NBC's John MacVane, one of the reporters on the scene, "this sort of talk made something less than a sensation among Hemingway's rather cynical audience." Hemingway's posturing proved too much for the *Chicago Times*'s Bruce Grant, who told the middle-aged writer to "stop trying to be a chickenshit general with your chickenshit little army." This had earned Grant a punch in the face. Army officials had little tolerance for Hemingway's shenanigans and ordered a full-scale investigation of his conduct.[6]

What is more, when French and US troops finally reached the city on August 25, six radio correspondents broadcast stories using the Radio France transmitter there without first submitting their scripts for censorship. SHAEF immediately suspended the six, charging that they had not gone to the Scribe for the required vetting of their copy. Their actions had angered those correspondents who had abided by SHAEF rules. MacVane had maneuvered to be first in line to have his copy cleared by the censors at the Scribe and so was particularly peeved at being robbed of his scoop. SHAEF's Public Relations Division (PRD) had recommended a sixty-day suspension for the broadcasters, which Eisenhower reduced to forty. That street fighting in Paris still continued on the day in question and that the broadcasts had contained no sensitive military information dissuaded authorities from imposing a stiffer penalty. For one PRD official, the culprits had "betrayed the other correspondents who had braved sniper fire to get to the censors at the Scribe" as well as "thrown the gauntlet down for SHAEF. Would we or would we not enforce regulations?"[7] Don Whitehead, the Associated Press (AP) correspondent on the scene, cabled his office in New York:

> I WISH TO ENTER STRONGEST POSSIBLE PROTEST AGAINST UN-AUTHORIZED BROADCAST WHICH IN VIOLATION OF CENSOR-SHIP REGULATIONS TO WHICH OTHERS ADHERED. WE SIGNED AGREEMENT THAT WE WOULD NOT TRANSMIT COPY ANY SOURCE WITHOUT CENSORSHIP, WITH SEVERE PENALTIES TO BE INFLICTED ON THOSE WHO TRIED EVASION. OUR PARIS STO-RIES PASSED THROUGH NORMAL SECURITY CHANNELS AND WE PLAYED BY RULES WHICH ARMY SET UP. IF WE CANNOT BE AS-SURED OF THEIR ENFORCEMENT, THEN ARMY'S REGULATIONS ONLY BURDEN THOSE WHO THINK THEY ARE DUTY BOUND TO STICK TO RULES. I NEVER WANT PENALIZE INITIAL RESOURCE-FULNESS BUT I DO WANT TO KNOW ALL OF US ARE PLAYING BY SAME RULES IN SAME LEAGUE.[8]

The next month, Whitehead's boss, Kent Cooper, the managing director of the AP, wrote to the cooperative's members that he was certain "this incident will act as a deterrent to any other correspondent who is tempted to do the same thing. There isn't a newspaperman in this country who wants to see a war correspondent gain a temporary advantage by violating his pledge to the detriment of his fellow correspondents."[9]

Whitehead and Cooper's words would come back to haunt the Associated Press eight months later when the Scribe would again be the scene of great pandemonium, only this time more choleric than bacchanalian. On May 6, 1945, the PRD quietly assembled a select group of war correspondents, soon to be dubbed the Lucky Seventeen, in the lobby of the Scribe to report on an unspecified "event of historical importance." The Scribe had been on edge for days as word filtered in that German units throughout Europe were surrendering piecemeal. The war's end seemed tantalizingly near, especially after the forces arrayed against Field Marshal Bernard Montgomery's 21st Army Group—the bulk of the German army in the west—had surrendered the previous day. When a PRO arrived at the Scribe in the early afternoon he found "a hornet's nest of rumor." The officer charged with assembling the group was accosted by every reporter he encountered as "word spread like grassfire" that something was afoot. When those at the Scribe learned that only a select few journalists would be allowed to witness something momentous about to occur, mayhem ensued.[10]

As the Lucky Seventeen (sixteen actually, as one of the chosen was already at the destination) boarded a military bus on the crowded street outside the Scribe, they confronted a "seething mob" of their brethren outraged not to be part of the group, according to their conducting officer.[11] When told that the bus was taking them to Orly Airport some in the party speculated that they would be flying to Berlin. The reporters and their army handlers paused briefly for a commemorative photograph before boarding a C-47, the correspondents still unaware of their ultimate destination. The trip from the Scribe to the airport was about the only thing that would go smoothly in the next forty-eight hours, both for the PROs and for the reporters in their charge.

It was not as if SHAEF had not thought long and hard about how to handle press coverage of the war's end in Europe. In fact, the Planning Branch of the PRD had been doing little else for months, and the army planned for that end almost from the war's beginning. The Allies stepped up planning for Germany's defeat and occupation in early 1943, and shortly thereafter public relations officials turned their minds to press coverage of such an event.[12] The PRD brought renewed vigor to the task after the debacle surrounding the liberation of Paris, which neither officials nor reporters had any desire to repeat. Public relations officers began to consider how to manage coverage of Germany's defeat, which presumably would involve entering Berlin, without the chaos that he just occurred in Paris. The roots of much of the press's unhappiness with SHAEF at the time of the actual surrender in 1945 lay in some of these preparations, which also exposed the PRD's own indecisiveness, enlarged natural fissures within the press corps itself, and exacerbated national differences in attitude toward the press among the Allied militaries.

The high spirits following the liberation of Paris had barely receded when the chief of the Publicity and Psychological Warfare Division of Montgomery's 21st Army Group reflected the heady optimism of the moment and predicted that the Allies might well be in Berlin "quite soon." Brigadier Alfred Neville was convinced that every correspondent attached to his army group would flock to the conquered capital. To forestall a media rush into Germany, he recommended that SHAEF should select a small press party for the initial occupation of Berlin. If the press contingent grew much larger, then "all those left out will want to go" and would "all try and [*sic*] dash through the Russian zone to Berlin." In that case, there would be "the devil to pay" for public relations at every level.[13]

At virtually the same time, SHAEF also received a plan for press coverage from Omar Bradley's 12th Army Group reflecting a far different approach. With all of the confusion he had witnessed in Paris top of mind, Jack Redding presented a detailed press plan for Berlin. The US army envisioned an initial airborne landing of troops to join the Russians in the German capital before the arrival overland of any larger occupation force, and so Redding conceived of separate press groups to accompany both air and ground contingents. Redding focused on the press party to accompany the land force and solved the problem of unauthorized entry into the city by simply letting everyone in, identifying 284 correspondents currently accredited in Northwestern Europe.[14]

SHAEF officials were aghast at the number of correspondents Redding proposed. One staffer circled the number 284 in the memo and wrote two exclamation points next to it. Shortly after being named chief of the PRD in September 1944, Brigadier General Frank A. Allen agreed that 284 correspondents were far too many, but that much else in Redding's plan made sense. Throughout the fall PRD officials consulted with the press in an effort to reduce the size of this Berlin contingent. After "several conferences and much haggling with the various correspondents [*sic*] associations," Lieutenant Colonel Thor Smith could report that the number had been whittled down to 60. This had taken some doing as "there are more than 300 different organizations represented here by one or more individuals . . . all with a beautiful story of why they should be included."[15]

Smith was not exaggerating the difficulty in obtaining press assent to a smaller Berlin press group. Military officials had long been vexed by which news organizations should receive priority in restricted operations such as coastal raids or airdrops. This had been an issue at least since the Dieppe raid in 1942 and had dominated planning for D-Day. The War Department had long privileged those media organizations reaching the largest audiences, on the face of it a sensible proposition. As the war progressed, it developed a more granular approach. The three US news agencies (Associated Press, United Press, and International News Service) received the highest priority since their product appeared in the greatest number of newspapers and reached the most readers. The broadcast networks also received priority, given their national reach. Next on the list were mass circulation news magazines (including *Time*, *Life*, and *Newsweek*), followed by the major syndicates staffing foreign bureaus and selling foreign reporting to other papers. These included those of the *New York Times*, *New York Herald Tribune*, *Chicago Tribune*, and *Chicago Daily News*, as well as the North American Newspaper Alliance. Lower in the pecking order were individual newspapers, followed by general interest periodicals.[16]

Such a hierarchy accorded with the preferences of the reporters' group that SHAEF consulted most often.[17] The Association of American Correspondents in London (AACL) was dominated by journalists from the larger media companies, and its willingness—indeed eagerness—to support such a system provoked much ill-will from those veteran correspondents who worked for newspapers or magazines lower down the pecking order. Army officials had found it convenient to consider the AACL the official organization of US journalists when such journalists needed to be consulted.[18] Although a rational decision by the military, it did not sit well with those reporters who were excluded.

A. J. Liebling was particularly scathing about the cozy relationship between the military authorities and the AACL. He charged that the AACL, "dominated by the representatives of the large press organizations," had hoodwinked SHAEF PRD into agreeing that those "which had large London bureaus should have first call" whenever spaces were scarce. According to one agency reporter, Liebling "was absolutely enraged" that the AACL and army public relations "did not recognize him as a 'newspaperman.' . . . For some reason the *New Yorker* correspondent was regarded as one being on the very fringe of journalism—say, like a writer for *House Beautiful* or *Charm* magazine." Quentin Reynolds, who had witnessed the Dieppe Raid while on assignment for *Collier's*, found himself excluded from subsequent similar operations after the president of the AACL complained that he was not on the proscribed roster. At least some reporters, then, resented the military's reliance on the AACL for guidance on press affairs and SHAEF's presumption that the AACL represented the entire US press. That SHAEF was an Allied command posed another set of challenges to PRD planners. Any press contingent for military operations in Northwestern Europe could involve not only US and British reporters but also Canadian and other Commonwealth correspondents and, on occasion, French and Russian ones. That reporters covering all three separate military services—army, navy, and air force—also clamored for inclusion only further complicated matters.[19]

Given all of these considerations, PRD's proposal drafted in October 1944 for "complete, equitable and expeditious" news coverage of the anticipated victory envisioned two alternatives, depending on whether Berlin would be occupied over land or by air. Both privileged the news agencies and networks. Notably there would be no reporters from daily newspapers in the smaller airborne group. This airborne cohort formed the basis of much subsequent planning for coverage of the surrender and predictably caused hard feelings on the part of reporters whose organizations were excluded from its ranks.[20]

Another point of contention emerged as such planning continued. Reporters with the armies in the field, ever sensitive to being coopted by correspondents safely back at Allied headquarters, were anxious to prevent the press corps stationed in Paris from monopolizing coverage of such a surrender. Twelfth Army Group, for example, felt that if the Germans requested an armistice the press should be represented, particularly reporters who had been long serving with the armies. When PRD's planners met in late October, though, they concluded that if a general surrender, "the biggest story of the war," should occur it would likely happen with little warning, making it impossible to gather reporters from the field quickly enough to be part of the press "brick" (as they termed it) that would travel to witness the surrender. Said brick of some twenty reporters would be drawn from press covering SHAEF headquarters in Paris. Predictably reporters at the front thought little of this arrangement. Brigadier Neville protested to SHAEF, arguing that it "would cause intense indignation" among those British correspondents who had been covering the war since the battles in the North African desert and "have been in the front line throughout this campaign."[21]

Over the winter wrangling continued over the size and composition of the press brick or task force as it was variously called, with planning efforts singularly muddled. On January 20, officials in Paris contacted London about getting input from the AACL and from the British press regarding who might be assigned to the three possible press groups now being considered: a group of ten to accompany an initial airdrop into Berlin, all of whom must be prepared to parachute in or land by glider; a second drop of thirteen to follow; and a larger contingent, Thor Smith's sixty correspondents, to accompany a land force moving into the German capital.[22]

Yet four days later the Planning Branch, evidently having been ordered to reduce the size of the press contingent, submitted for approval three plans reducing the number of correspondents in the Berlin force from eighty-eight, a number seemingly drawn from thin air, to alternately twenty-three, nineteen or eleven, the latter two figures never appearing in any other planning documents. Then a week later another officer in the Planning Branch suggested that since it now seemed likely that the Russians would capture Berlin without help from the Western Allies, the PRD should revert to its idea for a smaller press contingent acceptable to the Russians; in this case, a public relations brick of just twelve, including only four actual reporters. When officials contacted the AACL, its newspaper members balked at their exclusion from the various iterations of the press contingent.[23] Thus planning for the surrender had followed a crude pattern, with British officers arguing for a smaller task force, US officials for a larger one, and newspaper reporters wary of the entire process.

By late March, and with all these plans in limbo, General Allen proposed what he now termed a "press flying squad," described as "a highly mobile unit of War Correspondents, equipped with its own radio communications, which can move at short notice to any desired location." Only such a squad could assure "balanced and expeditious coverage of important historical events." Those events were now not limited to an entry into Berlin but had been broadened to include any armistice meeting in Germany. The press contingent would include six agency correspondents, two radio broadcasters, and two photographers. This number "had been very carefully worked out to provide balanced and complete Press, Radio and Pictorial coverage" and would be "difficult to improve upon." These ten members of the press would be accompanied by military personnel and all necessary equipment. Two C-53 aircraft outfitted with transmitters would be used for transport.[24]

In late April, with the Russians on the outskirts of Berlin and German resistance on all fronts collapsing, none of the PRD's various plans for press coverage had been approved. At the last minute, the PRD abandoned all its previous work and created a new scheme "for the coverage on short notice of a news break of transcendent importance" under the codename JACKPLANE. It called for a small group of correspondents and public relations personnel to constitute a flying squad, with all copy "to be submitted on a world pool basis." It identified a press party of twelve, six from news agencies (three US, two British, and one Canadian or Commonwealth), a US broadcaster and one from the BBC, and four photographers. If time allowed, the flying squad would use the transmitter-equipped transport planes Allen had proposed, but on short notice the squad would depart in regular transports. Reporters then would either fly back to Paris to file or have their copy, negatives, and recordings returned to Paris by courier.[25]

While SHAEF thus had been planning for months to cover the German surrender, in the event most of this effort was tossed out the window, and arrangements were made on the fly. What to make of all of this largely futile planning activity? For one thing, it highlights the competing constituencies and pressures bearing on the PRD. The conflicting agendas of different types of news organizations and the tension between headquarters and field correspondents all whipsawed planners. Moreover, with a war to be won and a tricky endgame to play on the battlefield, press coverage was hardly the main concern of Eisenhower and other SHAEF leaders at the time, who never got around to acting on any of the public relations plans. Finally, it reminds us just how contingent any such planning was given how little SHAEF knew of Russian military and political intentions. The Western Allies felt the need to accommodate the Russians at the end of the war, but Russian thinking and actions often remained opaque.

Once the C-47 (and not one of the intended C-53s) had taken off from Orly, the reporters clustered around General Allen as he sought to be heard above the engine noise. Allen revealed that they were going to SHEAF's forward headquarters in Reims, a flight that would take less than an hour. He explained that German emissaries were also in transit to Reims. It was thought that they would attempt to negotiate an armistice and possibly a surrender but that in either case an immediate agreement was unlikely. Such negotiations would be sensitive if only because of Russian suspicion that the Germans would make a separate peace with the Western Allies. In consequence Allen pledged the reporters to secrecy. All on the plane agreed that they would not discuss the trip with anyone else, much less write about it, until SHAEF authorized them to do so. The meaning and merit of this "pledge on the plane" would come to be hotly contested in the days and weeks to come.

The Paris bureau chief of the Associated Press, Ed Kennedy, was one of the Lucky Seventeen on the plane. Kennedy had been reporting from overseas for almost a decade and had been covering the war since the invasion of Poland in 1939. The Associated Press had rewarded him over the years with constant raises and assignment to successively more important posts. This had culminated in his taking over as chief of the Paris bureau, supervising the agency's coverage of the war in Northwestern Europe. Wiry, dark-haired, and often intense, Kennedy fit the stereotype of the hard-drinking and chain-smoking reporter. Although he did not write with a distinctive or memorable style—such was a near impossibility for agency work—he was a master of the clear, accurate spot news story, news of events reported at the scene and in the moment. He had extensive experience reporting both from the front lines and from various headquarters. During his career he had not been afraid to tangle with officials when he thought they were overstepping their authority or unfairly preventing him from pursuing a story. None on the plane had his breadth of experience reporting the war, although his agency competitors—Boyd Lewis of the United Press (UP) and James Kilgallen of the International News Service (INS) in particular—came close. Even Lewis and Kilgallen did not approach Kennedy's breadth of experience dealing with military public relations officials of varying nationalities and temperaments. As such, his career provides great insight into the challenges, including confrontations with military officials, faced by war correspondents as they went about their jobs in Europe.

Ed Kennedy was approaching his fortieth birthday in May 1945 and had spent half those years as a journalist. Kennedy had moved from his native Brooklyn to Pittsburgh in his late teens to study architecture at the Carnegie Institute of Technology. His college career was short-lived, likely due to lack of funds. Either in a doomed effort to pay his tuition

Figure 1.2. Ed Kennedy in a photo released by the AP when announcing his appointment as Paris bureau chief in Paris in September 1944. The photo itself is dated 1943 and might have been used when Kennedy was promoted to bureau chief in Algiers that March. Courtesy AP Images.

bill or shortly after leaving Carnegie Tech, Kennedy began working on the *Canonsburg Daily Notes*, a small-town newspaper in nearby Washington County. He held a succession of jobs with newspapers in the Northeast over the next nine years, among them the *Syracuse Journal*, the *Newark Star-Eagle*, and the *New York Sun*. He usually moved from one paper to another after a year or so, a common trajectory for young journalists at the time. Kennedy paused his burgeoning career in 1927 to go to Paris to study French, and he seems to have had only two passions in life other than reporting—architecture and Paris. After a stint as the *Newark Ledger*'s city editor, Kennedy returned to France in 1930, working on the Paris edition of the *Chicago Tribune* for six months after his savings ran out.[26]

Kennedy went to work for the Associated Press in 1932, joining arguably the country's preeminent news organization. He spent the next thirteen years working for the AP within the competitive world of agency reporting. The Associated Press was admired by some journalists and loathed by others. Both the intense competition among the major news agencies and the resentment of many newspaper and magazine reporters toward the powerful and at times overbearing agency would ultimately factor into the surrender controversy in 1945. That resentment was grounded in the agency's history.

The Associated Press traces its roots back to 1846, when six New York newspapers joined forces to defray the costs of obtaining news about the distant war in Mexico; they had then expanded their collaboration to include any telegraphed news from the entire country. An exclusive agreement reached with the Western Union Telegraph Company proved mutually beneficial. The New York cooperative quickly developed regional networks of papers that agreed to buy the news it collected. The Associated Press also began buying more local news from its clients for redistribution, but whether buying or selling, the transactions occurred on the Associated Press's terms. It marketed its service as quick, accurate, and impartial, and these would remain the pillars of its brand.[27]

In short order the Associated Press in New York was able to control the flow of news throughout the country even as resentment surfaced over its business practices. As the number of newspapers multiplied in the last decades of the nineteenth century, many begrudged the New York press's control over the national collection and distribution of news. Many came to decry the Associated Press as monopolistic, providing franchises to newspapers that assured them exclusive rights to the AP's services in their local markets. Rival papers so excluded therefore had some incentive to build an alternate agency, which they did with the founding of the United Press Association in 1882.[28]

The late nineteenth century witnessed battles within the newspaper industry just as titanic and tawdry as those occurring elsewhere in the US economy. Neither the original New York Associated Press nor the United Press Association survived a scandal when AP executives were caught forwarding stories to its rival in return for a share of the profits in reselling them. In 1893, a year after the kickback scandal broke, Melville Stone took over as general manager of the Chicago-based Western Associated Press. One of Stone's first moves was to broker a deal with a cartel of European agencies led by Reuters for exclusive use of its dispatches, effectively muscling out the United Press Association from much international coverage.[29]

In 1900 the Illinois courts ordered the Western Associated Press to revise its membership contracts to allow for competition. Shortly thereafter the Associated Press reincorporated in New York, which had laws more favorable to its business model. In 1907, E. W. Scripps started a second iteration of the UP as a purely commercial venture rather than a cooperative, attracting to it many evening and Sunday papers that had been excluded from the Associated Press. Not to be outdone and after constant feuding with the AP, William Randolph Hearst also established a news service in 1909 to sell wire copy outside the stable of his own papers. The next year he named it the International News Service.[30]

By Kennedy's time, all three agencies were well established. Kent Cooper had replaced Stone in 1921 as general manager of the Associated Press and immediately took steps to modernize it. He also developed the AP's own foreign bureaus rather than pay the Reuters cartel. Under Cooper's leadership, the AP clearly dominated the field, serving the most newspapers and employing the most staff, but critics complained that it had grown complacent and somewhat stodgy.[31] The UP, under the energetic leadership of Roy Howard, remained a leaner and scrappier operation, embracing its underdog status. INS was smaller still and never bettered its third-place status. The three agencies served more than two thousand newspapers by the First World War, and they competed fiercely over the next four decades.[32]

In addition to shaking up the business side of the newspaper industry, the Associated Press also established the style of writing that would come to dominate newspaper journalism in the century to come. Much nineteenth-century reporting had been plodding and verbose, taking paragraphs to set a scene or introduce a subject. For its part the Associated Press adopted the formula of "lead first, details later." It privileged verbal economy since telegraph companies charged according to wordage. The Associated Press also adopted the practice of having reporters file a short bulletin summary with the lead and then await approval before sending lengthier (and costlier) details if the story warranted, this again to reduce costs. Associated Press reporters toiled in anonymity, given that Melville Stone disdained bylines, and they wrote in its dry, stripped-down house style. Kent Cooper's modernizing efforts included introducing bylines on some prominent AP stories and eventually expanding AP's coverage beyond spot news to sports coverage and a range of feature stories.[33]

All of the agencies placed a premium on speed—the story that came into the newsroom first would most often be the one a newspaper used—sometimes to the detriment of writing quality and detailed accuracy.[34] Later the complaint would surface that the agencies were draining away good reporting jobs on individual papers since publishers found it more economical to fill their papers with dry wire service stories than to hire reporters to write more vibrant local ones. For good or ill, the agencies dominated US journalism of the day.

Whatever the AP's attraction for Kennedy, his decade of varied experience and some glowing reference letters made him attractive to it and landed him a position in its Pittsburgh bureau. He quickly moved to the District of Columbia when the AP began supplying stories from Washington to member papers in the West Virginia-Maryland-Delaware area, a service similar to other regional ones it had established. For all of his restlessness earlier in his career, he insisted to Kent Cooper that by the early 1930s he had finished with such "job-changing and would like to remain with the AP for good, not only because I like it, but because I believe it offers the opportunities I am after." The opportunity he most desired, he told Cooper, was to work as a foreign correspondent, preferably in Europe.[35]

Kennedy lobbied New York several times for a foreign post. When an opening came up in the Paris bureau, Kent Cooper wrote to Byron Price, then the AP's Washington bureau chief, asking if he thought Kennedy might be ready for the position. Price assured Cooper that Kennedy was doing an excellent job in Washington. "He is much better than average as a reporter," offered Price, "writes well, is industrious and dependable." Cooper did not dither over this decision, and before the end of the month Kennedy was aboard the SS *Deutschland* heading for Cherbourg.[36] With only the occasional home leave, he would remain overseas for the next decade.

Kennedy arrived in Paris on September 3, 1935. He found a more somber city than when he first visited in 1927. The economic depression had taken its toll, and French politics were increasingly dysfunctional; the foreign news was dominated by Mussolini's invasion of Ethiopia and Adolf Hitler's increasing belligerence. Kennedy spent the next year in the AP office near the Paris Bourse, where the routine work consisted of following the domestic and European news as reported in French papers, then writing bulletin summaries for distribution to AP members.[37]

In 1936, Kennedy was assigned to track down Wallis Simpson, the US divorcee who had fled London for France to escape the scandal over her relationship with Edward VIII, the newly crowned English king. Kennedy left Paris on what was thought to be a one-day assignment; he would not return to the city for a full year. Simpson headed not to Paris as expected but rather to the Riviera where the press found her secluded in the villa of US friends. After weeks of waiting even as other reporters tired and left, Kennedy's patience was rewarded when he was among the select few admitted into the villa's garden in mid-December for Simpson's first formal press conference. Kennedy's superiors were impressed.[38]

They ordered him directly to Rome, where Pope Pius XI was thought to be near death. This proved to be a false alarm, though, and after six weeks the AP reassigned Kennedy to Spain, then in the midst of civil war, his first experience of conflict reporting. He established himself in the loyalist wartime capital of Valencia where conditions were grim. The city was suffering a desperate food shortage, and Kennedy reckoned he lost twenty pounds in his months there. Reporting was made difficult by Spanish authorities who kept a tight rein on foreign correspondents. Kennedy supervised the AP's bureau in Madrid for several weeks, his first managerial responsibility, before briefly returning to Paris. He spent the better part of the next two years on assignment in Rome, where among other stories he covered Hitler's state visit to Italy in May 1938, for which Mussolini prepared, in Kennedy's words, "as gaudy and elaborate an organized spectacle as the Eternal City has ever seen." Kennedy was also part of an AP reporting team that converged on the Sudetenland in September 1938 to cover the Czechoslovakian crisis. If Hitler had appeared somewhat nonplussed by the pageantry during his visit to Italy, his triumphal entrance into the Sudetenland was another matter. The rapture of the adoring crowds convinced Kennedy that Hitler enjoyed a hold on the German people unlike anything Mussolini had managed in Italy.[39]

After the German invasion of Poland marked the beginning of actual combat, the AP reshuffled its European correspondents, sending Kennedy to Budapest, the hub of the AP's coverage of southern Central Europe. In the next year Kennedy would report from Rumania, Bulgaria, Turkey, Syria, and finally Greece. While no fighting had begun in the region, everywhere he found people fearful and disoriented, with governments maneuvering frantically to avoid being drawn into the war. Soon after arriving in Budapest, Kennedy also connected with Cyrus Sulzberger, the favored nephew of *New York Times* publisher Arthur Hays Sulzberger. Sulzberger's presence assured that even without actual fighting to report, Kennedy's time in the Balkans would be anything but uneventful.

Cy Sulzberger was working for the *Times* at the beginning of what would be a distinguished career as a foreign correspondent. Sulzberger and Kennedy became friends and professional allies, and in December they took an extended reporting trip together. Their destination was Slovakia, the eastern portion of the dismembered Czechoslovakia, then a German protectorate crawling with Gestapo. After hiring a car and a voluble Hungarian whom Sulzberger judged "the worst driver in all central Europe," the two reporters barreled off toward Bratislava along treacherous winter roads. Once in Slovakia they were promptly arrested by three Slovak troopers. The Gestapo representative in the area accused them alternately of being smugglers or English spies. Then the Slovaks brought in a local informant who denounced Kennedy as a Magyar terrorist. "This allegation was too much," Sulzberger recalled. "We burst into roars of laughter. Even the Gestapo man began to look embarrassed." After several hours, the two correspondents were released to be followed amateurishly for the rest of their time in the country.[40]

Kennedy was in Athens when the war's first months of unnerving calm, the Phoney War, ended with the German invasion of Holland and Belgium on May 10, 1940. Shortly thereafter, Kennedy recalled that when he had arrived in the Balkans the previous year he had thought there would be "some real fireworks" there, but such had turned out not to be the case. "This is not an orthodox war," he ventured, "every prediction has been wrong." Frustrated that the action seemed to be in Western Europe, Kennedy wrote that he "would like to get somewhere nearer the center of things."[41] However, the AP ordered him not to France but to Cairo, just as the Italian forces in Libya and Ethiopia eyed the Suez Canal. Kennedy's real war was about to begin.

Kennedy arrived in Cairo on August 30, 1940. Cairo proved to be Kennedy's important if frustrating post for the next two and a half years. For one thing, Kennedy found that British authorities there regarded correspondents, "especially American correspondents, as necessary nuisances who had to be held in check but handled politely."[42] Kennedy also encountered a bewildering array of overlapping and overweening censorship organizations that would bedevil reporters in Egypt throughout the war.

Just as Kennedy arrived in North Africa, five Italian divisions had advanced into Egypt from Libya and occupied the coastal town of Sidi Barrani, three hundred fifty miles west of Cairo. There the Italians inexplicably dug in and moved no farther east for months. During this lull in the fighting Kennedy attended maddeningly uninformative briefings in Cairo when not taking the occasional junket to visit a ship recently docked in Alexandria or to witness the trooping of the colors as new forces arrived. On one occasion reporters were allowed into the field to visit the 7th Armoured Brigade near Matruh. Even the army's conducting officer noted that the trip had "served little useful purpose from the press point of view," since censors forbid mention of either place or unit names despite official communiqués having revealed both. The small press corps in Cairo finally rebelled in early November, complaining to the British authorities about their exclusion from the front and about a censorship regime they deemed ludicrously restrictive.[43]

Kennedy's frustration was temporarily interrupted in November when he and Alan Moorehead, the respected Australian journalist then working for the (London) *Daily Express*, were chosen to accompany General (later Field Marshall) Archibald Wavell on an inspection tour of Crete, where the British were stiffening defenses and reinforcing the garrisons protecting their naval bases. The episode earned Kennedy praise from his employers in addition to a rare byline. "NICE CRETE STORY" the New York office wired, and Cooper himself cabled shortly thereafter, "FINE COVERAGE EXCELLENT COLOR KEEP AFTER IT AND THANKS." Kennedy would later infer that he and Moorehead had been brought to Crete as part of a British deception plan, with Wavell's publicized presence in Greece disguising British preparations for an offensive against the Italians in Africa. Kennedy took note of how the British military had not thought twice about using the press for its own purposes, even for such an understandable end.[44]

Kennedy was one of only six reporters on the scene when the British had routed the Italians from Sidi in early 1941. After the capture of Tobruk, Kennedy reported that so many Italians were surrendering that they had become an annoyance not only to the army but to the press corps. "I am the only American covering the campaign," he explained, and so was often "mistaken for a British officer. Consequently dozens of Italians have surrendered to me."[45] Kennedy remained in the field for much of this first desert campaign as the British routed an ineptly led force many times its size.

Kennedy returned to Greece in late March accompanying British forces being rushed there to check the German divisions massing at the Bulgarian border. The Germans were coming to the rescue of their Italian allies faltering in the Balkans as in North Africa. Here again Kennedy encountered the military's controlling hand. The British isolated Kennedy and the other correspondents in Athens for several weeks. He was not even allowed to inform his editors that he was in the country. This was done ostensibly to keep the British presence in Athens a secret, even though British troops roamed the streets in uniform and the German embassy remained fully staffed.[46]

In the ensuing weeks, Kennedy filed gripping accounts of the invasion and the subsequent evacuation of more than forty thousand British troops. His stories of the Greek king fleeing Athens, of fierce fighting near the Thermopylae Pass, and of retreating with British forces (when he had to dive into a ditch to avoid German strafing), all earned him front-page bylines. His final dispatch described fleeing Greece on a small steamer crowded with Australian troops, German prisoners, and civilians of all nationalities. One of the last ships to leave Piraeus, it crawled out of the harbor, where "the waterfront was a mass of twisted wreckage—the work of waves of German bombers."[47]

Upon his return to Cairo Kennedy found the British situation in the region bordering on the desperate. Greece had fallen, opening the door to the Near East. Many of the gains Wavell had made against the Italians had been reversed once Hitler decided to reinforce Mussolini's forces in North Africa. Field Marshall Erwin Rommel's Africa Corps had pushed well into Egypt and threatened to capture the Suez Canal, essential for British control of its empire. Kennedy was soon on his way to Syria, Lebanon, and Iraq to report on the British effort, ultimately successful, to thwart the German ambition to capture oil fields in the region. At virtually every stop on this trip he encountered censorship bordering on the absurd. For example, while in Syria, where the British were claiming that the Vichy French forces there had not resisted their incursion, censors deleted all mention of French opposition.[48]

In the months to come Kennedy had more on his mind than British censorship, though, as he assumed responsibility as the de facto head of the AP office. Kennedy was not officially named bureau chief because the Cairo staff was so small; the British there would only accredit two correspondents from each agency. After the United States entered the war at the end of 1941 and as the US military presence in Egypt ramped up, Cooper again praised Kennedy's work. "Indeed I am so grateful that I don't know how The Associated Press can ever adequately repay you," Cooper effused. "In my sentimental moments, I have felt like saying that you could write your own ticket." Kennedy could only respond that "outside of one or two love letters, I don't think I ever received a letter in my life that made me feel as good." Combined with frequent pay raises, such messages establish just how much the AP valued Kennedy's contributions at this crucial early stage in the war. In May 1942 and after the British relented and allowed more correspondents into theater, Kennedy was formally named chief of a Mideast bureau headquartered in Cairo and expanded to include all of Asia Minor.[49]

Although his managerial duties usually grounded him in Cairo, Kennedy did manage to make several reporting forays into the desert in 1942. On one of them, Kennedy found himself at the center of yet another censorship fracas, one that earned him a reputation for sharp practices with at least some in the press corps. In May Rommel attacked British forces in Libya. The Germans drove the Eighth Army back to El Alamein, within seventy miles of Alexandria, and were threatening to expel the British from Egypt. While attached to the British army, a tank squadron became the first US unit to engage the Germans in combat. The unit was under the command of Senator Henry Cabot Lodge Jr. of Massachusetts, a reserve officer assigned to the First Armored Division, and the US tankers had acquitted themselves well. Kennedy had the story. Like other correspondents who learned of the incident, he wanted to report on it, but the news was held up for release by the War Department.[50]

Lodge agreed to carry a copy of Kennedy's account of the action back to the United States for delivery to the Associated Press after Washington made its official announcement. When released, Kennedy's story appeared on the front page of the *New York Times* and scored a significant beat. The same day as the tank story appeared, Lodge praised Kennedy as "one of the most capable newspapermen in the Middle East battle zone" and emphasized that he was "highly regarded" by military officials there. At the Associated Press offices in New York, an editor told John Evans that Kennedy was "so consistently good that we might be inclined to forget it."[51]

Kennedy's competitors and the army begged to differ. The press corps resented being scooped, unfairly to their minds, on such a vital story. The army itself was furious that Kennedy had made an end run around censorship in Cairo. "RELATIONS WITH OTHER CORRESPONDENTS STRAINED BY RELEASE BY WAR DEPARTMENT OF KENNEDYS AP STORY," the US commander in Cairo cabled Washington. "THIS STORY NOT SUBMITTED CENSORSHIP HERE. OTHER CORRESPONDENTS STORIES HELD MY REQUEST PENDING BREAK BY WAR DEPARTMENT. REQUEST IN FUTURE NO STORIES WRITTEN HERE BE RELEASED UNLESS FORWARDED."[52]

Kennedy's gambit in this instance actually led to a change in War Department policy. "SUGGEST YOU INSTRUCT RETURNING OFFICERS NOT TO BRING BACK UNCENSORED STORIES FOR CORRESPONDENTS," the War Department replied to Cairo. "ALSO ADVISE CORRESPONDENTS NOT TO ATTEMPT TO GET UNCENSORED MESSAGES OUT OF AFRICA UNDER PENALTY REVOCATION OF CREDENTIALS WHICH IS WITHIN YOUR POWER."[53] Evidently from the official perspective, Kennedy had violated a policy that did not yet exist.

Such resourceful reporting, though, delighted the AP front office. One story, in particular, Kennedy's account of a massive bombing raid over Navarino Bay in Greece from his position in the last heavy bomber over the target, earned him a front-page byline and another round of commendations from New York. Cooper's executive assistant, Alan J. Gould, declared that Kennedy's story "ranks with the best of the many great descriptive war stories we have handled." Gould deemed it "brilliantly written by a staff man who has consistently shown his capacity for first-rate production and fine leadership in the field."[54]

Some evidence suggests that the pace of such work might have taken a toll on Kennedy. Don Whitehead had arrived in Egypt in October 1942 at the start of what would be a distinguished career as a front-line war correspondent. Kennedy first instructed his new reporter in the art of writing "headquarters stories," plausible accounts of battles at the front based on briefings, handouts, and maps distributed well behind it.[55]

Although the men got along well, Whitehead began to worry about his boss, especially after Kennedy confided that he was in love with the wife of a *New York Times* correspondent stationed in Teheran and planned to kidnap her and bring her to Cairo as his secretary. (One wonders if Kennedy might have been pulling his young colleague's leg when he told this bizarre tale.) Another reporter, George Tucker, had also recently been assigned to the Cairo bureau, and despite liking Kennedy, he too, according to Whitehead, was confounded by the bureau chief's behavior. "You never know where you stand with him," Whitehead quotes Tucker as saying, "One minute he is laughing and joking, everything is hysterically funny. The next he's sullen and moody." Whitehead suspected that Tucker might have resented Kennedy for not yet sending him out in the field. In any case, Whitehead agreed that "Ed is unpredictable and going to pieces."[56]

One might ascribe the Southerner Whitehead's reading of the Brooklynite Kennedy to regional misunderstanding if others over the years had not also noted Kennedy's drinking and occasional mood swings. The black Irishman could be volatile. However, if Kennedy was "going to pieces" in Cairo, he took a long time to shatter, since he would work at a high level under the greatest pressure for three more years. And if a love of drink and bouts of distemper were hanging offenses, then the gallows would be crowded with Second World War correspondents.

Figure 1.3. The AP captioned this photograph "AP staffer Don Whitehead, left, settles an affair of honor with fellow staffers Ed Kennedy, as George Tucker looks on in horror, March 8, 1943. Weapons were captured in desert during first Wavell campaign in 1940 by Kennedy." The three were in Cairo at the time, and may have been celebrating Kennedy's recent appointment to Algiers. Whitehead would soon follow. Courtesy AP Images.

The British Eighth Army, now commanded by General (later Field Marshall) Montgomery, counterattacked the Africa Corps at El Alamein in late October 1942. On November 8, an Allied force led by Eisenhower (in his first Allied command) landed in Algeria and Morocco. Operation TORCH aimed to catch the Axis troops between the two Allied forces in North Africa and drive them from the continent. By February 1943, the Eighth Army had advanced nearly one thousand miles to the west and had been attached to Eisenhower's headquarters, so the Associated Press decided to combine its Mideast and North Africa bureaus. Cooper directed Kennedy to proceed to Algeria to head the merged offices. He arrived in Algiers in early March. There he led an accomplished staff that included Wes Gallagher (who later headed the agency), Dan De Luce, Noland (Boots) Norgaard, Don Whitehead, and Hal Boyle, who would become the best-known AP reporter of the war. By the end of March Alan Gould was pleased that "Kennedy clearly has stabilized staff operations since taking charge" and also had "turned in fine writing himself."[57]

In June, while Allied Force Headquarters (AFHQ) planned for the invasion of Italy, Kennedy took home leave, his first in four years. This break proved short lived, as the Allied invasion of Sicily on July 10 signaled the start of a major campaign in Italy. Given Kennedy's experience, Cooper exhausted his contacts in the Bureau of Public Relations trying to get the reporter back to the Mediterranean, but it took weeks to arrange transport across the Atlantic. Kennedy flew back to North Africa in late August and crossed to the US beachhead at Salerno. For the next several months he divided his time between reporting from Italy and running the AP bureau in Algiers, where AFHQ remained until mid-1944. He continued to battle censorship, especially after Eisenhower left in late 1943 to take command of the Normandy invasion and was replaced by Field Marshal Henry Maitland ("Jumbo") Wilson. Less as a reporter and more as bureau chief, Kennedy became a thorn in the side of the public relations staff in AFHQ's Information and Censorship Section (INC). As early as September, for example, INC alerted Washington that the Associated Press had formally complained to officials that the British Eighth Army favored British correspondents. In fact, the army in the Mediterranean had long been "troubled by its [AP's] constant complaints which exceed those of any other agency."[58]

In January 1944, the Allies landed a force on the coast at Anzio, leap-frogging German defenses and aiming to break the stalemate that had developed in Italy. There they would hold a shallow beachhead for several months in the face of constant German shelling and attack, as Anzio proved to be one of the most dangerous battle zones of the war and a serious Allied misstep. Kent Cooper had frequently expressed his concern for the safety of correspondents in the field, directing bureau chiefs in 1943 not to assign reporters to cover routine bombing missions and similar operations that had little specific news value. Mindful of Cooper's instructions, Kennedy was hesitant to order any of his staff to Anzio given its danger. That said, Kennedy pushed against what he found to be the AP's excessive concern for the safety of its war correspondents. Although he agreed that "no story is worth the life of a man," Kennedy insisted that "this is a total war and we have a part in it. Our part is to tell the story of what the troops are doing. I have found no better way of doing this than being with them when they do it." Kennedy was also certain that the troops noticed the presence of reporters in the field, and he worried about their morale "if correspondents run out on them when they are in a tough spot."[59] It would be hard to find a more succinct expression of the war correspondents' credo.

Kennedy concluded that the only way to protect his staff would be to go to Anzio himself. He later called the three weeks he spent on the beachhead "the most moving of my life." He never forgot the camaraderie he encountered: "There probably never have been 50,000 men who lived together with greater devotion and consideration toward one another."[60] His experience at Anzio was so intense that it effaced his usual combative attitude toward military censorship. In this case, he was happy simply to report what he could of that devotion and consideration.

Sid Feder, who replaced him on the Anzio beachhead, reveals just how much respect Kennedy had earned from his staff. Kennedy was "just about the greatest guy I've ever worked for," Feder affirmed, "as competent a newspaperman as there is in the Mediterranean." Kennedy was "the perfect chief of bureau, for my money," Relman (Pat) Morin, who later was on Kennedy's staff in Paris, wrote to an editor in New York: "You can't help but be devoted to him. I think you'll agree that the coverage from there [Italy] in the past year says all this better than I can."[61]

After leaving the Anzio beachhead, Kennedy returned to the AFHQ Public Relations camp near Naples and from there coordinated the AP's coverage of the painfully slow advance up the Italian peninsula. The Allies entered Rome on June 5. As the United States Fifth Army neared Rome, Kennedy went to the press camp that had been set up a few miles outside the city. Dan De Luce had sent Kennedy a dispatch from the city itself describing Rome's capture, and Kennedy was able to get it cleared by the field censors and transmitted to Naples. Moments later, a German plane disabled the transmitter, delaying the dispatches of the other correspondents in the field for several hours.[62] The Associated Press had scored another scoop. The next day the Allies landed in Normandy, shifting the focus of the war to Northwestern Europe. Kennedy's time in the Mediterranean was nearly over.

In mid-August the US and French troops of the Seventh Army landed on the southern coast of France in support of the forces in Normandy. The aim was to move up the Rhone valley to join with the Allied forces in the north. Kennedy did not participate in the landings themselves but flew to southern France several days thereafter. Once there he would again prove himself to be a resourceful reporter and, to some, a scofflaw. He earned his first formal investigation by the army after he, with three other correspondents, traveled beyond the boundaries of the Seventh Army zone in search of French resistance fighters in the area. The first trip took them to the Swiss border, the second all the way to Paris.

They arrived in Paris in the middle of the night to find that SHAEF deemed their presence in northern France unauthorized. The reporters were brought before Colonel Ernest Dupuy, then the senior public relations officer in the city, who faced a dilemma. The reporters were without orders, but Dupuy admired their initiative. Kennedy was quite vocal, Dupuy recalled, "full of reasons why they should stay." Dupuy fashioned what he considered a fair compromise: SHAEF would censor and allow transmission of their dispatches, but then the reporters would have to return to the Seventh Army press camp.[63] Upon their return they faced the ire of Brigadier General Tristram Tupper, in charge of public relations for the Seventh Army. Tupper was a World War I veteran who had enjoyed some success writing screenplays in Hollywood between the wars. He was also George Marshall's brother-in-law. One reporter described Tupper as a "strange, unmilitary character," and few were impressed with his abilities.[64] Tupper's prominence as a senior public relations officer, then, hints at the dearth of able PROs throughout the theater. In this instance, Tupper was incensed that Kennedy and the others had flouted his directive not to leave the area of their accreditation. He suspended them and ordered a court of inquiry. The reporters returned to the press camp on September 14 to face their hearing two days later.

Summoned to the Carlton Hotel in Lyons, they were questioned by Tupper himself. Kennedy protested that he had done nothing improper. He argued that the Seventh Army boundaries had not been defined for the correspondents. "As far as I'm concerned," he told Tupper, "I made a trip in performance of my duties as a war correspondent, reached a point where PR facilities were available, submitted a story for clearance and left it up to SHAEF for censorship and transmission." After the War Department warned him off a harsher penalty, Tupper determined that their punishment would be limited to the suspension already imposed, in effect to time served. He reinstated them, then closed the case. Tupper's superior noted with relief that Kennedy was going to Paris as AP bureau chief and that another of the miscreants, Philip Jordan of the (London) *News Chronicle*, had been reassigned to Switzerland as a political reporter, "thereby removing from Theater two extremely uncooperative individuals."[65]

After some wrangling with military officials over the appropriate quota of personnel in each theater, the AP succeeded in accrediting Kennedy to SHAEF. He assumed responsibility for the AP's operations in Northwestern Europe in early October.[66] Over the next months Kennedy in Paris oversaw the AP's coverage of a growing number of Allied armies in the theater, working with Wes Gallagher, who was in the field, to shuttle personnel from one locale to another depending on the military situation. With a small staff in Paris Kennedy himself also covered SHAEF headquarters as well as France's reconstruction and political rehabilitation. Throughout these months, he chafed at having to spend much of his time as what he derisively called a "headquarters *wallah*," cut off from the front and enmeshed in the metastasizing military public relations bureaucracy. "I was never able to find out the total number of public relations personnel in the European Theater," he later wrote, "I know it ran into the thousands." In Paris alone, PRD not only controlled the Scribe but had also commandeered the American Express Building for its own offices, another large hotel, the Chatham, to house its officers, and two other hotels to billet the enlisted men in the division. Kennedy was not the only correspondent appalled by the mushrooming of the army's public relations operation.[67]

As a "headquarters wallah" in the months to come, Kennedy sometimes locked horns with SHAEF officials, with his competitors in the other news agencies, and even with his colleagues in the AP. One can detect notes of both weariness and impatience in the seven months between his arrival in Paris and the German surrender. He was hardly alone in this. The letters and diaries of both journalists and PROs from the period contain similar emotions. Nerves frayed as the war dragged on even as its end loomed so near.

Part of the pressure on Kennedy came from the second-guessing of the New York office when it thought one of the other agencies had beaten the AP on a story, even when only by a few minutes. If anything, the competition between the news agencies grew fiercer as the war progressed. In late November, in one instance, the UP issued a story quoting Eisenhower to the effect that the only sensible course for the Germans was to fight to the bitter end west of the Rhine rather than retreat farther into Germany. Editor Glenn Babb in New York cabled Kennedy in Paris demanding to know why he had not filed a similar story. Kennedy replied that New York needed to calm down, since the UP story to his mind "REPRESENTS UNDUE STRIVING FOR SPECIAL ANGLE WHICH FARFETCHED." While the Germans were indeed fighting west of the Rhine, Kennedy had learned that German units were also withdrawing across the river, and all indications were that the Germans expected to use the waterway as a defensive boundary.[68]

Competition between the agencies was exacerbated not only by the prospect of the end of the war but also by the frostiness between Kennedy and Boyd Lewis, the UP's chief in Paris at the time. Lewis recalled that

> Early in my days at the Scribe, I had an experience with Ed Kennedy of the AP, my most important rival, which I should have remembered the following May, but did not to my great disadvantage. The first time I ran the footrace against him [to file] we were neck and neck at the first turn when he stumbled. Instinctively I reached down, took his elbow and helped him to his feet. To my astonishment, Kennedy used that advantage to shove past me

on the stairs and beat me to the window. I should have known I could never expect that man to compete by any but dog-eat-dog rules.[69]

Allied authorities targeted Kennedy personally in February after he published a story indicating that if Franklin D. Roosevelt stopped in France after the Yalta Conference, the president would inquire about problems surrounding the relief of French civilians. "It is reported that White House directives for more of this relief have not been fulfilled," Kennedy wrote, noting that aid to the French, or its absence, might become "one of the war's greatest scandals." He explained to New York that he had not been able to include further details because censorship had stopped them. Several influential editors, including the *Kansas City Star*'s Roy Roberts, contacted the AP in New York shortly after the story was put out on the wire, eager for more information. The *Washington Post*, for its part, editorialized that it had also heard reports of problems with French relief, and that the government owed the public candor about any such problems. It quoted Kennedy's line about the relief issue possibly turning into "one of the war's great scandals."[70]

That line in Kennedy's story had also sounded alarms in the War Department, which asked SHAEF to investigate Kennedy's sourcing on the story and what he had meant in using the word "scandal." SHAEF in reply forwarded a statement from Kennedy who stressed that the gist of his story, that the program for food relief for France had not been carried out as planned, had been based on a variety of credible sources. Several of those sources had thought the situation was grave enough to warrant use of the word scandal. He pointed out that he had not included any specific allegations of army corruption, and "any interpretation of the word 'scandal' in the dispatch as involving a suggest of corruption is *incorrect*."[71] The issue continued to percolate for the better part of a month.

As the year ground on, Kennedy tangled with the PRD's Thor Smith in April at the Hotel Chatham, where most SHAEF public relations officers lived. Smith was eating in the dining room with two Army Air Corps officers, friends from his time as a PRO with the Eighth Air Force. Kennedy rushed into the room and sat down at their table. Apologizing to the others, Kennedy lit into Smith for PRD's denying the AP an additional reporter with a particular army group even though it had approved rival UP's request for the same. Smith replied that the UP's increase had been a mistake and had been corrected. According to one of the visiting officers, Kennedy then complained that PRD "instead of helping correspondents, was impeding them." He also complained about the number of correspondents from lesser publications swamping the theater. The other officer asserted that "Smith's responses were in good humor until Mr. Kennedy voiced the threat" to write about PRD's shortcomings, "of which he indicated there were plenty that had not been recorded for public consumption." Smith then told Kennedy he was free to write whatever he liked. After this, Kennedy seemed to cool down, but Smith was evidently concerned enough to ask his two friends to write up their accounts of the incident. "Col. Smith handled the matter neatly and in no way used threatening language," one attested, while the other vouchsafed that Smith's "attitude was tolerant in the extreme under the conditions and provocations existing."[72] That Smith requested these formal statements alerts us to the growing strain between PROs and reporters in Paris at the time.

Thus Kennedy, as well as so many others, seemed short-tempered and on edge in the weeks before the war in Europe ended; soldiers and journalists alike were truly sick of the war and desperate for it to end. The prospect of transfer to the Pacific after a German surrender increased everyone's anxiety. Despite these obstacles, Kennedy continued to enjoy the support and encouragement of the AP leadership. Cooper and others at the AP in New York continued to praise his skill while coordinating coverage of what had expanded to nine armies housed in three separate army groups. Few if any bureau chiefs for the Associated Press bore such responsibilities.

Not many of the war correspondents at the Scribe that spring had participated in the raucous celebrations there following the liberation of Paris. Few knew much, if anything, about SHAEF's scattershot planning for the German surrender, although fewer still would have been shocked by the army's bureaucratic wheel-spinning. Kennedy's own encounters with military public relations throughout the war mirrored those of other veteran war correspondents. Even as the army was able to service correspondents at the front with increasing efficiency and transmit copy back to readers in the United States with increasing speed, during the later stages of the war censorship issues continued to rankle, and the tensions between correspondents and military public relations, never far below the surface, threatened to boil over. In large part this was because as the threat from

Germany dissipated with it went much of the solidarity forged by Pearl Harbor and the fascist menace. The mood at the Scribe, even before the surrender controversy, had grown as somber and tense as it had been joyous and unleashed after the liberation of Paris.

By April, Kennedy and many other correspondents rarely left the Scribe. Given that his bedroom adjoined the sitting room the agency used as an office, he spent most of his hours in the AP's suite of rooms on the fourth floor of the Scribe. Kennedy would go downstairs for briefings, to the hotel's dining room to eat, and to the basement bar for drinks with other correspondents. He evidently had little time to get out into the city he most loved in those springtime weeks. Kennedy's war was about to end. Whether his estimable career as a war correspondent ended in a blaze of glory or under a cloud would be debated for years.

2

THE MILITARY'S APPROACH TO THE PRESS

Ed Kennedy and other reporters approached the German surrender after a war-long slog, and so did those in the army responsible for dealing with the press. The media controversy that occurred in May 1945 was predicated on and conditioned by how the press traditionally interacted with the military. That relationship was defined at heart by the contradictory information imperatives of the two institutions; as a general rule, armies try to divulge as little as possible as late as possible, while the press publishes as much as possible as soon as possible. Both the media and the military throughout the war struggled to assure that the public had sufficient access to reliable war information while still safeguarding military security. The inherent tensions in the relationship would never completely disappear, even in a war so widely supported.

Prior to the twentieth century, military officials tended to think of reporters as irritating but inconsequential nuisances, when they thought of them at all. The rancor between the press and the army can be traced as far back as the Revolutionary War, when George Washington complained that loyalist newspapers undermined the morale of his troops. During the Civil War, General William Tecumseh Sherman spoke for many officers of his day when he complained that "now to every army and almost every general a newspaper reporter goes along, filling up our transports, swelling our trains, reporting our progress, guessing at places, picking up dropped expressions, inciting jealousy and discontent, and doing infinite mischief."[1]

Before the twentieth century, war correspondents were invariably civilians without official sanction or status, who traveled to battlefields on their own, and who were responsible for their own shelter, provisions, and communications. They moved about freely and without military control. The public came to think of war correspondents as dashing and romantic figures, intrepid souls who risked discomfort and danger to provide readers with eyewitness accounts of distant battles. Richard Harding Davis was the most prominent such US correspondent, reporting on the Spanish-American War, the Boer War, and the early years of the First World War.[2]

For decades historians posited that official controls on war correspondents began in the First World War, but in 2019 Michael Sweeney and Natascha Loft Roelsgaard determined that the actual source of such control was Japanese practice in its war with Russia a decade earlier. During the Russo-Japanese War (1904–5), Japan implemented a system of accreditation that required foreign correspondents to abide by strict regulations under the threat of punishment; it instituted a severe censorship regime and limited reporters' access to transmission facilities; and it required that correspondents be accompanied by conducting officers wherever they went. The Japanese were so effective in restraining the press and shaping the journalistic narrative of the war that such measures became a template for governments and militaries during the First World War and beyond.[3]

Both the military and the press defaulted to their nineteenth-century attitudes toward each other as the First World War began. By its end, that relationship had changed irrevocably. When war broke out in 1914 correspondents initially resumed their free-roaming habits, making their way to Belgium and elsewhere that fighting might occur. During August and September correspondents from neutral countries could travel back and forth between the belligerents. In consequence reporters were habitually detained on suspicion of espionage (e.g., Richard Harding Davis by the Germans at one point), and British war correspondents were even arrested by their French allies.[4] Military officials adopted Shermanesque attitudes toward the press in the field. Even their own army "treated British war correspondents as pariah dogs," one such reporter complained.[5]

This period of the freelancing adventurer-correspondent did not last long. Static trench warfare descended by October, and the territory between the opposing armies in which reporters could shuttle back and forth disappeared. Both sides increasingly adopted the Japanese model. By the Battle of the Marne, the British and French had all but banished correspondents from the front, with the British threatening to prosecute any correspondents found in forward areas. Absent independent correspondents, war news came in the form of eyewitness accounts written by Allied officers reflecting the army line rather than from reports by independent journalists.[6]

The Central Powers proved more accommodating at first, feeling confident after conquering Belgium that they were winning the war. The Germans initiated a system of tours for reporters, supplying free transportation, conducting officers, and convenient communications links for small groups of reporters who wanted to visit the front. While correspondents found it difficult to turn down such opportunities, the public was understandably skeptical of reporting based on such supervised tours. The Austrians went their German allies one better, as foreign correspondent William G. Shepherd recounted. Promising a tour of the front, the Austrians offered reporters free transport to a Hungarian spa town where they were installed in plush resort hotels and plied with Hungarian wine. Each was assigned a personal batman, and the reporters were free to write, swim, and hike as they wished. The trips to the front lines never materialized. The reporters received everything they wanted, Shepherd noted, except news.[7]

Under pressure from the press, both British and French armies relaxed their grip somewhat by adopting the German system of conducted tours. These limited correspondents' movement required them to travel with a military escort, and mandated they submit all correspondence and copy for censorship. Officials also devised written accreditation agreements that required reporters to obey military instructions as a condition for access to the front. They then restricted such accreditation to just a handful of reporters; initially only five British correspondents and one American, Frederick Palmer, were accredited to the British Expeditionary Force, with Palmer filing for all three US news agencies. In sum, the Allies had adopted the Japanese system fully.[8]

From that point on, the press operated in the information environment of total war that would obtain in both world wars. Such conflicts as conducted by modern industrialized societies were not confined to the battlefield itself; popular support was essential to sustain the required war effort. The need to maximize production and manpower in total war led governments to deem civilian morale essential to the war effort, and thus countries involved in total wars developed complex strategies to bolster public opinion.[9] That meant governments must generate propaganda, both for domestic and foreign audiences, as well as control the dissemination of information through the censorship of news, and above all military news.

When the British and French did permit reporters to tour the front in the spring of 1915, correspondents hoped they would be able to report in detail, but they were frustrated when British officials imposed severe restrictions on what could be written. In protest, correspondents refused to write a word until the worst restrictions were eased. This shocked the British command into a compromise.[10] Such compromises would be rare during the First World War because all the combatant nations, following the Japanese model, imposed rigid military censorship protocols. Reports of mutinies in the French army and the British navy, for example, were ruthlessly suppressed. Trench warfare was considered so unsettling to home audiences that front-line photography was all but banned. Virtually nothing of the gruesome conditions on the Western Front reached home audiences through their newspapers.[11]

When the United States entered the war in April 1917, the War Department claimed that the army's need for security trumped the people's right to know, and it demanded authority to control any news emanating from the theater of war. As a result, military censorship began the moment United States troops reached France that summer. Even before reporters arrived overseas they had to navigate the War Department's costly and cumbersome accreditation process. Would-be war correspondents were required to provide proof of their physical fitness, post a $10,000 bond against any future rules infractions, and pay $1,000 in advance toward their expenses overseas. Reporters were also compelled to swear that their stories would contain neither demonstrably false information nor report rumors, with such to be defined by the military. In return, accredited correspondents received military identification cards and travel passes; they were issued uniforms without insignia and were required to wear a green armband with a large C for correspondent on it, all necessary for access to the front.[12]

General John Pershing, the commander of the American Expeditionary Force (AEF), had little time for the press and did not allow correspondents to accompany troops on their voyage to France. At first, Pershing wanted a mere eight reporters accredited to his command, all from the news agencies. The Wilson administration convinced him that the press would oppose such a restricted pool, and so Pershing reluctantly allowed twenty-five reporters to attach to the AEF. There would be hundreds of US correspondents in France by the armistice, a small number (never more than thirty-five) formally accredited to the AEF headquarters, a larger number of correspondents accredited to divisions, and a still larger group of "visiting" reporters who were housed in Paris (and not with the army) and typically stayed only for short durations. Once in France, the US army adopted large pieces of the system of press relations used by the French and British, limiting front-line access to infrequent tours with conducting officers, for example, but in time the US correspondents did gain some greater freedom of movement.[13] Even at war's end, most copy moved slowly from France through congested transatlantic cable heads or even more slowly by ship.

Censorship control took place through a division of the Intelligence Section (G-2) of the AEF. In a deft move, Pershing hired an old acquaintance, the journalist Frederick Palmer, awarded him the rank of major and placed him in charge of the Press Censorship Division. Palmer hoped to act as a good-faith intermediary between the army and the press; he respected the security needs of the army, but he had also experienced firsthand unreasonable censorship prohibitions. He also understood from his reporting days that senior officers were tempted to use the press to promote themselves, and that censorship had been misused to cover up military mistakes and scandals.[14]

Although Palmer succeeded in convincing censors to allow criticism of the military's actions as long as that criticism was constructive, he was less successful in other areas. The Press Censorship Division began scrutinizing every story written, rating correspondents according to their willingness to hew to the army's line. The army also insisted on suppressing stories that might injure morale. This was vague enough to cover almost anything that might embarrass the military, and the morale clause would prove the bane of reporters in two world wars. Pershing disaccredited Westbrook Pegler, for example, then a young United Press reporter, for his aggressive reporting on equipment shortages. Heywood Broun, for another, wrote a series of exposés of the army's general lack of preparedness for actual warfare; he waited until his return to the United States to publish them in the *New York World*, knowing they would be stopped by censors in France. Exhausted by the wrangling between censors and reporters, Palmer left the censor's post as the war wound down.[15]

Regarding the quality of the journalism itself, in the years the United States was still neutral, several US correspondents had been able to file memorable stories. Shepherd, for one, wrote vivid accounts of a poison gas attack at Ypres and also of a Zeppelin raid on London.[16] Davis wrote eyewitness dispatches of the German entry into Brussels and the destruction of Louvain. Once restricted to supervised tours and particularly after US troops went into battle in early 1918, however, US reporting turned undistinguished, dominated by rehashes of army communiqués and briefings at headquarters. At such a remove from the troops in the trenches, US war correspondents developed the same distanced, spectatorial vision as John Dos Passos, Ernest Hemingway, E. E. Cummings, and the others who volunteered as ambulance drivers during the First World War.[17]

Military public relations and censorship were but one aspect of the US government's information strategy in the First World War. After declaring war in April 1917, Woodrow Wilson recognized the need to win over a skeptical public. He created the Committee on Public Information (CPI), headed by Colorado journalist George Creel, to enlist the public in the war effort. Creel became one of the more controversial figures of the day.

Creel set up a domestic censorship regime that was nominally voluntary; it provided guidelines to the press but did not require that copy be submitted to government censors prior to publication. Those guidelines prohibited unauthorized disclosure of any military information and banned publication of rumors and deliberate falsehoods. Even without an apparatus for compulsory press censorship, the federal government still found ways to control speech. A series of federal laws—the Espionage Act, the Sedition Act, and the Trading with the Enemy Act—all criminalized statements that were considered disloyal and sanctioned those who sent them through the mail (as were most magazines and many newspapers). Creel also used his sweeping powers to squeeze any publications he deemed subversive, for example by denying them newsprint.

The Creel Committee also provided a steady stream of press releases promoting the war effort and demonizing the German enemy. Creel himself was both prickly and mercurial, alternately aggrieved and aggressive. Creel's heavy-handedness, his encouragement of crude propaganda, and his stifling of dissent brought many complaints. That said, on the whole the Committee on Public Information did its job: the press followed the CPI's guidelines and disseminated the desired messages.

George Creel and the US military might have been pleased with their efforts to shape attitudes toward the war, but neither the press nor the public shared that satisfaction. The Creel Committee left journalists and many of their readers deeply suspicious of all governmental efforts to manage information and bend the truth. "Creel had oversold his product," in one historian's view.[18] Complaints focused on two areas: a censorship regime thought to have been unwieldy and mismanaged, and a propaganda program that relentlessly beat the drum for the government. Censorship and propaganda had been so excessive by every government during the First World War that people on both sides of the Atlantic were convinced that they would learn what had actually happened only after it had ended. "The truth is about to be unmuzzled," wrote the *London Daily News* in 1918.[19] A raft of postwar books by former war correspondents now freed from censorship disclosed the horrors of industrialized warfare and life in the trenches, feeding the consensus that the war had been badly reported and the public poorly served, a feeling that lingered for years.

The unfortunate experiences of the First World War were much on the minds of government officials and the press as war again loomed two decades later. Whatever these misgivings, all fully understood that information was now essential war matériel. Germany's extensive use of propaganda in the 1930s crystallized this understanding. The British, in turn, created a massive new agency, the Ministry of Information, responsible for censorship and propaganda. In the United States, the armed services at first proposed to recreate the structure of the Committee on Public Information by combining publicity, propaganda, and censorship in a single agency, the Public Relations Administration, but this time with the military in control. Aware that the public disapproved of the Creel Committee's overreach, President Franklin D. Roosevelt rejected this plan.[20] Roosevelt resolved to separate censorship from propaganda, although none of the different bureaucratic frameworks for information he tried before Pearl Harbor functioned well.[21] In the days after the Japanese attack, the Roosevelt administration created the Office of Censorship, charged with domestic censorship. It then built a second agency, the Office of War Information (OWI), to act as a clearinghouse for all government information about the war effort, to promote civilian morale, and to disseminate US propaganda overseas. In May the various bureaus with possible jurisdiction over press reports from overseas—the State, War, and Navy departments and the Office of Censorship—agreed that news stories originating from abroad would be vetted by the military authorities in the region and not by officials in the United States, an approach known as censorship at the source.[22] However ungainly the process had been, Roosevelt finally arrived at a structure that might avoid the problems of the Creel Committee by separating domestic censorship from military censorship, then isolating them both from any propaganda activities.

President Roosevelt appointed Kennedy's former boss in the Washington bureau, Byron Price, then the AP's executive news editor, to run the Office of Censorship. It was given the enormous task of security censorship of communications going out of the country by post, cable, and telephone, and the lion's share of its resources and personnel were devoted to that effort. Price resisted calls, especially from the military, for compulsory censorship of the domestic media and instead opted for a voluntary system based on lists of prohibited and sensitive topics, in essence steering the press away from information that might compromise security. Journalists and broadcasters could query the Office of Censorship for guidance when they had questions about a story's status under that code. If a journalist could cite the proper controlling authority, by which Price meant the relevant government agency, as the source of information in a story, then it could be published. The Office of Censorship also mediated when journalists protested the military's tight grip on information about its activities in the United States. Price's deft hand running the Office of Censorship and his effectiveness at mediating disputes between the press and the military led voluntary censorship during the war to be judged on the whole a success.[23]

The OWI's performance was considerably more uneven. Headed by Elmer Davis, the respected CBS commentator and, like Price, a straight-talking Midwesterner, the OWI never enjoyed the support that Price and the Office of Censorship did. Congress always suspected the OWI of acting as a cheerleader for the Roosevelt administration, an unwarranted extension of the aggressive public relations effort that had accompanied the New Deal. Moreover, the OWI was wracked by ideological infighting, with frequent charges from Republicans that the left-wing was controlling its messaging. Finally, the OWI never succeeded in corralling the public relations operations in every agency and department in Washington, all of which resented and resisted its authority.[24]

The third leg of the government's war information regime, and the one of most concern in the surrender controversy, was military public relations and censorship. When the United States entered the Second World War, the army had been as ill-equipped to deal with the press as it had been to fight on the battlefield. The reasons for this included the military's habitual mistrust of journalists, its ignorance of the burgeoning field of public relations, and its internal divisions with separate military bureaucracies competing for public favor and funding. Moreover, career officers considered public relations and military censorship as backwater assignments to be dutifully performed on the path to more important postings.

When the Roosevelt administration implemented conscription in 1940, the War Department awoke to the need for popular support for this expansion and so created a Bureau of Public Relations. Its chief throughout much of the war, Brigadier (later Major) General Alexander Day Surles, was a capable administrator who took as his main brief protecting the secretary of war and the army chief of staff from public criticism.[25] The few regular officers with expertise in media relations were insufficient to staff its press offices, so the army then turned to draftees and volunteers, only a small number of whom had been actual journalists. Even those who had worked for newspapers often had not been reporters or editors. For example, Thor Smith, generally credited as one of the more competent public relations officers in Europe, had worked for newspapers in San Francisco and elsewhere for more than a decade but always on the business rather than the editorial side. As far as can be determined, he had never published an article in his life. As the war progressed and the army public relations staff grew, veteran reporters often found themselves dealing with junior officers with little understanding of journalism and a fear of making mistakes that would upset their superiors. Beyond this, army public relations focused more on getting out the military's story than aiding independent reporters in getting out theirs.

The early action in the war had been in the Pacific, where public relations was largely the province of the navy. Given the vast distances and poor infrastructure in the region, reporters were reliant on the navy itself for transportation and communications, and the navy was historically cautious in the extreme about security and consequently wary of reporters. Those suspicions only ramped up after *Chicago Tribune* reporter Stanley Johnson inferred in an article that the navy must have broken a Japanese codes (which was indeed the case and one of the most closely held secrets of the war). The Japanese either discounted or disbelieved the story, while the navy invoked it whenever defending its strict censorship. Throughout the war, war news from the Pacific was doled out parsimoniously: details of the Doolittle raid on Tokyo, for example, were withheld for months; ship losses, even when known to the Japanese, were not announced in the United States; and nothing approaching the full extent of the damage at Pearl Harbor was revealed before the end of the war. Ground forces in the Pacific were commanded by General Douglas MacArthur, a notorious publicity hound who thought the role of the press in the theater was to inform the public of his exploits rather than those of his troops. For these and other reasons, reporters in the Pacific faced even greater challenges than those in Europe.[26]

The first campaign for the US army in the European and Mediterranean theaters followed the TORCH landings in French North Africa in November 1942. It had revealed the army to be ill-prepared to accommodate the press. By the end of the campaign in Tunisia seven months later, the basic framework within which war correspondents and military officials would interact for the rest of the war had been established. Planning for press coverage of the landings themselves was done at the last minute and largely by one officer on the staff of AFHQ. Following the model from the First World War, Eisenhower had housed AFHQ's Public Relations Section in the Intelligence (G-2) branch of his command.[27] He selected a career officer who specialized in psychological warfare and who had been serving as the military attaché in London, Brigadier General Robert A. McClure, to be his intelligence chief and to oversee the unit. In turn, to plan for press coverage of TORCH, McClure relied heavily on Major (soon to be Colonel) Joseph Phillips, a former foreign correspondent who at the time of Pearl Harbor was an editor at *Newsweek*.

Twenty-six war correspondents accompanied Allied troops when they landed in Algeria and Morocco in November 1942; dozens more would follow. All were formally accredited to AFHQ, a process that began with a general background check in Washington to identify any security risks. Correspondents then signed an agreement to abide by military regulations and to furnish military censors with all outgoing copy and business messages. AFHQ developed censorship guidelines and procedures based largely on British practice but also influenced by prewar US field manuals and refined by what little experience the fledgling US army in Britain had gained in dealing with reporters.[28] AFHQ established its headquarters in Algiers, where it remained for the duration of the campaign in North Africa and beyond. There, public relations took a distinct back seat to intelligence and psychological warfare in G-2's priorities, and the handful of public relations officers and censors in Algiers struggled to accommodate the needs of the press. Communication delays proved an enormous problem as cable and radio links to London and to the United States were scarce and slow.

Conditions for those reporters who made it to the front, some hundreds of miles east of Algiers, were even worse. The army had made virtually no provision for reporters in the field. The intrepid few journalists who made it to these forward areas, Wes Gallagher of the AP and Drew Middleton of the *New York Times* among them, had to buy their own cars for transportation and to arrange for their own food and shelter. Even if they obtained a newsworthy story, it proved all but impossible to file, as the army had not put in place any system to censor or transmit copy from the field. All of the censors remained at AFHQ in Algiers. John D'Arcy-Dawson of the British Kemsley newspaper chain was only one of the reporters frustrated by his inability to get reports back to Algiers, let alone to his readers: "The chaos was incredible," he complained.[29]

Eisenhower sought to ameliorate some of these problems by separating propaganda and censorship from military intelligence. He formed the Information and Censorship Section (INC) and summoned McClure from London to Algiers in early 1943 to head it. McClure and Phillips were able to ameliorate some of the dire conditions reporters faced in the field by adopting the British model of mobile press camps, arranging for the army to transport, house, and feed reporters at the front while also relaying their dispatches to Algiers through military teleprinters and couriers.[30]

Because of these conditions, news coverage of the North African campaign, especially in late 1942, was poor by any standard. Reporters at the front were constantly frustrated by the transmission delays that dated their stories by the time they reached Algiers, let alone the United States. Spot news written from headquarters in Algiers relied on terse official communiqués and largely told the story as the army wished it told, with few details and little mention of shortcomings. Even these stories took days to reach the public. Reporters complained to AFHQ that their editors, desperate for any information, were actually publishing items picked up from Vichy-controlled Radio Maroc rather than from AFHQ.[31]

Coupled with a ban on reporting about the political situation in French North Africa that Eisenhower imposed, such difficulties led to a rocky start to relations between the press and military authorities. Reporters blamed the military for the inadequate communications facilities, vague briefings and communiqués, shoddy staff work, and arbitrary censorship. Alan Moorehead, the respected Australian war correspondent who had accompanied Kennedy to Crete in 1940, arrived in January and was shocked to discover that the British and US publics "had only the wildest misconceptions of what was taking place" in North Africa. There were many difficulties, but foremost was the military's penchant for secrecy, "which was often expressed in fretful and overcautious censorship." From the army's side, McClure decried what he considered to be unfair criticism when he vented to a colleague that "our difficulties of transmission, censorship, providing news and otherwise wet-nursing this bunch of temperamental prima donnas, are sufficient without being distorted."[32]

Although correspondents largely admired Eisenhower throughout the war and the general handled the press deftly, he had faced several significant challenges in press relations by 1945. Each, in its way, served as a backdrop to the fiasco that May. The first involved political censorship in French North Africa. The TORCH landings were nominally undertaken at the invitation of General Henri Giraud, whom the Allies hoped to install as the head of all French resistance forces. After the landings, the Allies' plans for Giraud immediately fell apart. Amid great confusion,

Eisenhower's deputy on the scene, General Mark Clark, had agreed to recognize a new administration in French North Africa. It was headed by Admiral Jean Darlan, commander of all French military forces and Marshal Philippe Pétain's first political deputy in the Vichy government. This agreement, referred to by its critics as the "Darlan deal," left in place much of the authoritarian Vichy regime in North and West Africa, including the repressive criminal justice system and its anti-Semitic legal code. Scholars portray Darlan as more a Machiavellian intriguer than a reactionary ideologue, but either way he was firmly entrenched on the French right wing. The announcement of Darlan's appointment as head of government prompted howls of protest.[33]

In the weeks after the landings, the small Allied press corps made the rounds in Algiers. Wherever reporters went in the city they heard much the same story—the deep sense of betrayal felt by those who had aided the Allied landings only to be jailed or otherwise persecuted by the Vichy regime the Allies had left in power. The harshest of the Vichy laws remained on the books and vigorously enforced, leading many to despair that one authoritarian regime had merely been replaced by another.

In response to this unrest and the roiling criticism of the Darlan deal at home, Eisenhower had abruptly banned war correspondents from any mention of the volatile political situation in North Africa. Stories alluding to politics that did pass censorship invariably reflected the official line put out by Robert Murphy, the diplomat serving as AFHQ's political adviser. In sum, the US public received only the sketchiest reporting from North Africa and virtually no information about the political crisis there. NBC's John MacVane wrote shortly after leaving North Africa that "to a man we, correspondents and censors alike, disagreed with the decision to bolster up a Fascist regime in North Africa by stifling the truth that all of us knew."[34]

The situation in Algiers reached a crisis on Christmas Eve when Darlan was assassinated by a young Frenchmen of opaque political views. Uncertain how Algerians would react to Darlan's death, AFHQ prevented journalists from dispatching news of the killing. On Christmas Day reporters learned that the young assassin, Bonnier de la Chapelle, was to be abruptly executed by the French. CBS commentator Cecil Brown in New York informed his listeners that "censorship at Algiers is very severe" and so he could offer them little more information about Darlan's death.[35]

In the days after the assassination, the Allies finally got their wish and designated Giraud as Darlan's successor. The general promptly jailed some dozen Algerians, including several who had aided the Allied landings, accusing them of involvement in the assassination. News of the arrests had emerged when Giraud held a contentious press conference, claiming that all those imprisoned had been "making trouble." He confided to a skeptical press corps that police had uncovered a plot to assassinate both himself and Ambassador Murphy. The *New Yorker*'s A. J. Liebling, who was at the conference, estimated that there were about thirty correspondents in Algiers at the time, and not one of them accepted the official explanation. When Frank Kluckhohn of the *New York Times* gave Giraud a list of the reported prisoners and asked Giraud to verify it, the general dismissed the list as fiction. Disbelieving and furious, most of the press corps filed critical stories about the conference only to have censors excise all reference to the political prisoners. Alarmed by what he saw as a virtual rebellion on the part of the press, Murphy invited correspondents to his villa for New Year's Eve and, in Liebling's phrase, "tried to pour gin on the troubled waters."[36]

It fell to Ernie Pyle early in the new year to break the censorship stranglehold on the political situation in North Africa. Pyle generally avoided delving into policy or politics, but in early January he managed to send a dispatch critical of censorship in North Africa. "Because the campaign at first was as much diplomatic as military," he wrote, "the powers that be didn't permit our itchy typewriter fingers to delve into things international, which were ticklish enough without our comments. I believe misconceptions at home must have grown out of some missing parts of the picture." AFHQ publicly claimed to be rooting out Axis sympathizers and then turning them over to French authorities for prosecution. "The procedure was [to be] that we investigated, and they arrested," Pyle had been told. "As it turned out," he discovered, "we investigated, period." Pyle concluded simply: "Our policy is still appeasement."[37]

Pyle's column prompted an outcry in both the United States and Britain when it appeared. Soon other stories of the repression in North Africa began to surface, and newspapers editorialized that such a policy toward the Vichy government in North Africa violated Allied war aims. Commentators on both sides of the Atlantic charged that the installation of Darlan had sent a chilling warning of what might happen under the Allies to those opposing the Nazis throughout continental Europe. Eisenhower relented and lifted political censorship in mid-January. By the spring of 1943, the most reactionary civil authorities had been removed from office, the right-wing paramilitaries had been dissolved, and much of the most pernicious Vichyite legal framework had been dismantled in French North Africa.[38] Eisenhower later admitted that his decision to impose political censorship had been "an error, even though from a good motive."[39] However, the entire Darlan episode left the press corps in Africa, most of whom moved on to Italy and France as the war progressed, deeply skeptical of official rationales and on alert for the reappearance of such political censorship.

Eisenhower's relationship with reporters and the public's confidence that it was getting accurate reporting, first put to the test in North Africa, were further strained by the Patton slapping controversy in August 1943. The notorious episode underscored a different source of tension in the military's working relationship with the media—the accusation that reporters in the field had grown too cozy with military authorities and were now only too willing to do their bidding. The bare facts of Patton's actions and the army's reaction are well-known, but less familiar is the story's impact on the media's relationship with the military during the war.[40]

The slapping episode was, in fact, two separate incidents that occurred in early August as the Allies were poised to expel the Germans from Sicily. Both involved General George S. Patton berating wounded soldiers in field hospitals. The second incident, similar to the first, was the more egregious. While touring a ward in an evacuation hospital, Patton approached a patient who was huddled up and shivering. Patton asked what was wrong, and Private Paul Bennett explained, "It's my nerves." Bennett began sobbing. Patton then shouted at Bennett to repeat what he had just said. When Bennett did, adding that he could not stand the shelling anymore, Patton, as recounted by the base's commanding officer, "yelled at him 'Your nerves Hell, you are just a goddamned coward, you yellow son of a bitch.'" Patton then slapped Bennett and told him to "shut up that God damned crying. I won't have these brave men here who have been shot seeing a yellow bastard sitting here crying." He struck the soldier yet again, knocking off his helmet liner. Patton turned to a medical officer and ordered: "Don't you admit this yellow bastard, there's nothing the matter with him." Turning back to Bennett, who was trying to stand at attention even as he shook uncontrollably, Patton ordered him back to the front lines. If he did not go, Patton threatened, he would have him shot by a firing squad. Reaching for his own pistol, Patton then said, "I ought to shoot you myself, you God damned whimpering coward." Patton was still yelling as he was hustled from the tent, while doctors and nurses gathered outside, drawn by the commotion.[41]

Alarmed by reports from hospital staff, the chief surgeon in Sicily investigated further.[42] His report quickly reached AFHQ's surgeon general, Frederick Blessé, in Algiers, who brought it to Eisenhower's attention. Patton's outbursts forced a real crisis. On the one hand, his actions were both indefensible and impossible to keep under wraps given that so many people had witnessed them. On the other, Patton was considered the army's most effective combat commander, whom Eisenhower was desperate not to lose.

Eisenhower ordered Blessé to Sicily to make his own investigation and sent with him a private letter for Patton. In it, Eisenhower called the chief surgeon's report "shocking in its allegations." He could not condone or excuse "brutality, abuse of the sick, nor exhibition of incontrollable [sic] temper in front of subordinates." Eisenhower warned Patton that "no incident of this character can be reported to me in the future," and he ordered Patton to apologize to the soldiers and the hospital personnel involved.[43] For all that, Eisenhower withheld the report and his letter from Patton's official file, and Patton remained the commander of the Seventh Army.

Eisenhower's prediction that the incidents would not stay under wraps was quickly borne out. Reporters in Sicily soon heard rumors of the second incident. The Seventh Army press corps could not descend en masse to interview the wounded soldiers and personnel at the evacuation hospital; however, four of them—Demaree Bess of the *Saturday Evening Post*, Merrill (Red) Mueller of NBC, John Charles Daly of CBS, and Albert Newman of *Newsweek*—went to the hospital to investigate. Bess wrote an account based on his interviews with patients and staff there and circulated it to the other correspondents. The group agreed not to report the story until AFHQ could be confronted with the facts.

This occurred when Bess, Mueller, and *Collier's* Quentin Reynolds flew to Algiers with Bess's report. They insisted that Patton had opened himself up to "general court martial by striking an enlisted man under his command." News of the hospital episodes had also swept through the Seventh Army. Reynolds warned Eisenhower that "there are at least 50,000 American soldiers [in Sicily] who would shoot Patton if they had the slightest chance." Bess assured Eisenhower that he was making the report on behalf of the other correspondents "in the hope of getting conditions corrected before more damage had been done."[44]

Eisenhower nonetheless resolved to do what he could to save Patton for the battles to come. To that end, he instructed Patton to apologize to his entire army if he wished to weather the storm. Patton did so, with the bizarre explanation that his reaction stemmed from an incident in the First World War. A friend who was suffering from battle stress had killed himself, and Patton believed the friend might have been saved if "more stringent measures" had been applied, which was what he had been trying to do in Sicily. Patton then wrote to Eisenhower after his contrition tour to apologize for the problems he had caused.[45]

Eisenhower also lobbied the press. Some reporters, including Kennedy, had urged the commander to allow release of the news from Algiers as the best way to manage the crisis, given how many people knew of the incident. Eisenhower had agreed in principle but feared that the Germans would make propaganda hay out of the episode. Although he did not directly ask reporters to kill the story nor explicitly instruct censors to stop it, Eisenhower's position was clear. According to an aide, the reporters who met with Eisenhower at the time, including Mueller, Kennedy, Bess, Reynolds, and Clark Lee, then of the INS "all seemed to feel, as he did, that Patton's great military record made him so valuable that he was worth saving."[46] However reluctantly and out of respect for Eisenhower, if not Patton, the reporters agreed to suppress the story.

There matters rested until late November when syndicated columnist Drew Pearson in Washington learned of the episode. In his weekly NBC broadcast Pearson ventured that the reason Patton had recently been out of sight was that Eisenhower had "severely reprimanded" him for striking a soldier in Sicily. "I don't think he will be used in combat anymore," Pearson concluded. While some in the public excused Patton's behavior, the same could not be said in the halls of Congress nor in the press. Members of Congress from both political parties demanded an investigation.[47]

When word of Pearson's broadcast reached Algiers, Major General Walter Bedell Smith, Eisenhower's gruff chief of staff, at first issued a blanket denial. Patton had not been reprimanded, Bedell Smith claimed, and still commanded the Seventh Army. Though it was technically correct that Patton had not received an official reprimand, the press in Algiers, many of whom knew the particulars, were outraged. "It would be difficult to imagine a more dishonest statement," Kennedy later wrote. Even Eisenhower insisted that Bedell Smith walk back this blanket denial, and so the next day he held a press conference at AFHQ to do just that. While he insisted that Patton had not received an official reprimand, and thus his statement of the previous night had been accurate, Bedell Smith assured reporters that Eisenhower personally had "taken the hide" off Patton.[48]

Bedell Smith's conference calmed the waters in Algiers to an extent, but some correspondents in Algiers were unmoved by his performance. They seethed over having held an important story in good faith only to find it reported stateside. Meanwhile, if the response at the Associated Press is any measure, many in the press were upset less at the army's original treatment of the matter than that a domestic radio commentator had scooped the print media on a foreign story. R. B. Chandler, the publisher of the Mobile (AL) *Register*, was especially pointed in his criticism of the Associated Press on this point. Chandler's paper editorialized on November 24 regarding the initial suppression of the story: "Here the American people have a flagrant example of how war news is withheld from them. Here is an illustration of the hush-hush that can be practiced—and is practiced—under a wartime censorship arbitrarily administered." The *Register* added: "This country's mothers and fathers did not watch their sons march off to war with the expectation that these soldiers would be cuffed about, slapped and abused by commanding generals after falling ill or wounded." The managing editor of the *Hartford Times* wrote directly to Kent Cooper to complain that trust in the AP's war reporting "has been badly shattered." Pearson's revelation had merely confirmed suspicions that the public was not being told the truth.[49]

To meet this rising chorus of complaints, Cooper instructed his deputies to investigate how the story had been handled. Joe Morton, who reported on the air war in Sicily, was certain that AFHQ censors would have stopped any dispatch about Patton, "even as a 'confidential note to desk,'" without Eisenhower's approval.[50] Ed Kennedy added that whatever the situation in August, once the Pearson story broke in November, censorship had been "very rigidly imposed." Correspondents had been allowed to report Bedell Smith's statement but little else.[51]

Charged with responding to the chorus of members complaining about the AP's "suppression" of the Patton story, Alan Gould often cited Morton's insistence that AFHQ would not have passed the story if submitted. Once Pearson's broadcast had aired, "all of us feel the Army blundered and, at the very least, displayed an appalling lack of understanding of the necessities for telling the truth."[52] Thus Gould sought to shift focus from the AP's initial failure to report the slapping incident to the army's more recent dissembling.

What did correspondents take from the Patton slapping episode? Certainly it highlighted the difficulty for the press in balancing their duty to inform the public with the desire to help (or at least not hurt) the war effort. It laid bare as well how the competitive pressures of the news business endanger the working relationship with military officials. The Patton episode also fed public suspicions that the press was manipulating or suppressing war news. Those suspicions had lingered from the days of the Creel Committee and the public remained on guard against any manipulation of information, regardless of whether through excessive censorship or through the press's self-censorship.

The Patton episode and the blowback from their bosses stateside only made reporters more skeptical of pleas to withhold stories that the army, for whatever reason, did not want released. They grew even more sensitive to how censorship (or even the threat of it) could be used to bury embarrassing facts and shield the upper echelons of the military from criticism. Although historians generally praise the fullness and accuracy of reporting during the Second World War, the Patton episode exposes persistent concern that military malfeasance, incompetence, and setbacks were being hidden. Eisenhower may have succeeded in keeping Patton as a possible field commander, but most of the press corps would never again bury a story of such importance at his behest. Eisenhower himself also redoubled efforts to make sure that reporters remained on board with the war effort. He would soon begin referring to them as "quasi-staff officers" in an effort to bring the media even more tightly into the military fold.

Eisenhower arrived in London in January 1944 to assume command of the Allied forces massing to invade the continent. At SHAEF he did not face a public relations crisis as fraught as those caused by the Darlan deal or the Patton episode, at least not until the surrender fiasco. Instead, public relations at SHAEF proved to be a low grade but chronic administrative headache, with Eisenhower never able to put in place a stable structure or the right personnel. As the army's public relations staff snowballed over time, turf wars and bureaucratic infighting became more troublesome than any direct conflict with the press. The press itself complained more about the bloated publicity bureaucracy and its shortcomings than it did headquarters strategy or battlefield performance.

In the months before D-Day, there were no less than nine overlapping US military public relations organizations in England. In addition to SHAEF (an allied entity) and ETOUSA (European Theater of Operations United States Army, the administrative headquarters for all forces in Europe), each numbered army, army group, air force, and naval fleet had its own public relations staff. They were often at odds, defending their own turf while encroaching on that of others and constantly competing for the attention of the press corps. SHAEF's public relations shop was conceived in theory as a small policy-making unit within the Publicity and Psychological Warfare Division, with most actual press supervision occurring at the operational level. However, defining the boundary between policy and operations in practice proved difficult. Almost from the start SHAEF clashed with ETOUSA, which handled public relations for the Services of Supply (SOS), the massive wing of the army that included all noncombat support units—ordinance, transport, medical, and the like—and encompassed most of the US troops in the UK. SHAEF and ETOUSA PROs constantly wrangled over who would supervise which correspondents.

Few in SHAEF had much time for ETOUSA's chief public relations officer, Colonel Justus "Jock" Lawrence, a former press agent for Samuel Goldwyn in Hollywood, who frequently claimed that since SHAEF was responsible merely for setting policy at the highest level, he was in fact in charge of everything else, including management of all the accredited correspondents in theater. SHAEF officials, and especially Colonel Ernest Dupuy, thought Lawrence had "delusions of grandeur" and was "crazy as a bedbug." Attempting to lure reporters away from SHAEF, Lawrence at one point had set up a Reporter's Service Room in Grosvenor Square serving free coffee and doughnuts at all hours and staffed by a PRO who hawked possible Service of Supply stories to all in the room. SHAEF officials were even more suspicious of the Service of Supply's chief of staff, Colonel (later Brigadier General) Royal Lord, whom Dupuy disparaged as "the Headless Horseman" and whom he thought schemed relentlessly to

Figure 2.1. Army public relations officers Thor Smith and Jack Redding playacting in front of a Christmas tree in their cottage in London. The pose suggests not all was stressful work for PROs in the long run-up to D-Day. Courtesy Eisenhower Presidential Library, Thor Smith Papers.

enhance his authority. For example, Dupuy was certain Lord was behind the effort prior to D-Day, in the end unsuccessful, to create a Public Relations Advisory Council that could, and presumably would, direct press policy and dilute if not coopt the authority of the SHAEF Public Relations Division in this area.[53]

So army public relations officials in England battled less with the press than with each other, much to the bewilderment of some reporters. To Liebling, Lawrence and Lord "tried to horn in on everything else" beyond their bailiwick.[54] Antagonisms and rivalries stretched far and wide. In fact, the diaries and letters of many public relations officers and correspondents suggest an essentially bureaucratic experience of the war. They call to mind Anthony Powell's wartime volumes of *A Dance to the Music of Time*, based on his experiences as a London-based British soldier and which, as one critic aptly stated, captured "a side of military life we seldom hear about, one of bureaucracy and back-stabbing and angling for preferment—like working for a corporation only more boring and with bosses who are more inept."[55]

While fighting these turf wars, SHAEF's Public Relations Division also suffered from conflict within. It had been created less than two months before D-Day, when Eisenhower determined at last that because of their competing missions, it made little sense to house both psychological warfare and public relations in the same unit. Having commanded the combined Publicity and Psychological Warfare divisions for Eisenhower, first in North Africa and then in London, General McClure grudgingly agreed to the change and remained as head of psychological warfare, his long-standing interest. Eisenhower then tapped a trusted friend, Brigadier General Thomas Jefferson Davis, to head up the new Public Relations Division. Davis was a highly efficient staff officer, well-liked, and an Eisenhower confidant. Although he had little actual experience in journalism, Davis proved a welcome choice and effectively oversaw the complex planning for press coverage of D-Day. Crucially, Davis was hospitalized with a severe infection just a week before the Normandy landings and was out of action for much of the summer.[56]

Acting in his stead was Colonel Dupuy who had been transferred from the War Department's Bureau of Public Relations to London to reinforce Eisenhower's staff. However, Dupuy served in Davis's place without general officer rank and the clout it carried. Public relations rivalries also took on a national cast despite Eisenhower's insistence on Allied unity. For instance, although Dupuy worked well with Brigadier William Turner, the British officer who served as assistant chief of the PRD, he detested and distrusted Air Commodore Lionel Heald, Davis's initial deputy and later head of the PRD Planning Branch. Dupuy disparaged Heald as an "accomplished liar" and a "cantankerous barrister who is not and never will be a soldier."[57]

Moreover, Dupuy often clashed with Alfred Neville, the English briga-dier in charge of public relations for Montgomery's 21st Army Group. Dupuy thought Neville "a charming gentleman," but that he could be "stubborn as a mule," feared reporters, and thought the press needed to be kept in its place. Melding British and US public relations staffs into a smoothly running organization proved difficult, nor was the PRD ever able to resolve the conflicting needs of the British and US press. Tim-ing of the daily communiqués, for example, turned out to be a particular bone of contention. The range of press deadlines for papers in British and North American time zones meant that this conflict was irreconcilable.[58] Shortly after D-Day, for another, the British began to complain of favor-itism, charging that the Americans had, against agreed policy, allowed a commercial radio transmitter onto the US beaches. For their part, the US reporters assigned to 21st Army Group headquarters complained that Montgomery's press operation seemed to run at the pleasure of the BBC.[59]

General Davis had returned to duty in August, which promised to re-store some stability to the PRD, but within twenty-four hours he was back in the hospital after a mild heart attack. Dupuy scrambled to assume his duties yet again. Recognizing that the PRD was close to crisis, Eisenhower loaned his close aide Commander (later Captain) Harry Butcher to the division. Butcher is best remembered for the detailed diary he kept for Eisenhower throughout the war and which he published in 1946 as *My Three Years with Eisenhower*. He had been a vice president of CBS be-fore the war, acting as the network's chief lobbyist in Washington. There Butcher had come to know Milton Eisenhower and, through him, Dwight and Mamie Eisenhower. Butcher and Dwight Eisenhower grew so close that their wives rented an apartment together during the wartime hous-ing shortage in Washington. A bon vivant who assured that Eisenhower's personal quarters were always well-stocked with liquor, Butcher also met with visiting dignitaries when Eisenhower was too busy to do so and ar-ranged diversions for Eisenhower in his infrequent downtime. Behind the scenes, Butcher also advised Eisenhower on press matters, often serving as an unofficial go-between with the press as during the Patton controversy. Walter Bedell Smith did not think much of Butcher, whom he considered a rival for Eisenhower's ear, and so was more than happy to release him temporarily to the PRD once it was clear that Davis's health would make it impossible for him to return to such a high-pressure job.

Meanwhile Eisenhower shopped around for a new permanent director for the troubled division. Public Relations "has been one of my hard problems of the war and I deeply regret that General Davis is incapacitated," Eisenhower confided to General Surles at the War Department.[60] Butcher, for one, admired Dupuy as an effective briefer but thought he was "showing the strain" after the strenuous summer and was at fifty-five too old for the rigors of the permanent post.[61] Surles recommended General Frank Allen who had recently been named to head the Intelligence Division for the Sixth Army Group in southern France. Eisenhower wrote to General Jacob Devers, its commander, to ask for Allen. Davis's heart attack had left the PRD in a "most critical" situation, and Eisenhower was willing to transfer the best intelligence officer he had at SHAEF to Devers as a replacement if he would give up Allen.[62] Allen took up his duties leading the PRD in October, quickly oversaw yet another staff reorganization, and

Figure 2.2. General Eisenhower meets with General Frank Allen in the Hotel Scribe in October 1944, soon after his appointment as Director of SHAEF's Public Relations Division. Allen was brought in to bring some stability to the PRD after months of uncertain leadership. Courtesy National Archives (111-SC-443081).

remained in that position until the end of the war without ever fully gaining the trust of the press corps.

Despite the upheavals, the PRD did succeed in erecting the systemic framework through which correspondents reported the war. Accredited reporters fell into two categories—those remaining in England and those assigned to forces on the continent. Those who remained in England were subdivided into those accredited to SHAEF and those only accredited to ETOUSA to report on the SOS and other US troops stationed in the United Kingdom.

SHAEF's press operations moved from Grosvenor Square to a wing of Senate House at the invitation of the Ministry of Information a month before D-Day. The University of London's nineteen-story art deco landmark would remain the hub of press activity for the remainder of the war and served as SHAEF press headquarters until the PRD moved to Paris in September 1944. From the run-up to D-Day until the end of the war, SHAEF PROs met routinely with a small group of correspondents to iron out policy and technical issues. What disagreements surfaced often had to do with how many and which reporters were permitted to cross the Channel to the war zone.[63]

Many of the procedures developed for press coverage of D-Day from headquarters in London were to remain much the same for the remainder of the war. In the preparations for D-Day authorities had focused on assuring that there would be sufficient cable capacity and personnel to handle the enormous traffic expected from London to the United States. After D-Day, PRD issued communiqués twice daily, held background briefings, and staffed an Information Room in Senate House with maps, biographies of the principal Allied commanders, descriptions and occasional models of war equipment, and other background materials useful in writing the daily headquarters story. Correspondents were also provided a large work room adjacent to the censorship station to facilitate conversations with censors when issues arose. Once cleared, copy was then sent to commercial cable companies by dispatch rider. "Mailers," or feature stories that were less sensitive, were sent to the United States on air force flights. Correspondents with the news agencies and larger newspapers also worked out of permanent offices on Fleet Street, where censors were stationed at the direct lines to cable heads.

The working lives of those correspondents who did make it across the Channel to cover the armies in the field centered on the press camp. The system that McClure and Phillips had adapted from the British and instituted in North Africa became the basis of field reporting from Europe. While each camp included lodging, workspace, messes, censors, and a motor pool for correspondents to use, the key component was access to a high-speed radio transmitter either in or adjacent to the camp, usually supplied and staffed by a commercial wireless company. Such transmitters were considered portable, but it required several large trucks to transport all the gear needed for both Morse and voice transmission to London or the United States. Access to and the effectiveness of these transmitters often seemed more of a concern to the war correspondents and PROs in Northwestern Europe than the contents of the stories those transmitters sent.

To begin there were two press camps in Normandy, one with the United States First Army and the other with the British Second Army, which also serviced Montgomery's 21st Army Group forward headquarters. As additional armies poured into France, beginning with Patton's Third Army in July, new press camps were added. By the end of the war the Allies fielded nine armies arrayed in three army groups, each army and army group running its own press camp. The first press camps in Normandy were situated within a few miles of the front lines due to the cramped lodgment area; given the speed of the Allied advance into Germany in 1945, though, during the last months of the war press camps were often stuck well behind the front, leading correspondents to complain of spending most of their time in freezing jeeps driving to and from the front line. Occasionally reporters would spend a night or two in the field with troops, but the presence of the transmitter kept them more closely tied to the press camps. The image of reporters, especially field reporters, stoically typing away in their muddy foxholes is a misleading one. Even Ernie Pyle would typically go to the front only for short stints, then return to camp well behind the lines to write his columns.

Camp comfort and efficiency varied considerably, depending on the nature of the facilities, the quality of the PROs running them, and even the season. Most were located in hotels or chateaus, often with tents in adjacent fields used as sleeping quarters. Returning to Normandy ten years

Figure 2.3. Lieutenant Colonels Jack Redding (left) and Thor Smith, in battle dress, while on a tour of forward press camps in 1944. This was a rare trip away from SHAEF headquarters. The two were close enough to write several books together. Courtesy Eisenhower Presidential Library, Thor Smith Papers.

after the war, Liebling remembered the First Army press camp at Vouilly as almost idyllic. It was located on a prosperous farm, with a moated manor house known locally as "le Chateau," reached by a long tree-lined lane. The press room was in the Chateau's salon and was larger than the city room of the *Providence Journal* where Liebling had worked years before. The reporters slept in large tents that the army had pitched in an adjacent cow pasture: "Every morning during the fighting for St. Lô, we would have a large, hot breakfast in the mess tent and then climb into jeeps, two or three correspondents to a driver, and take off for the battlefield. The mess tent was our ace good-will builder with the farmers; it was run cafeteria style, and all of us generally left a lot on our plates. The swill was of a magnificence unparalleled in that thrifty countryside, and the farmers carted it away for their young pigs."[64]

Later in the war, PRO Barney Oldfield did his best to entice reporters to cover the Ninth Army by operating a press camp at the four-star Hotel de Lévrier et l'Aigle Noir in Maastricht. Having attracted a contingent of reporters from Paris, he then had to instruct the chef to make his food less appetizing so that the correspondents would be less reluctant to leave for the field.[65] Major James Quirk, Third Army's PRO after the liberation of Paris, had a similar experience in Germany months later. He wrote to his wife that the press camp was a beehive of activity, "like election day," and that although the camp frequently moved he usually enjoyed electricity, hot water, a dry bed, and plentiful food. Conditions were so comfortable that he had to coax some of visiting press junketeers (he mentioned Lowell Thomas by name) into leaving the camp to tour the front line.[66]

Covering the First Army as it entered Germany, NBC's George Hicks painted a bleaker picture of press camp life. Returning to the camp after a leave "was like taking on a burden again when you've been rid of it for

Figure 2.4. General Frank Allen, Brigadier William Turner, and Colonel Ernest Dupuy at the Hotel Scribe. Turner and Dupuy had been involved in SHAEF PRD from the beginning; Allen came in after the liberation of Paris to bring some discipline and organizational coherence to the Public Relations Division. Allen, who had little experience in public relations, relied heavily on Turner and Dupuy, fellow career officers, to deal with the press corps. Courtesy United States Army Heritage and Education Center, Richard H. Merrick Papers, Carlisle, PA.

a while . . . it is like a tired runner who again has to start running." Hicks was certain "we are going to pay the price for this thing—all people, in the fatigue and despair which is bound to come afterwards." Two days later, Hicks apologized in a letter home for "just sort of mumbling out loud because I am tired and dirty." The next day he confided that he was "writing again by candlelight in our broken battered house. But it is all a lot better than being at the front itself. All the newspaper guys sitting around and talking a little and the censors in conference and some dope coming over the field telephone about the latest movements for the news stories."[67]

In whatever circumstances, from D-Day until the German surrender reporters and military officials had established a basic working relationship that seemed to satisfy the requirements of both groups. Unlike in any previous war, Allied officials felt free to confide in reporters, so confident were they that censorship at the source would catch any damaging leaks. It also helped that Generals Eisenhower and Bradley were unusually accommodating to the press. For example, Robert J. Casey of the *Chicago Daily News* was pleasantly surprised when just before the offensive that finally broke the German defense in Normandy, Bradley laid out his entire plan to the First Army reporters. Casey was even more impressed the next day, when after Allied planes had mistakenly bombed their own lines and stalled the attack, Bradley made no excuses. "We tried it and it didn't work," he told the correspondents. "I am sorry, gentlemen. We shall try it again."[68]

There were occasional bumps in the road. These came in the form of stories suppressed, from the pointless Allied bombing of Caen in July virtually destroying the city, to the news blackout imposed during the first days of the Battle of the Bulge. A nasty spat broke out between General Montgomery and the press when he imposed a similar news blackout in Normandy during an Allied offensive. Later that summer Eisenhower accused the press of creating dissension in the Allied ranks when reports surfaced that Montgomery had been effectively demoted as commander of all Allied ground forces with the activation of the US 12th Army Group, which was not under his command. At least once, with the rush into Paris, the military's supervision of the press seemed to break down entirely.

One contentious issue throughout the war was the inconsistency rather than the severity of censorship rulings. Information that was passed at one location was often stopped at another. If SHAEF, for example, allowed release of a story that one of the field armies was holding, then headquarters reporters could and would beat reporters in the field to the story. Those field reporters then blamed the army. The AP's Ed Ball, for one, was furious when officials at SHAEF held up for twelve hours release of his account of the Third Army's crossing of the Rhine, losing him an important beat.[69] Such skirmishes only highlight the different experiences of and occasional conflicts between the war correspondents who covered headquarters and those in the field.

Was the Second World War the "best reported war in history," as Kent Cooper and others claimed at the time? It certainly represented an improvement over the First World War. The sheer volume of news dwarfed any previous war. Technological changes also improved the speed with which information could move. Foremost among those was the widespread use of radio broadcasting and messaging. The first made it all but impossible to withhold news of major events from the public; the second made it possible for correspondents to use transmitters far from actual cable heads to dispatch stories. While clearly there was a greater volume of news, whether it was more accurate and informative than in past conflicts remains a question. Many reporters accepted the notion, albeit with some misgivings, that in the era of total war journalism needed to aid the country's war effort. John Steinbeck, for example, looked back on his dispatches from Italy during the war with some regret, not for what he reported but for what he chose to omit. "It is in the things not mentioned that the untruth lies," Steinbeck wrote, a sentiment that would have been shared by those reporters who had buried the Patton story, for instance. Fletcher Pratt's provocative assessment immediately after the war was that such journalistic self-censorship combined with strict military censorship had left the country with the sense that "the war was won without a single mistake, by a command consisting exclusively of geniuses."[70] Few shared Pratt's mordant view, but he did capture the widespread conviction that much had been withheld from the US public during the war.

However great the common cause, the media and the military could never escape entirely the frictions caused by their conflicting information imperatives—the press's to reveal and the military's to conceal. More than any personal enmity, this institutional tension accounts for the greater share of what wariness existed in the relationships between reporters and PROs. Certainly, individual journalists and military officials became friends or continued friendships established before the war. Harry Butcher, for one, had many friends in the press corps, as did the PRO Barney Old-field. Photojournalist Robert Capa's best friend during the war was the air corps PRO Chris Scott. A correspondent even served as the best man at a PRO's wedding in England. Still, it remains a curious fact that while correspondents and PROs often came from the same background, traveled in the same social circles, and even had worked for the same companies before the war, they kept their distance. There are surprisingly few references to PROs by name in reporters' memoirs, for example, and vice versa. By May 1945, and with the war all but won, the ties that bound the military and the press together to fight the country's enemies were beginning to unravel.

3

Reims

Various German officials had been quietly extending peace feelers to the Allies by January 1945. In February, German commanders in Italy arranged secret meetings with US and British representatives to explore a possible surrender, but the Soviets, always wary of such a separate peace, objected when they got wind of the meetings and such contacts came to nothing. There matters remained until early April when Heinrich Himmler's staff made similar overtures in Northwestern Europe. By the middle of the month the US military alerted the Soviets that they expected any number of localized surrenders shortly. The Germans maneuvered to pit the British and Americans against the Soviets, hoping at a minimum that stalling for time would allow German soldiers and civilians to move westward ahead of the advancing Russians. Eisenhower alerted forces in the field that while they could accept local surrenders, anything more comprehensive needed to be cleared through SHAEF.[1]

As it became clear that the question was when precisely and not if Germany would surrender, officials throughout the government tried to squelch any premature peace rumors. The United Press's notorious misreporting of the World War I armistice still weighed on the minds of many in the press, and especially in the agencies, some twenty-seven years after the embarrassing miscue. A similar mistake would mortify the Associated Press in 1945 and affect its handling of the Kennedy surrender story.

The UP in Paris had cabled New York on November 7, 1918 that the Allied commander, Marshal Ferdinand Foch, had negotiated an armistice with German military envoys. The cable was signed by Roy Howard, the president of the United Press Association, who happened to be in the French capital. The flash dispatch was carried in the late editions of afternoon newspapers even though Secretary of State Robert Lansing had denied the story.

However, it soon became clear that Howard had cabled the flash an hour before Foch and the German envoys had met, apparently mistaking for a general armistice the temporary cease-fire called along a section of the front to allow the German emissaries to cross. The UP had also received a second wire from Howard describing crowds celebrating in Brest and took this as confirming the first report. This message had reached New York shortly before noon and was quickly retransmitted to subscribers. By mid-afternoon, extra editions proclaiming the armistice hit newsstands, and celebrations erupted across the country. In New York, office workers tore up wastepaper and threw it from office windows in what might have been the first such ticker tape display in that city's history.[2] The public, already weary of the war, was more than happy to believe the news and so ignored the State Department's denial.

The next day the United Press grudgingly admitted its mistake after the British and French conceded that no armistice had been agreed. The agency blamed Vice Admiral Henry B. Wilson, the commander of US naval forces in France, who had informed a newspaper in Brest that the armistice had been signed, only later to discover that this information had not been confirmed. The UP wire carried Wilson's statement that he had made his initial announcement believing it to be true, and that the United Press had "acted in perfect good faith" and thus was not responsible for the error.[3]

The damage had already been done. Newspapers that had not picked up the story were more than happy to decry the UP's mistake. Several claimed that Howard, as an accredited war correspondent in uniform, should be court-martialed. Others labeled the UP's actions traitorous.[4] The Associated Press reveled in taking its rival to task. "Millions of Americans realized today that they had been hoaxed into celebrating the end of the war," it observed with barely repressed glee. "The Associated Press did not receive nor distribute any of the dispatches which misled the American people into celebrating the greatest hoax of recent years." The AP gloated that its own reporting had exposed the UP's mistake.[5]

Memories were long and so after the liberation of Paris in 1944, the War Department alerted SHAEF that the Office of War Information had met with all the US news agencies and radio networks in an attempt to forestall a repeat of the "abortive celebrations such as obtained at the end of the last war." Washington had decided that the best way to avoid a repeat would be to designate SHAEF itself as the controlling authority on such an announcement. Harry Butcher in Paris instructed correspondents to check with SHAEF PRD to confirm any peace rumors that came their way. Little more was said about the issue throughout the winter. With the war's end in sight and not wanting to be caught out as the United Press had been in 1918, Kent Cooper warned AP members in mid-April that "with further major military developments obviously imminent there are bound to be rumors and reports leading to erroneous or premature conclusions." The New York office would do everything "within its capacity to keep matters in focus."[6]

That focus was lost within weeks. On the morning of April 28, with German units surrendering daily and anticipation of victory at a fever pitch, the *New York Times* reported that Washington believed that a general surrender was imminent. That afternoon the AP released a story written by Flora Lewis of its Washington bureau stating that administration officials were expecting peace in Europe at any time. A *San Francisco Chronicle* reporter covering the United Nations conference then in session in that city shared Lewis's wire story with Secretary of State Edward Stettinius, who then passed it on to Senator Tom Connolly of Texas, the vice chairman of the US delegation.[7]

Jack Bell was the AP reporter covering the conference. Bell was in the press area on the mezzanine and noticed that Connolly and Stettinius scurried off the floor after receiving the note. Bell intercepted them in a hallway to ask what was happening. According to Bell, Connolly said that he expected the Germans to surrender at any moment. Bell filed a dispatch that evening with the news that a high US official had stated that the war in Europe was over. This was truthful but misleading. President Truman announced an hour and a half later that the Germans, in fact, had not yet surrendered, but the AP flash had already prompted many newspapers (the *New York Times, Chicago Tribune,* and *New York Herald Tribune* among them) to publish extra editions with banner headlines proclaiming the surrender. The flash was also broadcast on the radio, sparking celebrations across the country.

The AP quickly apologized for its mistake in not seeking confirmation before putting the story on the wire. It insisted, though, that its reporting had been accurate. Connolly, for his part, denied ever saying that the Germans had surrendered, and the UP played up the premature celebrations after the AP's report. In a message to Kent Cooper the day after the erroneous story, Gillis Purcell, director of the Canadian Press news agency affiliated with the AP, wrote that the United Press was "BITTERLY ATTEMPTING TO SMEAR" its rival. Purcell mentioned the *New York Herald Tribune*'s jibe that the United Press "has been waiting since 8 P.M. Nov. 7, 1918" (the date of the UP's armistice mistake) for the chance to blame the AP for such a blunder. German propagandists could not resist reporting that the police intervened in New York to break up the wild celebrations. "Today American journalists described the whole affair as the biggest stupidity in American history," bloviated a German radio propagandist.[8]

Word of the San Francisco debacle quickly reached Paris. Ernest Dupuy wrote to his wife that he had been up half the night ("we had quite a party," as he sarcastically phrased it) dealing with questions from the press in the wake of the "San Francisco canard about unconditional surrender."[9] Taking place just days before the actual surrender, this gaffe only contributed to the AP's defensiveness after the Kennedy release.

Just as things were coming to a head, yet another incident caused SHAEF additional headaches and further complicated its planning. On April 24, SHAEF had asked the Russians for permission to send a press contingent to Berlin after its capture. Twenty-three correspondents would be needed at a minimum, but more would be desirable to cover "one of the world's greatest news events."[10] The next day US and Russian forces made contact at the Elbe River near Torgau, splitting Germany in half.

Two reporters heard of the Allied link-up at the Elbe while covering the capture of Nuremberg a few hundred miles to the south. They, together with other enterprising journalists, headed toward Torgau, on the east bank of the Elbe, for the official ceremonies marking the event.

Andrew Tully was a young reporter for the *Boston Traveler* attached to the Third Army's 26th Division; Virginia Irwin worked for Joseph Pulitzer's *St. Louis Post-Dispatch* and was attached to the Ninth Air Force. Irwin had arrived in France in July 1944 and with the handful of other women correspondents in theater had proved a thorn in the side of public relations officers, protesting against and occasionally defying the army's insistence they confine themselves to reporting on uniformed women all of whom served behind the front lines—Women's Army Corps personnel (WACs) working in office pools, nurses assigned to hospitals, and the like.[11]

Neither Tully nor Irwin had permission to be in the First Army zone let alone travel into Russian-controlled territory, but on the morning of April 27 they and their G.I. driver left Nuremberg. Hours later, they cajoled some Russian troops into ferrying their jeep across the Elbe to witness the historic handshake and join in the raucous festivities.[12] After any number of vodka toasts, Tully impulsively suggested that they carry on to Berlin, and Irwin agreed. They again set off with their driver, this time for the German capital, some seventy miles away. Tully admitted that their situation "was at least bordering on the illegal. Although there had been no direct order forbidding American correspondents to go to Berlin, we also had no official permission to do so."[13]

With only their SHAEF cards for identification and fearing they would be mistaken for spies, the reporters were guided by a road map which very quickly proved useless, if for no other reason than the German-language signposts had already been replaced with Cyrillic ones. Neither reporter spoke nor read Russian. They alternately encountered empty roads and ones crowded with Russian troops in a motley collection of vehicles, from US-made trucks to horse-drawn carts. The Russians were heading toward Berlin. Masses of refugees headed in the opposite direction. Gunfire occasionally crackled in the distance. Tully later admitted it was "the craziest thing I have ever done."

Tully and Irwin mounted a makeshift US flag on the jeep and shouted "Americanski" to any Russian soldier they happened across. The first thirty miles of the trip passed without incident, but eventually they were flagged down by a "very stern" Russian MP who scrutinized their SHAEF identity cards for several minutes before allowing them to proceed. In another town they were stopped by a Mongolian sergeant, but Irwin "smiled her best and most charming smile," and the sergeant waved them forward. "Keep smiling," Tully urged Irwin. A flat tire late in the afternoon caused even more anxiety as "a group of Russian soldiers . . . gathered around us," Tully later recounted, "fondling wicked looking riot guns."

That evening Tully and Irwin reached a Russian outpost within the city limits and became the first Americans to enter Berlin, three days before Adolf Hitler's suicide. A Russian lieutenant took them to his commander, a young major with snow-white hair. Tully and the commander were able to communicate in broken French and before long the US reporters found themselves in their jeep careening toward the commander's headquarters. The Americans were treated there to their second Russian banquet of the day, again accompanied by a stream of vodka as they toasted the late President Franklin D. Roosevelt, Premier Joseph Stalin, the other Allied leaders, and even the Americans' jeep.[14]

The next day Tully and Irwin made two forays toward the city center, first on their own and then accompanied by a Russian guide, but both times were driven back by sniper fire. After several hours of this, they decided that they had seen enough. Tully and Irwin headed back toward the US lines, eager to cash in on their scoop. The reporters reached the Elbe as the light faded, then spent the night hiding near the river with two British soldiers who had been liberated from a POW camp nearby. At daybreak, and after Russian troops manning a ferry had refused them passage, Irwin hailed some US soldiers on the west bank with the plea, "I'm an American woman, come across and get me from these Russians."[15]

When Tully and Irwin made it back to the nearest press camp at Weimar, censors there refused to process their stories. Public relations officers with the Ninth Air Force whom Irwin had befriended were able to get the reporters aboard a plane bound for Paris, where they planned to cable their stories directly to the United States. Once they reached the Hotel Scribe, however, a furious Dupuy suspended them on the grounds that they had strayed from the zone to which they were accredited. He also impounded their copy as "CAPABLE OF EMBARRASSING RELA-TIONS BETWEEN ALLIED NATIONS."[16]

Tully and Irwin's Berlin trip quickly proved "a ring-tailed snafu" for Dupuy, especially when others in the SHAEF press corps came to the re-porters' defense. More than one correspondent complained that Tully and Irwin's stories had been unfairly withheld since even PRD acknowledged that the dispatches did not violate any announced censorship stop. Dupuy himself disparaged their stories as of "no news interest; they were travel-ogs with no pertinent facts about conditions in the city itself."[17]

The two correspondents pleaded with army officials either to pass the stories or, in a sign of their increasing desperation, to disaccredit them and send them home, in the mistaken belief that they could there publish their dispatches free from censorship. By the time the stories were eventually re-leased on May 8, they had been overshadowed by the German surrender. Tully and Irwin were summarily disaccredited and ordered back to the United States. Of SHAEF's response to her trip to Berlin, Irwin could only fume that "it has been the greatest exhibition of bungling I ever saw in my life. They treated you as if you were a half witted child."[18]

The only people more irritated by Tully and Irwin's misadventure than Dupuy and his PRD colleagues were the Russians themselves. Moscow was further angered when four other US reporters—John Groth of *Parade*, Seymour Freiden of the New York *Herald Tribune*, Ernie Leiser of *Stars and Stripes*, and Mack Morris of *Yank*—made a similar foray into Berlin days later. This was particularly galling to SHAEF PRD since two of the reporters were soldiers working for army publications. Groth and Freiden were disaccredited with Tully and Irwin on May 8 and ordered home; presumably Leiser and Morris were disciplined by their army supe-riors.[19] The Russians thereafter demanded to vet each individual reporter intending to go to Berlin rather than the news organizations for which they worked.[20] When presented with that list, the Russians further stalled on the Allied request until US occupation forces actually arrived in the city in July. In essence, all of the PRD's planning for press coverage of the fall of Berlin came to naught. Moreover, a restive press corps was increasingly undeterred by SHAEF admonitions. For their part, Dupuy and others in the PRD were losing patience with any perceived press misbehavior or boundary pushing.

By the first week in May, all at the Hotel Scribe were on edge. Kennedy, for one, had been working without much rest for more than a month. Tension over the anticipated end of the war was mounting, in Dupuy's words, "like the slow but inexorable winding of a spring." The PRD had installed a klaxon system in the hotel, dubbed the hog-caller, to alert reporters when information was about to be issued—one blast for a routine announcement, three blasts for anything major. By May Dupuy was noting "the jitteriness of correspondents when they rush to a 3-honk alarm."[21]

While the PRD continued to work from Paris and the bulk of the sprawling SHAEF bureaucracy remained at the Trianon Palace Hotel and other buildings in Versailles, by May 1 Eisenhower and most of the senior leadership had moved to SHAEF's forward command post in Reims, the cathedral city ninety miles northeast of Paris in the heart of the Champagne region. SHAEF had requisitioned the Collège Moderne et Technique de Garcons, a technical training school for boys, which the Germans had also used as a headquarters. SHAEF came to refer to the school as the "Ecole Professionelle" after one of the programs within the college (Ecole Professionelle et Ecole Practique de Commerce et d'Industrie). Because it was clad in red brick, many reporters could not resist calling it the "little red schoolhouse" even though the three-story structure built in 1931 filled a city block, could house as many as fifteen hundred students, and contained more floor space than SHAEF's headquarters in Versailles. SHAEF personnel had begun occupying the building in February 1945; by the time of the surrender it housed upward of two thousand SHAEF staffers.[22]

There, too, nerves were strained. The first week in May at Reims was the "most hectic of the war," Walter Bedell Smith recalled. "Scarcely anyone left headquarters. We ate when we felt hungry, slept when we could no longer keep awake. Twelve o'clock on the dial of a watch might mean noon or midnight. A man looked toward the window to find out." Butcher was shuttling between Reims and Paris; on May 1 he noted that "rumors of peace are sweeping Allied capitals," increasing the strain on Eisenhower, his staff, and the correspondents in Europe.[23]

Concerted German resistance had all but ended everywhere except the Eastern Front, and each new day brought word of increasingly sizeable German forces agreeing to cease-fires or outright surrenders. The German

Figure 3.1. A platoon of German prisoners is marched past the front entrance of the Ecole Professionelle in Reims two weeks after the surrender. The school was the site of SHAEF's forward headquarters and of the German surrender. Reporters often referred to the building as the "little red schoolhouse," but it filled a city block. Courtesy National Archives (111-SC-374878).

command structure had virtually disintegrated, with German generals stumbling over each other in their haste to surrender. On May 2, Field Marshal Albert Kesselring alerted the Allies that he was prepared to capitulate in Italy. He requested, though, that any announcement to that effect be delayed by forty-eight hours. After consulting Washington, Eisenhower cabled Harold Alexander, the commander in Italy, ordering the "earliest possible announcement that does not jeopardize consummation of the surrender." Eisenhower surmised that Kesselring had requested the delay because he anticipated a change in the German government or else wanted to alert all of his forces before the surrender was announced publicly. In either case, less than a week before the Reims ceremony, it was clear that none of the Allied military leaders in either Europe or Washington wanted to delay announcement of a major German surrender. At the same time, Washington had cabled Eisenhower warning him that "in connection with the possible over-all surrender of the German Forces, the Joint Chiefs of Staff desire that every precaution be taken to prevent the release of any information of such an event prior to its announcement simultaneously by the 3 Governments." The next day the Joint Chiefs repeated this warning to Eisenhower directly. Evidently even the Allied high command was not of one mind about how best to handle the collapse of the Third Reich.[24]

Also on May 2, Admiral Karl Dönitz, successor to Hitler as head of the German state, assessed the shrinking Reich. In mid-April he and the remnants of the Ober Kommando der Wermacht (OKW), the German army's high command, including its chief, Field Marshal Wilhelm Keitel and its chief of operations, General Alfred Jodl, had fled Berlin heading north. They eventually stopped at Flensburg, the northernmost German town bordering Denmark. Flensburg was reasonably close to Hamburg, the last major city still under German control. From there the admiral clung to the hope that he could surrender to the Western Allies to escape the wrath of the Soviets, even as the futility of further resistance became harder to ignore by early May.[25]

At midday on May 3, envoys from the German forces arrayed against Field Marshall Bernard Montgomery's 21st Army Group arrived at his headquarters on the windswept Lüneburg Heath in northwestern Germany. Dönitz had sent four officers, led by Admiral General Hans-Georg von Friedeburg, his successor as head of the navy, who all sat in their field car "waxen-faced, tense and bolt upright," according to the *Daily Express*'s Alan Moorehead, "the perfect caricature of the Junker officer on parade. Monocles, thin, tight contemptuous lips, jack-boots, long gray belted coats, a general atmosphere of pent-up defiance." Friedeburg proposed surrendering to the British the three German armies hundreds of miles away facing the Russians, an offer Montgomery rejected out of hand, insisting that those armies must surrender to the Soviets. Montgomery inferred that Dönitz would not have sent such a high-ranking delegation if he had wished merely to negotiate a local agreement, and so the British commander countered that he would accept the surrender of all the German forces facing him in northern Germany. When Montgomery sent his account of this meeting to Reims, Eisenhower again reiterated that any such surrender must include the Russians.[26]

Montgomery's offer surprised Friedeburg, who was forced to admit that he did not have the authority to accept it. Ever the showman, Montgomery then produced a detailed battle map of the front and suggested that the Germans may not have grasped their precarious situation. Given the chaotic state of German communications and the wishful thinking of OKW in Flensburg, the extent of the German collapse detailed on the map came as a shock to Friedeburg. Montgomery advised the Germans to have a meal and consider their options, or lack of them. Friedeburg was heard to weep uncontrollably while dining, Montgomery's map having had its desired effect.[27] After lunch Montgomery stressed again that a surrender of those troops opposing 21st Army Group needed to occur before starting negotiations on a more comprehensive agreement.

Friedeburg then drove back to Flensburg to consult with Dönitz. He warned his superiors that the Western Allies' patience with German delaying tactics had ended and that they rejected out of hand an overall surrender unless it included the Russians. A forlorn Friedeburg returned to Lüneburg Heath the next day, May 4, to signal the Germans' agreement to a surrender limited to those forces opposing 21st Army Group. Documents were signed in a ceremony carefully choreographed by Montgomery in a rainswept tent described as being "lit like a Hollywood film set." Relishing the moment, Montgomery conducted the ceremony personally, in Moorehead's view "rather like a schoolmaster taking [giving] an oral exam." The Germans sat stone-faced and uncomprehending as Montgomery spent several minutes reading aloud an English version of the surrender document. The cessation of hostilities was to occur the next morning, five years and eight months after the war between Britain and Germany had begun. Once this was agreed, Friedeburg let it be known that General Jodl was on his way to Lüneburg to discuss the surrender of all German forces. Montgomery told the Germans that if so they would need to deal with Eisenhower as Supreme Commander.[28]

News of the Germans' appearance at Montgomery's headquarters had reached the press corps in Paris, and by mid-afternoon on May 4 both the press and their military handlers were on tenterhooks. In fact, the hog-caller at the Scribe had been going off repeatedly alerting reporters to a succession of local surrenders. To Dupuy, that day "the Nazi world was ripped apart, chunk by chunk." Butcher had returned to Paris from Reims but almost immediately had an "uneasy feeling that somewhere something was happening that I was missing." After learning from a censor who had been in touch with 21st Army Group that something significant was happening on Lüneburg Heath, Butcher decided to head back to SHAEF Forward.[29]

While he was en route, official word of the German surrender to Montgomery was released at the Scribe, prompting the typical mad rush by the news agencies to be the first to file. Dupuy was puzzled by Ed Kennedy's nonchalance in joining this race. He had noticed similar behavior in other AP reporters at recent read-outs, but he knew AP reporters in the field at that point in the war often could file directly to New York well in advance of announcements in Paris. The AP in New York would then contact Kennedy as bureau chief to alert him that such stories had already been received, and so he could avoid the demeaning scramble to file. However, in this case, Dupuy knew that the Lüneburg surrender had not yet been announced by 21st Army Group. He wondered how the AP had been well ahead of its competitors with the wire story even though both the UP and the INS reporters had actually filed in Paris before the AP. "Censorship began to scratch its head; how could AP do it?" Dupuy made a mental note to investigate but soon was overwhelmed by the rush of events.[30]

Cables in the Associated Press archives coupled with the testimony of one of Dupuy's colleagues yield a likely answer to Dupuy's question, one that lingered for years. According to the PRD's Thor Smith, the Signal Corps had succeeded after many delays in laying a cross-channel telephone cable connecting Paris to London in late April. It was intended for military use, but the trunk line was tied in at both ends to civilian as well as military exchanges. Before long army operators in Paris were using this line to contact girlfriends and others in England. In theory these transmissions should have been censored, but SHAEF security authorities had grown lax as victory approached and so had yet to put such monitoring in place.[31]

Robert Bunnelle in London sent a service message to Kennedy in Paris congratulating him on the Paris bureau's scoop of the German surrender to Montgomery:

YOUR FLASH TEN MINUTES AHEAD OF REUTERS FIRST AN-
NOUNCEMENT WHICH WAS INCOMPLETE THUS GIVING AP-
WORLD EVEN WIDER ADVANTAGE ON FULL STORY STOP PLEASE
CONTINUE USE PHONE SUCH BIG DEVELOPMENTS STOP CON-
GRATULATIONS FINE WORK.[32]

That Kennedy, in this instance, used the phone line described by Smith—evidently the only telephone connection between Paris and London not surveilled by military censors—is further indicated by a subsequent cable Kennedy received from the AP in New York:

> THAT TELEPHONE TIE WITH LONDON ONE WARS BEST JOBS PLANNING COORDINATION GAVE ASSOCIATED SMASHING BEAT SURRENDER STOP LEAST FOUR MINUTES AHEAD FIELD RADIO AND NETWORKS AND SEVEN TO TWENTY AHEAD OTHER PRESS SERVICES CONGRATULATIONS THANKS ALL CONCERNED.

A handwritten note on the bottom of this cable written by AP staffer Austin Bealmear hints that it was just this telephone line that Kennedy used three days later to get out the German surrender story: "All Hands—Suggest we keep this in the family so we can use it again without opposition getting wise."[33]

These cables indicate that several days before the German surrender the AP had discovered a means to bypass SHAEF censorship, had used it to scoop its competitors, and was at least anticipating doing the same again. As such, they support those who contend that competitive zeal rather than the public's right to know motivated Kennedy on May 7, even if much other evidence does not. At a minimum they provide further proof, if such were needed, of the intense competition fueling wire service reporting at the time, and the lengths to which the agencies would go to achieve even the smallest advantage. Even a sixty-second advantage could be valuable in an environment where the first story off the wire was the one a newspaper usually carried. At the same time he criticized Kennedy for the surrender story, J. C. Oestreicher, the foreign editor of the International News Service, crowed about the one minute beat the INS had scored on the Normandy invasion. That scoop had been achieved when the INS's Kingsbury Smith had used a coded message (such were expressly forbidden by military authorities) to alert Oestreicher of the impending invasion announcement, rendering the INS's charge that Kennedy had defied military authorities more than a bit hypocritical.[34]

The atmosphere was even more tense at SHAEF Forward when Butcher drove into Reims late on the afternoon of May 4. Eisenhower was awaiting a call from Montgomery with the latest word regarding the German maneuvering toward surrender. When the call finally came at seven o'clock, Eisenhower told Montgomery that Friedeburg and his party could proceed to Reims, but only if the German delegation had authority from Dönitz to negotiate an all-fronts surrender. Eisenhower left it to Bedell Smith to arrange transportation for the Germans from Lüneburg to Reims if such assurances were forthcoming.[35]

Eisenhower then returned to his quarters, his Scottish terrier nipping at his heels. As he sat down to eat, Eisenhower took a call from his chief of staff alerting him that the Germans were being flown to Reims and would arrive shortly before noon the next day, Saturday, weather permitting.[36] Montgomery believed that Friedeburg now had the authority to negotiate a surrender on all fronts. Although not certain of this, he advised that it was worth the effort to bring the Germans to Reims.

After dinner Eisenhower and Butcher drafted a brief public statement which Butcher dictated to Dupuy at the Scribe. Dupuy released this to the press at 10:30 p.m., announcing that German resistance on the Western Front had disintegrated. "On land, sea, and air the Germans are thoroughly whipped," the statement read. "Their only recourse is to surrender." Minutes after finishing with the press, Dupuy received a call from Brigadier Neville at 21st Army Group, who was furious that the British had not been allowed to make the announcement. Dupuy, who had locked horns with Neville more than once, could only reply that this had been by order of the Supreme Commander. Allied public relations personnel apparently continued to snipe at each other to the end.[37]

Butcher was also on the phone to General Allen in Paris several times throughout the evening of May 4. If the Germans were coming only to negotiate, there would be no need for the press to trek to Reims; if they intended to surrender, though, Butcher warned that SHAEF would catch hell if reporters were not on the scene. Shortly before midnight Allen met with senior staff outside his bedroom at the Chatham Hotel. Dupuy, Brigadier Turner, Lieutenant Colonel S. R. (Roy) Pawley, and SHAEF's chief censor, the British Colonel George Warden, arrived from the Scribe. Allen related to them the gist of Butcher's calls and stressed that he still did not know whether the army would allow any of the SHAEF press corps into Reims.[38]

Roy Pawley was the former news editor of the *Daily Telegraph* who represented British interests in the PRD's Press Policy Branch, and he fretted over the absence of journalists in Reims. The pool reporter covering

SHAEF Forward, the only journalist in Reims at the time, happened to be a serviceman, Sergeant Charles Kiley, of the army's own newspaper *Stars and Stripes*. Pawley reminded those huddled in the hallway that some weeks earlier he had advised that even if Eisenhower and Bedell Smith banned the press corps from the surrender ceremony, the PRD should at least make sure that PROs attended who were also experienced journalists and could report back to the press corps.

At this point PRD backbiting flared again. Dupuy interjected that the Planning Branch should have prepared for a formal surrender long ago but had not. "Now, it appeared, the unexpected had happened and there was no plan for it," he complained, pointing the finger at his nemesis, Anthony Heald, head of the Planning Branch. Dupuy warned that an irate press corps would make the PRD as a whole pay for Heald's mistake. After the war, Dupuy would bemoan the fact that the Planning Branch "in its ivory tower, had never worked out, as it should have done at the very least, a staff study affirming the necessity of world press coverage of a formal surrender." Had Bedell Smith been given such a plan to consider ahead of time, he "could have weighed it calmly" and "would doubtless have approved." The PRD would "pay through the nose" for this omission.[39]

Allen ordered Pawley himself to Reims to cover whatever might happen there. Pawley cautioned that the US press would distrust any such "one man account," especially if that one man happened to be British. He recommended that Burroughs Matthews, the PRD officer who had formerly been the editor of the Buffalo *Courier-Express*, accompany him. Allen agreed then telephoned Butcher yet again with the news that he was sending the two former newspapermen to Reims. Given their positions, Pawley and Matthews enjoyed access to SHAEF Forward denied the press corps. Sergeant Kiley could assist them. They would at least be able to document events as they occurred there and relay their accounts to the press at the Scribe when such news could be released. Butcher went to bed that night pleased that he had played his hunch and returned to Reims.[40] Still, if momentous events did indeed transpire, the presence in Reims of Pawley, Matthews, and Kiley would hardly mollify the press corps miles away in Paris.

For all of the effort that went into ECLIPSE, JACKPLANE, and the other such plans, the surrender caught the PRD flatfooted. Allen's scheme was definitely an improvisation, a stop-gap measure made in lieu of knowledge of what part of the press corps if any the irascible Bedell Smith might allow at such a ceremony. It was even made before Allen knew for certain that there would indeed be a surrender. What is more, Dupuy was correct to predict they would pay the price.

As dawn broke on May 5, the stage was set for the last act of the war against Germany. Low cloud and rain squalls dampened all of northern Europe. At eight o'clock the German units facing Montgomery's 21st Army Group formally surrendered, as had been agreed the day before. Admiral Friedeburg and the OKW's Colonel Fritz Poleck then left Montgomery's headquarters at Lüneburg and flew to Vorst, taking off again for Reims at 10 a.m. in worsening weather.[41]

In Paris, Matthews and Pawley woke early, requisitioned a jeep from the motor pool, and set out for Reims, arriving at about the time the Germans left Lüneburg. Later that morning, Allen, Dupuy, and Thor Smith huddled yet again at the Scribe. Having verified that the Germans were indeed on their way to SHAEF Forward, they realized that if a surrender did occur, PRD would be blamed if there was no visual or audio record of it. They quickly dispatched the British and US pool photographers, Signal Corps photographers, and a crew of recording engineers to follow Pawley and Matthews.[42]

In Reims itself, Eisenhower and his staff kept an eye on the skies while monitoring the progress of the two German envoys. The weather proved so dismal that at one point SHAEF considered using the Supreme Commander's personal train to fetch the Germans. Butcher asked if any reporters would be allowed on the train if it were used; Eisenhower responded that Butcher could "lay them in the aisles" if the Germans were indeed surrendering. Butcher took this off-hand remark as license to summon the reporters from Paris if and when he knew the Germans were, in fact, ending the war.[43]

Butcher also quietly called Mollie Ford to invite her to come to Reims as "things were about to pop." He arranged a car for her, and she drove up to Reims after lunch. Butcher had met the attractive young Red Cross official in North Africa and, at some point, the two had begun an affair. Ford would figure in the surrender story before its end, if only indirectly.[44]

Butcher and General Allen telephoned back and forth throughout the morning. Butcher also directed Sergeant Kiley to go to the Reims airport in case the Germans flew in, while Matthews staked out the Message Center awaiting any relevant cables arrived. Pawley checked in with SHAEF's Intelligence and Operations Divisions, while Butcher tried to glean updates from Eisenhower and Bedell Smith. All were looking for definitive word that surrender was in the offing.[45]

Meanwhile Allen's executive officer in Paris alerted Butcher that reporters there sensed that something big was afoot. Nothing could be done about bringing reporters to Reims, Butcher was convinced, until it was clear the Germans had come to surrender and not merely to negotiate or stall for time. Bedell Smith remained adamant that correspondents should be kept from SHAEF Forward and had even "looked at Pawley and Matthews with a questioning eye." At eleven o'clock Kiley called from the airport to say that the weather was still miserable and the plane carrying the Germans was now overdue. The storm forced the plane to land in Brussels shortly thereafter, and SHAEF arranged to drive the Germans the 150 miles south to Reims.[46]

SHAEF Forward learned this at noon, as well as that the Germans would have lunch at the RAF snack bar in Brussels (Spam sandwiches and locally brewed Kiltie Scotch Ale, as a subsequent SHAEF release overspecified) before proceeding to Reims. Their driver reported that an exhausted Friedeburg slept for most of the trip while Poleck, who did not speak English, "spent most of the time looking out of the window morosely" at the rain.[47]

Once SHAEF officials knew for certain that the Germans were on their way, Bedell Smith designated the War Room on the second floor of the Ecole Professionelle as the place for the possible signing. The War Room was roughly thirty feet square and used by Eisenhower for his morning staff conference. It featured a large wooden table in the center where teachers had formerly marked examination papers. The pale blue walls were covered with large maps, casualty lists, weather forecasts, and the like. Visitors often remarked on a large drawing of a thermometer atop a swastika on one wall measuring the growing numbers of German prisoners.[48]

Lieutenant General Harold R. Bull, SHAEF's Chief of Operations (G-3), and Bedell Smith reluctantly agreed early in the afternoon that if a surrender took place in the War Room, a limited number of journalists could attend. Still and newsreel photographers would be able to record the Germans as they entered, but if any substantive negotiations occurred then the press would have to leave. This seemed awkward, so Bedell Smith decided that any such talks would occur in his office; the principals would go to the War Room only to sign the surrender instruments.[49] The decision on whether reporters could attend would have to wait until German intentions were clear.

Butcher found Eisenhower subdued at lunch. The previous day the general had alerted the Russians through the Allied military mission in Moscow of the Germans' possible arrival, and he had reassured them of his commitment to accept no less than an unconditional surrender on all fronts. He had also invited General Ivan Susloparoff, the highest-ranking Russian officer in the Western theater, to come to SHAEF Forward. General Aleksei Antonov, the chief of the Red Army's General Staff, had cabled back that the Russians had no objections to proceeding as Eisenhower proposed as long as the Germans acknowledged they were surrendering on all fronts. However, when Eisenhower asked the Russians on May 5 whether they desired a second ceremony at a location where more senior Russian officials could attend, their response was delayed. Antonov was away from Moscow for the Russian Easter holiday, and the Allied military mission had difficulty contacting any other members of the Russian General Staff. This only ratcheted up tension as Eisenhower worried that Russian objections might still surface.[50]

Back in Paris, General Allen and his staff remained largely in the dark about what was unfolding in Reims. No definitive word had been received from SHAEF Forward other than that correspondents were still unwelcome there. Matthews and Pawley "kept passing back such scraps of information as they could gather, which did not total much," according to Dupuy.[51]

Meanwhile Butcher was dealing with yet another unexpected problem that menaced the PRD's most recent ad hoc plan. Even as Bedell Smith remained opposed to the presence of any reporters in Reims while a German surrender was less than certain, *Life*'s Charles Wertenbaker had arrived at SHAEF Forward. Kennedy later maintained that Wertenbaker was in Reims without permission and that he agreed to return to Paris once Matthews confronted him.[52] However, Butcher's diary for May 5 indicates that Wertenbaker was in Reims for an authorized interview with one of Eisenhower's aides, a meeting that had been arranged days before. Even so, Butcher knew well that "all the other correspondents would be sore" if Wertenbaker scooped them on the surrender story, albeit by accident. Butcher decided to tell Wertenbaker "straightforwardly the pickle we were in and ask him as a gentleman to leave headquarters and play dumb," although this seems a bit far-fetched. Wertenbaker had already noted the unusual number of SHAEF staff congregating at headquarters. Butcher revealed to Wertenbaker what was happening and told him of Bedell Smith's ban on reporters. As Butcher understood it, Wertenbaker then "agreed completely and wholeheartedly to leave the building" after his scheduled interview.[53]

While Allen and his staff marked time in Paris, Butcher was busy in Reims. The photographers and sound crew arrived and began to set up klieg lights and microphones in the War Room, which was soon laced with cables. The photographers also pushed the large table from the center of the room into a corner to improve their sight lines. As Butcher supervised this activity, Kiley, Matthews, and Pawley periodically touched base.[54]

Friedeburg and Poleck arrived at the Ecole Professionelle shortly after five o'clock that afternoon. Military protocol dictated that, since he outranked them, Eisenhower not deal with the German envoys directly before an actual surrender. Bedell Smith would instead meet with them and, if and when it came to pass, sign the surrender documents. More than a hundred staff had gathered to watch the Germans step out of their car and acknowledge the Allied officers with the traditional German military salute rather than the stiff-armed Nazi one. Poleck appeared tense but Friedeburg was humming softly, seemingly more relaxed. The Germans were then taken to Bedell Smith's office, passing through an anteroom where most of SHAEF's senior staff had gathered.[55]

When Friedeburg proposed a surrender of German forces on the Western Front only, Bedell Smith coldly informed him that Eisenhower refused to continue discussions unless they included the Eastern Front as well. To underscore to the Germans their desperate situation, Bedell Smith deployed Montgomery's trick of showing them up-to-the-minute battle maps. He went the British field marshal one better, however, by also brandishing maps charting imaginary Allied attacks soon to be launched. Bedell Smith presented Eisenhower's terms in writing: the surrender must be unconditional, it must occur simultaneously on all fronts, the Germans would freeze their forces in place, and the OKW would agree to obey all Allied orders.[56]

Figure 3.2. Admiral General Hans-Georg von Friedeburg entering the Ecole
Professionelle on May 5, 1945 to negotiate surrender terms. Friedeburg was
a part of last-minute German maneuvers to pit the Western Allies against
the Soviets. Courtesy National Archives (111-SC-205948).

A shaken Friedeburg pleaded that given the fractured state of German communications, it would take at least two days to alert all units
in the field to any surrender. Bedell Smith took this to be yet another
stall. Friedeburg also made a special pleading for the suffering of the civilian population. Finally, he confessed that he had not been authorized
to negotiate a general surrender, only to explore the terms for such. Bedell Smith sternly warned that the German people were still at risk and
would remain so until they capitulated; he put Friedeburg on notice that
the Dönitz government would be charged with unnecessarily prolonging
hostilities unless they agreed to terms quickly. Either Friedeburg received
written authority to surrender, or Dönitz would have to send someone else
to Reims who could. Friedeburg thus was desperate to contact Dönitz, but
he was embarrassed to admit that he did not possess the requisite codes or

prearranged radio frequencies to do so directly. With that, Bedell Smith ended the conference, which had lasted barely twenty minutes.[57]

According to Butcher, the admiral "took the terms back to the office assigned and asked for whiskey." Friedeburg composed a message to Dönitz relaying Eisenhower's conditions and Bedell Smith's options for signing. This was transmitted in SHAEF code to the British Second Army headquarters where it was deciphered and sent by dispatch rider to Flensburg. Bedell Smith went to the War Room to inform staff there of all that had just occurred. Blinded by the intense lights the photographers had installed and alarmed by the vast bank of microphones now on the table, the chief of staff told them everything would be paused until the Germans received a response from Flensburg.[58]

Bedell Smith proceeded to Eisenhower's office to bring him up to speed. They agreed that Friedeburg seemed in favor of an immediate surrender on SHAEF's terms, and they speculated that such a signing in Reims might be followed by a grander but symbolic ceremony elsewhere. Eisenhower again left the Ecole Professionelle for his personal quarters where he would wait until Dönitz had responded. Butcher remained at the Ecole before returning to Eisenhower's quarters for dinner. When he told the general that the War Room was lit like a Hollywood set, Eisenhower said that "he didn't give a damn so long as he got the formal and complete surrender."[59]

At dinner Butcher also took a call from Matthews, "who said that Charlie Wertenbaker was [still] hanging around the Ecole Professional [*sic*] interviewing persons who had seen the German officers."[60] According to Kennedy's acerbic telling, Matthews himself had spied Wertenbaker "lurking in the doorway" of the Ecole hours before Friedeburg and Poleck had arrived.[61] Matthews had told him that reporters were not allowed at SHAEF Forward, and Wertenbaker then agreed to go back to Paris. Kennedy makes no mention of Wertenbaker's prearranged interview nor of his earlier conversation with Butcher.

A few hours later, Matthews again saw Wertenbaker loitering outside the building. Wertenbaker had seen the two German officers enter, and he pleaded to be allowed inside. He offered to write a pool report, but Matthews and Pawley countered that they had been assigned to do. "Wertenbaker argued that the event was of such magnitude as to merit the talents of 'a great writer,'" according to Kennedy, "and nominated himself to fill that capacity." Matthews and Pawley well knew they could not agree to this without the rest of the press corps screaming favoritism. However, PRD's scheme to provide the press with its own account already had been compromised, given Wertenbaker's ability to write an eyewitness story was guaranteed to infuriate the other reporters. Matthews had never liked the idea of having army personnel as the sole journalists at the surrender, so when the Wertenbaker incident took place he called Allen and urged him to let the Paris reporters attend.[62] In short, Wertenbaker's appearance in Reims sent the PRD scrambling madly for yet another plan for press coverage. Butcher and Dupuy agree, though, that the actual decision to send a press contingent from Paris to Reims was not made until the next day, after they had finally overcome Bedell Smith's aversion to the press.

After a long and frustrating day, Eisenhower retired early. Mollie Ford relates that the small coterie around Eisenhower had a "pleasant evening" but that "everyone [was] tense waiting" for Dönitz's emissaries to hear from Flensburg. After Ford left for the WAC residence where she stayed with Kay Summersby, Eisenhower's driver, and Ruth Briggs, Bedell Smith's secretary, Butcher took a final call from Winston Churchill, who had been phoning throughout the day to check on progress. Friedeburg and Poleck, for their part, had been taken to the large townhouse used as a billet for visiting officers. The Germans asked for soap, then at 10:45 dined with their three escorts, according to SHAEF's narrative later distributed to the press, on pork chops and mashed potatoes. They drank red wine with dinner, followed by martinis. The Germans listened to the radio until 12:15 a.m. then went to bed. The PRD account does not mention how well they slept.[63]

As the Germans were preparing for bed, SHAEF Forward continued to fret over the possible Russian response to the German peace overtures, so General Bull sent yet another cable to the military mission in Moscow. Bull asked if the Russian High Command had any other conditions it wished to include in the surrender document.[64] The SHAEF high command's anxiety ratcheted up when there was no reply from Moscow as the hours passed.

Friedeburg's dispatch finally reached Flensburg in the early hours of May 6. Dönitz was shocked by Eisenhower's insistence that Germany surrender on all fronts, as he still clung to the hope that the Western Allies could be turned against the Russians. He found Bedell Smith's terms unacceptably harsh and decided to send a personal emissary to Reims to make that point. The obvious choice for such a mission was General Alfred Jodl, chief of staff of the German army. Jodl ferociously opposed any surrender on the Eastern Front; if anyone could explain to the Americans why the Germans could not possibly surrender to the Russians, Jodl was that person. Jodl's involvement would also provide convenient political cover for Dönitz if the Germans were forced to surrender on all fronts.[65]

The rain clouds lifted overnight and Sunday, May 6, dawned a beautiful day throughout Northwestern Europe. Friedeburg and Poleck were awakened at their request at seven that morning and breakfasted at the junior officers' mess (grapefruit segments, bacon and eggs, toast, and coffee). Friedeburg spent the morning thumbing through old copies of *Life* and recent issues of *Stars and Stripes* while listening to the radio and waiting for a response from Flensburg. At one o'clock, the Germans officers returned to the mess for lunch (fried chicken, mashed potatoes, corn, peaches, wine, and coffee).[66] Matthews and Pawley noted what the Germans ate as if these were their last meals before execution.

In Paris that morning Thor Smith brooded over the lack of a press presence at SHAEF Forward. The surrender story would likely break so quickly that it would be impossible to transport the press corps to Reims in time to cover it, and so he urged Allen to move the reporters immediately. Bedell Smith might growl at their presence, but he was always growling. Dupuy relates that Allen then directed a group of reporters to be transported to Reims without first consulting Bedell Smith or others at SHAEF Forward; Butcher claims that he himself actually made this decision later that day and communicated it to Allen's executive officer.[67]

In either case, Allen and his deputies in Paris early that day concentrated on how many and which members of the press corps to send to Reims, if Bedell Smith so allowed. They mulled over the various plans that had been developed, from the original ECLIPSE project to the more recently conceived JACKPLANE. In truth, for all of SHAEF's effort, none of its plans quite fit the situation: JACKPLANE, for example, called for only eight correspondents who would pool copy, which promised to elicit the reflexive protests from the press when pools were used; on the other hand, the ECLIPSE plan called for as many as sixty reporters, an impossible number to transport on such short notice. Dupuy and Smith both believed that the press corps had signed off on the use and composition of such schemes in their past meetings, but many reporters disagreed. After the surrender, PRD and the press corps continued their squabble over the nature of just such agreements, as they had throughout the war.

Thor Smith and the others eventually settled on a plan that would provide basic world press, radio, and pictorial coverage but, crucially, would not rely on a reporting pool or radio pool as JACKPLANE did. The contingent would include representatives from the three US and two British news agencies, plus one agency reporter each from Canada, France, Russia, and Australia (a late addition). The four US radio networks were included, plus the BBC and CBC. Reporters from two service newspapers, *Stars and Stripes* and the Canadian *Maple Leaf* rounded out the cadre. This "emergency newsgathering group," as Dupuy described it, seemed to assure the maximum coverage "for the man on the street" without having to resort to pooling other than that routinely used for photography.[68]

Smith agreed. Given that the story was breaking so quickly, there would be no way to get the press to Reims in time for a signing unless they moved them before it was clear such a signing would occur. In these circumstances the "basic Berlin list" for the airborne component of the ECLIPSE plan made the most sense. Smith, too, was convinced that an expanded list of some seventy reporters (including those from newspapers) would be unworkably large.[69]

Crucially, though, such a small group excluded correspondents, no matter how experienced, from individual newspapers, no matter how influential. At least fifty reporters from daily newspapers existed in the SHAEF press corps in Paris. As the surrender negotiations remained top secret, Dupuy worried about security with some seventy correspondents informed of a "news break of transcendent importance," as the JACKPLANE plan referenced.[70] Bedell Smith's continued opposition to any press attending a surrender also argued against any larger group. Moreover, choosing some newspapers over others would invite charges of favoritism. Thus, the decision to limit the press to what the PRD came to refer to as the Berlin group—roughly the group that would have been flown to Berlin as the first press wave in the case of a US occupation of that city—struck Smith and Dupuy as a reasonable and defensible compromise. In any case, Smith and Dupuy recommended it to Allen, who approved their plan. Allen considered the list "airtight," that is, not to be added to or subtracted from, arguing that as it was it assured at least indirect representation (through the news agencies and radio networks) for every newspaper and local radio station in the Allied nations.[71] No decision SHAEF PRD made during the war would cause it more grief.

Having decided it would be the "Berlin list" or nothing, the PRD then arranged for reporters to leave from Orly Airport on a C-47 transport later that afternoon and began to contact the bureau chiefs of the organizations allocated spaces in the press contingent. Kennedy himself recalled that one of Allen's aides, presumably Smith who was responsible for the US correspondents, woke him that morning with word that the Associated Press could designate one reporter to attend an event whose nature could not be disclosed. Kennedy assumed it must be surrender-related and determined to go himself. Smith contacted the other agencies and organizations on the Berlin list, instructing them to have a reporter in the lobby of the Scribe in short order. A problem immediately arose as those specific reporters who had been designated by their organizations to be a part of the Berlin list were not all on the scene, leading several news organizations to suggest substitutes. Besides Kennedy, the others who assembled were Boyd Lewis (UP), James Kilgallen (INS), Montague Taylor (Reuters), Price Day (Exchange Telegraph), Margaret Ecker (Canadian Press), Jean Lagrange (Agence France Presse), Michael Litivin-Sedoy (TASS), Thomas Cadett (BBC), W. W. Chaplin (NBC), Charles Collingwood (CBS), Herbert Clark (Mutual), Gerald Clark (CBC), and Sgt. Ross Parry (*Maple Leaf*). As Gerald Clark remembered it, he was in the bar at the Scribe chatting with a French woman when a public relations officer burst in, surveyed the room, and eventually spotted Clark. "Thank God I found you," he declared, "We need a Canadian." In short order Clark was on the bus. Osmar White, the veteran Australian correspondent who wrote for the Melbourne *Herald and Weekly Times*, learned from a sympathetic SHAEF sergeant that the press party had been formed without any Australian representatives. White cried foul to SHAEF officials and found himself added to the group. He turned out to be the only reporter to make a successful plea for inclusion.[72]

Exchange Telegraph's original designee could not be found, so was replaced by Price Day, who also reported for the *Baltimore Sun*. Similarly, Clark, representing the CBC, also reported for the *Montreal Standard*. These substitutions would prove to be a thorn in the side of the PRD before the day ended. These sixteen would join the *Stars and Stripes* Kiley, who was already in Reims with the four pool photographers PRD had sent from Paris.

In Reims, whether any press would witness the surrender story remained an open question. Earlier that morning Eisenhower had walked through the War Room still filled with technicians installing lights for the newsreel cameras. He had remarked that it looked like a Hollywood set, which Bedell Smith took to mean that Eisenhower shared his distaste for such an obtrusive press presence.[73] According to Butcher, shortly before noon Bedell Smith stormed into the office where Matthews and Pawley were working and demanded that all of the equipment in the War Room be removed. "This isn't going to be a show. There's going to be a surrender. Get it out immediately," he ordered.[74]

Butcher himself had picked up Mollie Ford from the WAC residence and walked with her to lunch at Eisenhower's mess, where Ford found everyone "silent and waiting." Butcher mentioned Bedell Smith's demand that all of the press equipment be removed from the War Room; Eisenhower replied that he himself had no objection to the press being present but that the surrender proceedings were Bedell Smith's responsibility. Then Eisenhower went off to his quarters to lie down.[75]

Butcher returned to the Ecole Professionelle. Word soon came that Jodl was on his way to Reims with an aide, Major Wilhelm Oxenius. Escorted by Montgomery's chief of staff, the party was aboard *Mary Lou*, the field marshal's personal airplane.[76] Friedeburg and Poleck were informed. Butcher then went to Bedell Smith's office, but was told by the staff that the general was resting and had left orders not to be disturbed until five o'clock. Worried time was running out, Butcher sought to discover what had prompted the chief of staff's decision to clear the press equipment from the War Room in the first place. He concluded that Bedell Smith had gotten wind of Eisenhower's "Hollywood set" comment and had taken this to mean that the Supreme Commander agreed that the press should not attend the surrender.

By his own account, Butcher then took the risk of calling PRD in Paris before he had spoken with Bedell Smith. He told Allen's executive officer that he thought fifteen or twenty correspondents should be sent to Reims immediately. Once at SHAEF Forward, they could be stashed in an office as far away from Bedell Smith as possible. By Dupuy and Smith's accounts, they had already decided to send a press group to Reims and had begun alerting reporters. Allen possibly took Butcher's call as the green light to proceed with the press flight to Reims. It is certain, though, that Allen, his staff, and the correspondents did leave the Scribe before Butcher was able to speak with Bedell Smith. Refreshed from his nap and much to Butcher's relief, the chief of staff was willing to reconsider his ban. Bedell Smith insisted, though, that the number of reporters remain small and that the bank of equipment that had been set up on the main table in the War Room be reduced to a single microphone.[77]

Dupuy found the Hotel Scribe a "hornet's nest of rumor" by early afternoon as reporters there feared that they were missing out on something momentous. Word that Thor Smith was contacting the Lucky Seventeen was spreading "like grassfire" among the SHAEF press corps, Smith realized, but "even then some of the correspondents thought it might be Berlin."[78]

When it became clear who was and was not part of the press party, the PRD faced a torrent of criticism. This was especially true once Charles Wertenbaker returned to the Scribe to announce that it appeared the Germans were, in fact, surrendering. The reporters working for daily newspapers and the news magazines were furious to learn that they had been excluded. Their rage only increased when it became clear that the substitutes Day and Clark, both newspaper reporters, were included in the group and would be positioned to write exclusive stories for their papers. Wertenbaker, Larry Rue of the *Chicago Tribune*, and Raymond Daniell of the *New York Times* confronted Dupuy about being left out. Daniell was especially upset that there were as many radio broadcasters in the press party as print journalists, voicing the disdain for radio news that many print reporters still felt at war's end. Smith extracted a promise from both Day and Clark not to exploit their positions in the press party by filing eyewitness accounts with their home papers, but this hardly mollified the rest of the press corps.[79]

Bedlam reigned at the Scribe as those who had been selected boarded the bus to take them to Orly Airport while those excluded shouted their displeasure. When Thor Smith arrived at the Scribe, he found that "the lobby was a seething mob of additional correspondents trying to chisel in on the trip." Shortly before the press cadre left the Scribe, Allen received vague word that although the surrender seemed likely to occur that night, by order of Washington news of that event could not be released until an undetermined later time. Allen briefed Dupuy about this, then he departed with Smith and several other PRD staff, leaving Dupuy to cope with the angry reporters left behind.[80]

Several of the participants dispute what actually was said on the plane to Reims once it was aloft. According to Allen, he recounted to the reporters the events of the past few days and stressed to them that while members of the German high command were indeed on their way to SHAEF Forward, what would happen after their arrival remained uncertain. He then told them: "This story is off the record until [the] respective heads of the Allied governments announce the facts to the world. I therefore pledge each and every one of you on your honor not to communicate the result of this conference or the fact of its existence until it is released by SHAEF." Twenty years later, Boyd Lewis recalled that Allen crouched in the middle of the plane, close to Kennedy and himself, as the briefing occurred. "This story is entirely off the record until the respective heads of government have announced it to the world," Lewis remembered Allen saying. "I pledge each one of you, on his honor as a correspondent and as an assimilated officer of the United States Army, not to communicate the results of the conference—or even the fact of its existence—until released by PRD, SHAEF." In an article in the *New York Times* published the day after the surrender, Daniell, who had not been on the plane, cites Lewis as conveying Allen's speech in essentially the same words. He also claimed that other unnamed reporters on the plane confirmed Lewis's account.[81] Whatever Allen's precise wording, this became the infamous pledge on the plane used as a cudgel against Kennedy in the weeks to come.

Kennedy had an entirely different take on what Allen said on the flight to Reims and its significance. In an interview granted when he returned to New York a month later, Kennedy insisted that the pledge on the plane was nothing out of the ordinary. "On boarding the plane we had no official information on the purpose of the trip," Kennedy said, "although we all had a pretty good idea that it would be the German surrender." Allen had told the group that "it was imperative that we not discuss this with anyone outside our group until the surrender was signed and we naturally agreed to this and to the holding of the story for its release, as in all such cases." In short, Kennedy had often in the past held a story for security reasons until authorized by the army. He harbored no reservations in doing so again because he had "naturally assumed [the hold] would

Figure 3.3. At Orly Airport, reporters and public relations staff pose before the C-47 about to take them to Reims on May 6, 1945. This blurry snapshot and figure 3.4 belonged to Thor Smith, but who took them is not known. Smith is standing third from the left. Courtesy Eisenhower Presidential Library, Thor Smith Papers.

Figure 3.4. This photograph is labeled "Inside the plane on the way to Rheims on way to Surrender of Germans, May 6, 1945." The snapshot is out of focus and grainy, but it is the only existing image documenting the plane ride to Reims. The reporters made their pledge on the plane to General Allen on this flight. Courtesy Eisenhower Presidential Library, Thor Smith Papers.

be a reasonable one" and expected the story to be cleared in the normal fashion. Several years later, Kennedy would add that Allen gave a "long and rambling talk" on the plane, difficult to hear "against the din of the propellers." Allen warned that the surrender negotiations might still fail and that if word of the talks got out it might have "disastrous effects." At Allen's insistence, the correspondents swore not to discuss the trip outside of the group itself, a pledge Kennedy thought reasonable, speculating that it was driven by the army's desire not to repeat the fiasco of the UP's premature armistice story in 1918.[82]

Kennedy did not recall Allen requiring all reporters to swear a specific pledge to remain silent about the surrender meeting until SHAEF released that information, but he did not dispute the point. His memory was of Allen being much less formal, saying something like, "Now does everyone here understand that this story is to be held up for SHAEF release?" All the correspondents on the plane, including Kennedy, agreed. Kennedy insisted that he did not attach great importance to this affirmation because (as he accurately claimed) "it was pure surplusage," since all accredited correspondents had signed individual agreements to abide by all military censorship restrictions, including release times.[83] In sum, he pointed out that there was no basic need for nor special weight to the pledge on the plane.

The reporters left behind seethed in Paris while the chosen few headed to Reims. At one point, Daniell, *Newsweek*'s Joseph Evans, Helen Kirkpatrick of the *Chicago Daily News*, and several others marched into Dupuy's office. He remembered them as "the angriest group of correspondents I have ever faced." Some worked for national news magazines. Others wrote for papers with long-standing foreign bureaus, syndication services, or both. All had been reporting on the war for years and had convinced themselves that they deserved to cover its end. Daniell demanded that Dupuy call Bedell Smith to have him authorize a larger press party. When Dupuy refused, Daniell went over Dupuy's head to SHAEF's administrative headquarters, the office of the Secretary of the General Staff (SGS). There he pleaded his case but to little avail. The SGS did grant the reporters permission to travel to SHAEF Forward, but it refused to add them to the official list of press witnesses. Thereafter Wertenbaker, Daniell, Kirkpatrick and several others set out for Reims by car.[84]

When the airborne cadre reached Reims, the reporters were taken to a classroom on the ground floor directly below the War Room. A large map of Europe hung on one wall. Osmar White noticed that someone had rearranged the colored pins representing troop locations into a large "V" for victory. There Matthews and Pawley briefed them about the events of the past twenty-four hours. For their part, Allen and Thor Smith faced a pressing issue. Butcher still believed that more reporters could be accommodated in the War Room; Allen and Smith were convinced that the Berlin list fairly represented the world press and that including a few more correspondents would only cause additional complaints from those still excluded. They were also aware that Bedell Smith was in no mood to deal with even more reporters on the scene. When contacted back in Paris, Dupuy agreed that it would be a mistake to expand the Berlin list.[85]

Jodl's plane arrived at Reims shortly after five o'clock. To one US observer Jodl was "completely expressionless" as "he strode arrogantly to the car waiting to take him to headquarters." During the fifteen-minute drive Jodl seemed to take little notice when the car passed two large detachments of German prisoners guarded by a handful of US troops. Jodl was taken to the office assigned to the German delegation, to be followed by Poleck and Friedeburg who arrived at 5:45. Shortly thereafter, Friedeburg came out and asked for coffee and a map of Europe. While Friedeburg seemed relieved that a surrender might be in the offing, Jodl was seen "marching up and down inside the room." At 6:15 the Germans were taken to Bedell Smith's office by General Kenneth Strong, SHAEF's head of intelligence, who translated.[86]

Jodl, like Friedeburg the day before, tried to stall for time, asserting that it would take days for the German high command to contact its units in the field. On Eisenhower's instruction, Bedell Smith rejected this request outright. Unless Jodl accepted the Allies' terms of an unconditional surrender on all fronts by midnight, Smith warned, Allied forces would seal the escape routes for those German civilians or soldiers fleeing westward. He left the Germans to consider his words.[87]

Bedell Smith and Strong summoned General Susloparoff to the Ecole Professionelle and then went to Eisenhower's office. Smith told Eisenhower that Jodl seemed intent on dragging out the negotiations. Eisenhower reiterated that either the Germans agree to stop all fighting within forty-eight hours or else he would carry through on his threat to seal the Western Front. Bedell Smith and Strong then returned to the Germans. Faced with Eisenhower's ultimatum, Jodl agreed to cable Flensburg for authority to surrender, advising Dönitz there was no choice but to accept Eisenhower's terms. To continue resistance would create unimaginable chaos within Germany.[88] At eight o'clock General Strong appeared in Bedell Smith's outer office to tell the waiting SHAEF officers that there would be at least a three-hour delay in receiving Dönitz's response. The two German officers and their aides then returned to their billet to await a reply from Flensburg.

Throughout the negotiations, such as they were, PRD officials periodically appeared downstairs to brief the press. At one point, Allen informed the reporters that if a surrender occurred, news stories they wrote would be held for release until after an announcement was made by the Big Three. Meanwhile Daniell, Kirkpatrick, Wertenbaker, and the other correspondents who had driven to Reims lurked outside the Ecole Professionelle. They spotted Allen and protested their exclusion. Daniell and Kirkpatrick complained once more that they represented newspapers with long established foreign bureaus who deserved to be included far more than the radio broadcasters. Allen remained unmoved and insisted that the press party would not be expanded. The line had to be drawn somewhere; besides, there was simply not enough space in the War Room. Still the reporters milled about outside the windows of the classroom where the Lucky Seventeen had been parked. The UP's Lewis went to the mess and grabbed a stack of hamburgers to pass through a window to the reporters outside. "This filled their stomachs," Lewis wrote, "but satisfied no one's appetite for the story."[89]

General Frederick Morgan, the respected British officer who had spearheaded early planning for the invasion of France, arrived at SHAEF Forward late in the day. The outsiders presented their case to Morgan, who remarked to Allen once he was inside that "something should be done" about the reporters waiting on the doorstep. Morgan meant this sympathetically, but Allen took it as a criticism and ordered MPs to remove the correspondents. Daniell wrote a few days later that the MPs told the reporters to "get the hell out of here," but then, on Allen's orders, allowed five of them, including Daniell, to remain so that Allen could speak with them, but Allen never made it outside for such a meeting.[90]

As eight o'clock neared, Butcher asked Eisenhower if he wanted to go to their quarters to await word from Flensburg. They both had been invited to a cocktail party hosted by Summersby and Briggs at the WAC house coincidentally scheduled for that night. Ford had also been invited after spending the afternoon at Eisenhower and Butcher's quarters reading magazines and playing with the dog.[91] Eisenhower seemed uninterested in attending the party until he learned that General Susloparoff and the French representative General François Sevez would be there. Eisenhower decided to stop at the party in the name of Allied unity before going home to eat.

Butcher, on the other hand, stayed at the Ecole Professionelle, where his phone rang time and again as Kirkpatrick, Daniell, Drew Middleton, and Evans all pleaded for inclusion as surrender observers.[92] Butcher finally left about nine o'clock, and went to the WAC house, where he found Eisenhower deep in discussion with Susloparoff. Ford earlier had surmised that something was afoot when Summersby, Briggs, and Butcher had not arrived for the party, so she had left for dinner at the quarters of T. J. Davis, who had stepped in as SHAEF's adjutant general, a less taxing post than directing public relations, after his health problems of the previous summer. General Bull shared a billet with Davis and appeared at 9:30, looking to Ford "tired and disgusted" because it appeared that the surrender would not occur that night. Butcher arrived a few minutes later, but he and Bull left almost immediately. The rest of the party sat distractedly through a screening of *Winged Victory*. Ford left to return to the WAC billet in the early morning hours.[93] The war simply refused to end.

When Admiral Dönitz received Jodl's message, he considered Eisenhower's threat to prevent the western movement of German troops and civilians to be "sheer extortion." Nonetheless, Jodl had recommended accepting the Allies' terms as Germany's only option. Dönitz agreed. Both Dönitz and Jodl were consoled by the fact that the surrender would not come into effect until midnight of May 8/9, and so both troops and civilians would indeed have forty-eight hours to head westward.[94]

When Mollie Ford returned to the WAC house she found several people still awake after the party had ended. She sat out on the terrace for a short while and was about to go to bed herself when Butcher walked in with Helen Kirkpatrick, one of the reporters who had trekked from Paris to Reims earlier that day. Butcher and Ford had known Kirkpatrick for some time, so when she had asked Butcher for help in locating a billet for the night, he had told the reporter that Ford was staying at the WAC house. If Kirkpatrick had a bedroll, she could bunk there.

All three had just sat down for a nightcap when the phone rang for Butcher. It was Ruth Briggs. "The party is on," she alerted him. Butcher then "picked up his cap and hotfooted it out," according to Ford. Ford asked a "Colonel Rosenfelt," a friend from North Africa who had also lingered after the cocktail party, if she and Kirkpatrick couldn't go over themselves "to see the proceedings from some dark corner." The colonel agreed to take them to the Ecole Professionelle, but he warned Kirkpatrick that she could not enter the building. Ford proposed that they could sneak her in by covering the correspondent insignia on Kirkpatrick's uniform. Lieutenant Colonel Abram H. Rosenfeld, whom Ford presumably meant, reluctantly agreed, and they headed for Davis's office just inside the front door of the Ecole. Ford later confided to her mother that from there "we saw everything. The arrival of all the participants."[95]

When Butcher reached the Ecole shortly before two o'clock, he found a "hornet's nest" of reporters swarming at the front door. They had already seen Eisenhower enter. Butcher immediately regretted not using the back entrance as the reporters beseeched him to let them in. While Butcher admired their initiative, he insisted that there was nothing that he could do. He briefed them on the events of the past two days and agreed to ask General Allen to meet with the reporters himself.[96]

Nor was Allen the only public relations officer stressed at that moment. Smith, Matthews, and Pawley, as well as Generals Bull and Allen, understood that Eisenhower much preferred releasing news of the surrender immediately, not so much to inform the Allied publics as to stop the fighting at the front and thereby save lives. At that point, though, while aware of the directive from the Joint Chiefs of Staff to withhold release until the Big Three had made their announcements, they expected those announcements straightaway. As he waited for word from Flensburg, Thor Smith had wolfed down a sandwich in the Officers Snack Bar before joining Matthews and Pawley to compile the chronological account later used to brief the entire press corps. While in the makeshift press room and between fielding queries from the reporters present, including Kennedy, the PROs discussed their options. Smith was concerned that if the story was released immediately, it would create problems with the press, given the dearth of transmission facilities in Reims. The press would have the story but not be able to send it.[97]

The PROs worried that if the news was released under these conditions, the press corps in Paris would break the story before those who had actually witnessed the ceremony could return there to file. The Reims reporters would be furious. Although Allen countered that those in Paris would merely have the outlines of the story while the reporters in Reims would be able to file detailed eyewitness dispatches, Smith doubted that this distinction would mollify the Lucky Seventeen. Ultimately, Smith and his colleagues agreed that it would be best to set a release time for some point after the Reims contingent had returned to Paris. "All of this was discussed quite openly with the correspondents in order to get an agreed procedure in case it was announced immediately," Smith later confided. "Of course, it never was, but that discussion was the basis of the 'confusion' which Kennedy used in his [subsequent] defense."[98]

Activity quickened at the Ecole Professionelle just before two in the morning. Cars and jeeps pulled up in quick succession, discharging both Allied and German officers. "An air of excitement spread throughout the building," the SHAEF record noted. Junior officers and enlisted men clustered in stairways and in the school's large courtyard, used as the headquarters' motor pool. Allen reappeared in the makeshift pressroom and announced, "Gentlemen, I think this is it." At 2:15 Kennedy and the others mounted the stairs to the War Room, now floodlit for the newsreel cameras. They joined the twenty or so photographers and technicians on the scene and the ten PRD officers who had accompanied the press party to Reims. The correspondents crowded behind a white line drawn diagonally across the floor to the right of the doorway as they entered.[99]

Kennedy wrote that the reporters were "roped off in one corner, but Signal Corps photographers buzzed around the table and mounted a stepladder placed next to it for 'angle shots.'" Bedell Smith had insisted on bare-bones staging for the surrender signing. The large wooden table with a cracked top had been placed near a wall covered from floor to ceiling with battlefield maps. The table had eight chairs placed on one side and two on the other. At each place was a name card, a small ashtray, and a pad of paper; a pen holder and one microphone stood in the otherwise bare center of the table.[100]

At 2:30 Allied officers began to enter led by General Bull, who moved across the room somber-faced as did those who followed. Each "shuffled from chair to chair looking for their place cards," according to Clark. Bedell Smith arrived a few minutes later. "He was never a robust-looking man," observed Osmar White, "but under the glare of the kliegs he looked ghastly, ill and exhausted." General Strong escorted in Jodl and Friedeburg, both looking haggard as well. They slightly bowed as they reached their chairs. Bedell Smith sat down, followed by the rest of the Allied officers and then the Germans. The chief of staff asked the Germans if they understood the terms of the surrender and were prepared to sign on behalf of the Reich, while General Strong leaned toward Jodl and translated the question. Jodl nodded. There were four copies of the surrender documents, Bedell Smith informed the Germans, as Strong passed the papers to them and explained each one. As White noted: "The film cameras made a low, whirring sound and dozens of small flash-globes popped as the official photographers, still bent double scuttled from point to point, ripping black papers from film packs and adjusting lenses. Pen nibs moved swiftly as aides passed copy after copy."[101]

Jodl then asked for permission to speak. Standing at attention and in a voice barely above a whisper, Jodl addressed Bedell Smith with a blend of arrogance and self-pity. His words were translated as: "General, with this signature the German people and German armed forces are, for better or worse, delivered into the victor's hands. In this war, which has lasted more than five years both have achieved and suffered more than perhaps any other people in the world. In this hour I can only express the hope that the victor will treat them with generosity."[102]

Figure 3.5. General Alfred Jodl, the chief of the Operations Staff in the German army, enters the War Room in the Ecole Professionelle to sign the surrender document. Jodl had fiercely opposed surrendering on the Russian front and was sent to Reims to try to buy time. He failed. Courtesy National Archives (111-SC-261108).

Figure 3.6. Lieutenant General Walter Bedell Smith, SHAEF chief of staff (at the center of the table), presides over the brief signing ceremony in the early hours of May 7, 1945. Flanking him are the other Allied representatives. General Jodl sits across the table in the middle. Courtesy National Archives (111-SC-205954).

Figure 3.7. General Alfred Jodl signs the instruments of surrender. Admiral Friedeburg sits on his left and Jodl's (unidentified) aide on his right. Photographers and newsmen can be seen in the background. Courtesy National Archives (111-SC-204260).

Figure 3.8. Lieutenant General Walter Bedell Smith, Eisenhower's long-serving
chief of staff, signs the surrender document on behalf of the Allies in Reims. Known
to all as "Beetle," Bedell Smith was a protégé of George Marshall, a gruff,
occasionally short-tempered officer who ran Eisenhower's headquarters
efficiently and, when needed, served as the Supreme Commander's enforcer.
Courtesy National Archives (111-SC-204259).

Bedell Smith stared coldly at Jodl from across the table and said nothing. The Germans, holding their hats, departed the room. There were no
cheers nor handshakes by the Allied officers. Bedell Smith simply said,
"Thank you, gentlemen," and the officers too left the room.[103] It was all
over in ten minutes. The official time of the surrender was set at 0241.

After the ceremony Allen directed the seventeen correspondents down
a crowded corridor toward Eisenhower's office. The German officers
were given a moment to compose themselves, then were ushered in to
see the Supreme Commander and his deputy, Air Marshal Arthur Tedder.
Eisenhower curtly asked if they had understood the surrender terms. Jodl
nodded and the Germans were summarily dismissed. Eisenhower then
called in his close associates for congratulations and photographs. The

press contingent was allowed to witness this scene through a doorway, and Lewis remembered that Eisenhower made a point to hug General Susloparoff.[104]

Both the official record and all the surviving first-hand accounts describe the proceedings in much the same way, but who had actually witnessed the ceremony came to be a major bone of contention between the press corps and the PRD. The next day, one of the reporters left outside of the Ecole, Raymond Daniell, wrote a scathing piece in the *New York Times* about SHAEF's handling of the surrender. He claimed that "20-odd girls and friends" had been allowed into the room even as General

Figure 3.9. Moments after the Germans had signed and left, General Eisenhower gathered the senior SHAEF and Allied leaders for pictures in his office. Here are left-to-right: Major General Susloparoff, Lieutenant General Morgan, Lieutenant General Smith, Captain Butcher (behind), General Eisenhower, Air Marshall Tedder, and Admiral Burrough, Allied Naval Chief. Eisenhower is holdings the pens used at the signing in a V-shape, an image that circulated worldwide. Kay Summersby is behind General Smith in this picture, barely visible, but is clearly present (in the back with Butcher) in others taken at the time. Courtesy National Archives (111- SC-205955).

Allen had cited lack of space as the reason why more reporters had not.[105] Even with these additional bodies, others had told Daniell that there still would have been space for another fifteen or twenty people, and this at a time when there were less than ten correspondents still camped outside of the Ecole. Daniell's piece was widely carried in papers across the country after the Associated Press picked it up, and it became the source of the widespread belief that many of the press were excluded from the surrender signing, though as many SHAEF officers had invited girlfriends to attend.

Conflicting evidence exists about Daniell's charge. Boyd Lewis, for one, later wrote that he saw Summersby at the signing. Kennedy, another eye-witness, later claimed that "various Headquarters officers managed to slip WAC and Red Cross girlfriends into the room to see the historic events." Thor Smith wrote to his wife less than two weeks after the surrender that the accusation that there were twenty girls in the room was "just snide tongue-sticking out." However, he admitted that an hour after the cere-mony he had seen Butcher accompany three women to the War Room just as Eisenhower had finished filming a statement for the newsreels. Smith's letter likely crossed paths with one his wife had written him after she had read Daniell's attack on the PRD. She asked if it were indeed true "that correspondents were chased away and there were ten or twenty pretty girls at the signing."[106]

Perhaps the most intriguing evidence comes from Mollie Ford, one of the "girls" in question. Ford recounted to her mother just a few days later that Colonel Rosenfeld at 2:30 a.m. "got us up into the War Room where we saw the whole show. Not the official signing but right after the peace was signed." She related that she was there "when Ike made his speech with Tedder for the newsreels," which would have placed her in the room at about 3:30. She wrote that all of the reporters from the press cadre were there, but that Kirkpatrick had been forced to stay outside the room "as she had no business being there in the first place." Ford recalled that French, British and Russian officials were all present, although there is no conclusive evidence that anyone from the SHAEF high command except Eisenhower and Tedder was in the room for the newsreel session. "It was tremendous and I was one of five women who saw it happen," Ford con-fided to her mother, who, the letter elsewhere indicates, was well aware of her relationship with Butcher.[107]

With its contradictory information, what to make of this letter is not entirely clear. Either Ford "saw it all," the surrender signing that was the only time all of the Allied military were in the room together, or she saw the newsreel filming an hour later. In either case, it seems almost certain that Ford and other "girlfriends" were shepherded into the War Room at some point. It also seems likely that there was space for additional correspondents during the signing but that the PRD had found the cramped space a convenient excuse for limiting the press party to the seventeen, as had been decided in Paris. While Butcher was convinced that the War Room would have accommodated additional correspondents, Thor Smith and the others concluded that it would have been problematic to allow those few correspondents camped outside the Ecole to attend the signing, for it would have penalized those reporters who had obeyed SHAEF's direction to remain in Paris. In any case, rumors of the presence of the "girlfriends" at the signing when so many of the press were excluded only fueled the press corps' resentment of the PRD for its mishandling of the surrender. Worse was yet to come.

After the signing, Kennedy returned to the makeshift press room with the rest of the Lucky Seventeen and got to work on his account of the surrender. When finished, he gave it to Lieutenant Colonel Richard Merrick, the PRD censor responsible for the copy of the US correspondents in Reims. Thor Smith later confirmed that Merrick had brought his censorship stamps with him, indicating that he was prepared to censor copy on site. According to Kennedy, the censor read his story and stamped it as passed. Later he claimed that Merrick then "asked me for the dispatch back and crossed out his okay, not because of any objection to any information in it but because the release, which had been expected to be almost immediate, was by that time uncertain." Lewis also recalled having several hours at the Ecole to work on his dispatch since the flight back to Paris would have to await daylight.[108]

By Mollie Ford's account, after the signing she met up with Helen Kirkpatrick and, as they passed an open window on the ground floor, "the excluded correspondents hissed at Helen to draw her attention." Kirkpatrick briefed them on what she knew and then called Ford to the window, asking her to "tell these men how much space there was in the War Room and about how many people were there," more evidence that Ford may actually have witnessed the signing itself. When Ford said that she did not know, Kirkpatrick was irritated and assured her that she would not be quoted directly by any of the reporters. Ford then conceded that there had been sufficient space for a few more people in the War Room. At some point thereafter, it seems that Allen finally relented and allowed Daniell, Evans, and the other unauthorized reporters into the building to view the War Room well after the signing. Kirkpatrick (who presumably had rejoined the group) even took a tape measure to prove that it could have accommodated more reporters. Those correspondents who had on their own initiative traveled to Reims and staked out SHAEF Forward would forever remain convinced that there had been space for them in the War Room.[109]

About four o'clock in the morning, a weary Allen met with the press to announce that while Eisenhower himself preferred an immediate release, the surrender story would be embargoed until at least three o'clock the following afternoon, May 8. The correspondents erupted at the news. Lewis followed Allen into the hall and pleaded with him for an earlier release time, but Allen said that SHAEF's hands were tied. He told Lewis that the Russians had agreed to participate in the Reims ceremony only if news of the surrender would be withheld long enough to convince them that the Germans had stopped fighting on the Eastern Front.[110]

When Allen announced the embargo, the press group objected that it was an act of blatant political censorship. Kennedy's exasperation was tempered by his sense that the news would leak out in the morning regardless of the stop: "the absurdity of trying to bottle up news of such magnitude was too apparent. I knew from experience that one might as well try to censor the rising of the sun." After the years of fighting, the war had finally ended, but that fact was to be kept from the Allied people for another thirty-six hours. To Kennedy, "it was as though the heads of the governments had jointly lost their minds at the last moment as a result of the strain."[111]

Eisenhower had gone to the War Room at about 3:30 to make the brief newsreel and radio recordings announcing the surrender. His irritation is clearly evident in the Pathé footage when Butcher requests a retake to substitute the word surrender for armistice, which conjured up unpleasant memories of the end of the First World War. Eisenhower cabled the Combined Chiefs of Staff and the British Chiefs of Staff in his understated style: "The mission of this Allied force was fulfilled at 0241, local time, May 7, 1945."[112]

Eisenhower next considered the vexing issue of the news release. Butcher alerted him to the reporters lurking outside the door of SHAEF Forward, and he warned that no matter what steps SHAEF took to prevent it, the story would leak once all of the press returned to Paris. Thus in a second message to the War Department, Eisenhower stressed his conviction that news of the surrender should be released "at the earliest hour coordination can be achieved." SHEAF officials also considered how to alert troops in the field. General Bull had prepared an order to be transmitted in the clear, but Butcher warned that such a radio message would be picked up by various monitoring services and would quickly become public, violating the commitment to wait for the Big Three's announcement. As a result, the message to military units went out in code and thus with some delay.[113]

Within the hour SHAEF also assured the Combined Chiefs of Staff, the British Chiefs of Staff, and the Allied military mission in Moscow that no release would be made to the press before the three governments had announced the surrender. SHAEF followed this thirty minutes later with a second message drafted by General Bull reiterating that SHAEF Forward would not release the news until after the announcements by civilian leadership. That said, Bull warned that "orders to troops in enemy commands will go in the clear and moreover it will be impossible to keep millions of individuals in France and neutral countries from learning the facts. It is believed hopeless to keep this secret until Tuesday." He then reinforced Eisenhower's earlier advice that an announcement of the surrender be made as soon as possible. Eisenhower sent a final message to the Russians alerting them that the Germans had acquiesced to a second, more formal ratification of the surrender to occur at a time and place chosen by the Allies. He stressed again that while troops in the field were to be notified, there was to be no release to the press pending the statements of Truman, Churchill, and Stalin. An exhausted Eisenhower finally left SHAEF Forward just before five o'clock and was quickly in bed for a few hours' sleep. Butcher, Ford, and a few others unwound at General Bull's billet before Butcher deposited Ford back at the WAC house just before six and then went to bed himself.[114]

When Butcher awoke at nine o'clock, he found Eisenhower already up and making phone calls to deal with Russian complications. Shortly after the ink was dry on the surrender documents, SHAEF Forward received an urgent cable from the mission in Moscow. The liaison officers there reported that responding to Eisenhower's cable of May 6 proposing language for the surrender, the Russians had withdrawn their assent to the Reims surrender after learning of radio broadcasts by Dönitz urging German troops to continue fighting on the eastern front while no longer resisting in the west. The Soviets also demanded a formal surrender ceremony in Berlin. This set off a flurry of messages from Eisenhower. He replied to the military mission that it should reassure the Russians that the Western Allies had not entered into a separate peace and that he would be happy to fly to Berlin for a second, more formal ceremony. He then cabled the Combined Chiefs in Washington that he had received the Russian message *after* the Reims signing, that he had told the Russians that he was prepared to go to Berlin, and that under the circumstances he now thought it unwise to make any announcement of the Reims surrender until the Russians were thoroughly satisfied.[115] Whatever chance that the news embargo might be lifted before the specified time the next day now seemed remote. As the Lucky Seventeen waited for first light, with their dispatches written and censored but held for release, one wonders if they felt that their luck had run out.

4

"Unmention Use Phone"

Just before dawn, the weary correspondents in the press party boarded army trucks in Reims for the ride to the airport. Boyd Lewis, who had hatched a scheme to be the first to file once they reached Paris, hung back so that he was the last to board. He would consequently be first off the truck and hence first on the plane. He could then sit nearest the door so that he would have the advantage in the race to file. Fog hugged the ground at the airport as day broke, shafts of sunlight piercing the low cloud. The full force of what he had just witnessed struck Lewis: "Soldiers could go home now. They wouldn't have to crouch in holes and fight like animals. . . . No more civilians scuttling down the road with their wealth in a bundle." The plane approached Paris just after seven o'clock in "the pale gold sunshine of an early May morning. I have never seen the city so beautiful as it was from the air that day," Ed Kennedy wrote, his spirits buoyed by what he had just witnessed.[1]

On the return flight to Paris, other reporters had crowded near the door hoping, like Lewis, to beat their rivals off the plane; the pilot cracked that "there were so many people in the tail that we came in almost like a pogo stick."[2] Once landed at Orly, the mad scramble of the agency men to be the first to file began in earnest. Here the story grows murky. Lewis claims that he jumped out of the C-47 and hailed the first jeep in line, bribing the driver with a bottle of brandy to ignore the thirty miles per hour speed limit in the race to the Scribe. He reached the hotel just before Kennedy who had shared a jeep from the airport with the INS's James Kilgallen. Lewis submitted his flash service message as well as his five-thousand-word story at the intake desk on the mezzanine of the Scribe. The clerk stamped it "No. 1," first to be transmitted. Lewis claims that Kilgallen filed next and ahead of Kennedy because "Jimmy had beaten him to the revolving door of the Scribe and 'accidentally' dropped his portable typewriter where Kennedy would fall over it." As Kilgallen and Lewis talked on the stairway, "Ed Kennedy puffed up almost audibly gnashing his teeth in frustration."[3] Lewis believed that Kennedy resorted to deceit hours later because he had been beaten fairly in the race to file.

Kennedy told a quite different tale, claiming that neither Lewis's dash nor Kilgallen's typewriter had in any way blocked him from filing. He pointed out that given the embargo, the typical agency race to file would be useless. There were five transmitters in the Scribe by the end of the war (belonging to RCA, Mackay, Western Union, Press Wireless, and the Signal Corps), each capable of sending at least seven hundred words per minute. On important stories, the army limited the length and sent in rotation the flashes and first takes from the three agencies. During the time the story was embargoed, the teletypesetters would have punched out the tape to feed into the high-speed transmitters, and as a result the agencies would have virtually simultaneous transmission. "I was well aware of the situation," Barney Oldfield, the Ninth Army's PRO quotes Kennedy as saying, "and was somewhat puzzled by the scrambling of Kilgallen. I did not see Lewis en route and did not know whether or not he had reached the Scribe before me. I lost no time in getting to the Scribe because I did not know what might be developing there, but there was no reason to be concerned whether any of us was a few minutes ahead or behind."[4] In this instance, the agency reporters could forgo the race to file.

Amid all this, Thor Smith and the other PROs also returned to Paris, silly with fatigue. After a bath and a shave, Smith joined Roy Pawley and

Burroughs Matthews to finish their account of the surrender. A conference was called for 10:45 a.m., when Pawley and Matthews distributed their narrative and Smith added additional eyewitness testimony. Ernest Dupuy stressed that the story would remain off the record until SHAEF authorized its release. Thor Smith thought that the conference had gone as well as could be expected, but Kennedy remembered it as an "angry meeting." Those correspondents who had been barred from the Reims signing were still grousing, their anger fueled by the thirty-six-hour hold. Dupuy admitted that as the reporters filed out of the briefing room, "everyone was tired, the majority of our news men disgruntled." However, "the flaming violence of the previous night" when reporters had howled at SHAEF's decisions, "had died down."[5]

Both Dupuy and Thor Smith remained as frustrated as the press by the hold on the surrender news. "To delay announcement of the fact by any artificial means was wrong," Dupuy had decided. "The story was held up artificially by the three Governments concerned. That was a matter of high policy with which SHAEF had nothing to do." When he had learned of the stop the previous night, Smith had pointed out "the foolhardiness of such a long embargo." Dupuy also thought that SHAEF had borrowed trouble by so limiting the press contingent to cover the surrender. He never accepted the argument that there was not sufficient space at SHAEF Forward to accommodate a larger press group, if for no other reason than "the surrender could have been held in the great quadrangle inside the headquarters building—a thousand spectators could have been gathered there." Three days earlier, Dupuy observed, Montgomery sensibly had held his surrender ceremony outside in a tent, witnessed by a full complement of reporters. Dupuy still believed years after 1945 that the press "were there to cover the war; they should have been able to cover its end—to cover it physically. It was the people's story; the more eyes and ears present to witness it, the better."[6] Thus even one of the few career army officers in the Public Relations Division had misgivings about the official effort to control such consequential news.

After the morning press briefing at the Scribe, Kennedy decided to take a rare walk to consider the situation. On the streets of Paris, people were buzzing with rumors of the German surrender and were puzzled that there had been no formal announcement. In the lobby of the Scribe, reporters were milling around "muttering their displeasure." Kennedy decided not to join them but rather to go up to his office on the fourth floor to check on the reports "coming one upon the other," chattering off the AP teleprinter. He also told his colleague Morton Gudebrod to prepare a story based on Kennedy's censor-approved copy to send to the French desk for translation, but with instructions not to release it until Kennedy gave the word.[7]

Kennedy tried to contact General Frank A. Allen shortly after mid-day to protest the news embargo, only to be told by his clerk that Allen was too busy to talk. He then went downstairs to lunch, stopping on his way at the office of Lieutenant Colonel Richard H. Merrick in the first of what would be two tense encounters with Merrick that day. According to an interview Kennedy gave a month after the surrender, he had asked Merrick, who supervised the censorship of the US press corps, if there was any chance of a quick release of the story. Merrick told Kennedy that there was presently no chance of an early release and that he doubted the situation would change. Merrick was silent when Kennedy declared that he now felt free to send the story.[8]

In the early afternoon Kennedy's belief that the story could not be contained for long, a belief shared by Dupuy and Thor Smith, was confirmed. The first hint came at 7:00 a.m. in New York (1:00 p.m. Paris time) when the AP's night editor left a message for the day crew that Admiral Dönitz had broadcast an order for German submarines to cease hostilities. There followed reports from Sweden that the Germans in Norway were about to surrender, and from London that shops there were hanging out flags for a celebration. "Unless somebody's kidding somebody," the editor concluded, "it looks like it's [the surrender] in the bag and the only questions is 'when.'"[9]

Likely Kennedy learned much of this from the messages he read when he went to the AP office after lunch. In rapid succession other reports began to reach the AP by phone or teleprinter: General de Gaulle's office announced that he was writing his VE address; General François Sevez, who had represented France at Reims, had written an eyewitness account soon to be published in *Le Figaro*; and papers hit the kiosks outside the Scribe with news that loudspeakers had been strung outside 10 Downing Street. Allied troops had been told that hostilities would cease at midnight, according to correspondents in the field. Kennedy even heard a rumor that "people in the know were reputed to be making

Figure 4.1. Lieutenant Colonel Richard H. Merrick in his office at the Hotel Scribe, February 1945. Merrick had chaired the Joint Censorship Committee responsible for all Allied military censorship on D-Day. He remained the chief censor for all material filed by US correspondents who were accredited to SHAEF headquarters, and he flew to Reims with the Lucky Seventeen. Merrick butted heads with Ed Kennedy in Paris on May 7 over the release of the surrender story. Courtesy United States Army Heritage and Education Center, Richard H. Merrick Papers, Carlisle, PA.

large sums of money in the markets," banking on a steep rise when the surrender was finally announced.[10]

As Kennedy mulled over his course of action in the Scribe that afternoon, he well understood the risk he would take in breaking the story. AP executives had been delighted with Kennedy's performance throughout the war and especially his direction of the Paris bureau; defying SHAEF might very well jeopardize his position with the agency. "I knew if I sent the story there would be fireworks and I would come out a marked man," he told an interviewer. He was sure that "the other correspondents would be highly indignant." Although in the past he had kept his agreements with authorities, especially those related to release times, "in this case I found myself confronted with what I believe was a conflict in rules and what I considered my duty."[11]

The final straw for Kennedy came just after 2 p.m. (Paris time) with reports that Count Johann Ludwig von Krosigk, foreign minister of the Dönitz government, had broadcast an address to the German people from Flensburg, which began: "After a heroic fight of almost six years of incomparable hardness, Germany has succumbed to the overwhelming power of her enemies. A government which has a feeling of responsibility for the future of its nation was compelled to act on the collapse of all physical and material forces and to demand of the enemy the cessation of hostilities." Von Krosigk's address was also picked up by British Ministry of Information (MOI) listening posts. In the Scribe, Kennedy listened as the BBC broadcast a translation of the statement a few minutes later. At 2:19 p.m. (Paris time), the London AP office cabled a bulletin to both New York and Paris alerting them to the broadcast, followed ten minutes later by a longer story.[12]

Kennedy assumed that since von Krosigk's broadcast was made from territory controlled by the 21st Army Group, it must have been sanctioned by SHAEF. To Kennedy, SHAEF had broken its own news embargo.[13] He instructed Morton Gudebrod to try to reach London by telephone while he returned with Relman Morin to Merrick's office. Kennedy showed him the Flensburg statement, declaring that his pledge to Allen on the plane had been to hold the story until SHAEF released it. Now that had happened. Kennedy would argue that in journalism: "It is a universal practice that when a story which is being held for release is inadvertently or deliberately released in advance of the time set by its source or by any news organization, other newspapers and agencies consider it then to be automatically and generally released and feel free to publish it without further delay. I followed this universally accepted practice. Any agreement is binding for all parties to it and it is obvious that the commitments made to us by the administration were as binding as our own commitments."[14]

According to Kennedy, Merrick told him that he would like to help, but he needed to follow orders. Kennedy again warned the censor that he was going to send the story. In Merrick's telling, Kennedy came to his office shortly before three o'clock and "ranted to me to the effect that there was no security in the story and that it was being held for no good reason and that he was going to 'bust' it if he had to send every one of his men to the Swiss and Spanish border." The lanky, bespectacled Merrick told Kennedy not to be foolish. The reporter "repeated something about being able to get the story out without its going through censorship," and he accused SHAEF of already allowing a United Press flash about the surrender. Merrick said he doubted this was true but that they should double-check. As the two walked down to the copy room, Kennedy repeated his claim that the Flensburg broadcast was in effect SHAEF's announcement of the surrender. Merrick said that he did not know who, if anyone, had authorized the German announcement, but that he held out hope that the release time might be advanced after all. With this, Kennedy left.[15]

Upon returning to his law practice in Chicago later that year, Merrick conceded that Kennedy's version of events was largely accurate, but he insisted that it did not capture the reporter's fury on the day. "Kennedy came storming into my office with his retinue," in Merrick's memory, and had "raged" that the surrender story had been released, "accused us of letting the United Press story go," and threatened to do what he could to get his story back out. "At the time I thought he was overwrought and didn't take him too seriously, especially as he seemed mollified after I proved we hadn't released his opposition's dispatches," Merrick recalled. "Later in the evening all hell broke loose."[16] Boyd Lewis claims that Merrick told him after the war that Kennedy had come in and "shouted almost incoherent threats to charter airplanes and send reporters to neutral sending points with the story if SHAEF did not release it." To which Merrick had replied that he should not do so but rather should "go to bed and sleep it off."[17]

Kennedy concluded that Merrick could only be so blasé about his threat to break the story if he assumed there was no practical way for Kennedy (or anyone else) to do so. Kennedy then went back to his own room in the AP suite to collect his thoughts and assess the situation one final time. He stressed in all of his subsequent accounts that he was well aware circumventing censorship would anger both army officials and the other reporters in Paris, but that he felt obliged to act.[18]

Gudebrod later testified that Kennedy returned to the AP suite within a few minutes of having left for the censor's office. In the interval, Gudebrod had succeeded in reaching the London bureau on the phone, even if on a poor connection. Kennedy handed Gudebrod a brief flash message. "Give them this," he said. AP staffers in London had been "sweating out peace news in [an] atmosphere loaded with rumor expectancy and cigarette smoke," according to a detailed AP service message that SHAEF intercepted, when the phone rang at 1:24 p.m. (London time), or just minutes after the Flensburg announcement. When editor Russell Landstrom answered it, he heard a faint "Paris calling" on the line. The voice faded, then returned. Landstrom heard the word Paris again and then gave the phone to another staffer, Lew Hawkins, who heard an unfamiliar voice state that Germany had surrendered unconditionally at Reims. Gudebrod identified himself, explaining that he was calling from the AP office in Paris. As Hawkins scrambled to take down details and query Gudebrod's authority, Kennedy himself came on the line, a voice that Hawkins recognized. "This is Ed Kennedy, Lew, Germany surrendered unconditionally—that's official make date[line] Reims and get it out."[19]

Hawkins immediately handed the flash to the censor to approve for transmission on the office's Western Union link to New York. The British censor in the office was unaware of the embargo, and since the dispatch had come from abroad with a Reims dateline, he assumed that it had been vetted at the source, and British policy was to forward such copy without additional censorship in London. This first flash with the Reims dateline was received in the AP's New York office at 9:26 a.m. and was marked "PBC" (passed by censor). It read simply: "Reims France Germany Surrendered Unconditionally."

Glenn Babb, the foreign editor on duty in New York, "handled the flash as one might pick up a firecracker whose lighted fuse appeared to have gone out," according to one report. Unsure of its provenance, Babb held the flash for eight minutes until the first section (or take) of Kennedy's bulletin began to arrive with his byline on it. No longer in any doubt of its authenticity, Babb assumed that Kennedy was reporting an official announcement, and so he and the cable editor added three fateful words to the flash, which read as it went out at 9:35 a.m. on the "A" wire reserved for the most urgent news: "Flash—Reims France—*Allies officially announced* Germany surrendered unconditionally." Kennedy was adamant that he did not state over the phone that the story was based on an announcement by SHAEF, only that he knew it was the "real thing" because he had witnessed it.[20]

The next few hours proved chaotic in AP offices on both sides of the Atlantic. In Paris, while Kennedy remained on the phone, often spelling out words slowly because of the poor connection, Gudebrod assumed that SHAEF had approved its release and so rushed down to the AP's French desk to see that it was dispatched to the agency's client newspapers in that country. There the editor showed him Kennedy's flash, which had been retransmitted on the AP's South American wire. Even as Gudebrod prepared to telephone the flash to the subscribing papers, translators had not yet begun work on Kennedy's longer story. Before they could do so, a liaison censor called the office to stop the flash and ordered that no other surrender news be released without permission. Gudebrod insisted that he only learned later that the AP flash had not been authorized by SHAEF.[21]

In London, bureau chief Robert Bunnelle was meeting with British newspaper executives in the Reuters offices when Gudebrod's call came in. Bunnelle asked Reuters's managing director if he had received a similar story and was told no. This was the first indication that something might be amiss, but his staff assured Bunnelle that there was no doubt that it had been Kennedy on the phone.[22] In the AP offices, it remained difficult to hear Kennedy as he dictated the longer bulletin report following the brief flash. After capturing the first take of the story, Hawkins turned the phone over to another staffer, Jim King, so that he himself could copy the bulletin and hurry it onto the wire. He sent this at 1:34 p.m. and included Kennedy's lead elaborating on the flash, adding that the Germans had surrendered unconditionally "to Western Allies and Russia at 0241 (French time) today in the big Reims red schoolhouse which is headquarters of General Dwight D. Eisenhower."[23] King then took the next two or three short takes of Kennedy's careful dictation, passing the penciled sheets across the desk to another staffer for copying.

After a hasty edit these first takes were sent to the censor for clearance and then to the cable transmitter. Kennedy's voice cut out several times before the bulk of the story had been received, edited, and transmitted to New York. The connection failed as Kennedy was describing General Alfred Jodl's postsurrender statement. In all, the first two hundred sixty of Kennedy's three hundred words were received. The line was lost thirty minutes after Kennedy had made first contact, and London could not reestablish the line. Having no special instruction to hold stories about

Figure 4.2. In August 1943, Robert McLean, the longtime AP board president, visited London and the AP bureau there. Pictured here, left to right, are Robert Bunnelle, the London bureau chief, Lewis Hawkins, a line editor, and McLean. Kennedy routed his dispatch through Bunnelle's London bureau, where it was handled by Hawkins. McLean would determine Kennedy's fate at the agency after the surrender story broke. Caption: Courtesy AP Images.

the surrender and adhering to MOI policy, the censor quickly passed the story as he had the flash, assuming both had been censored and approved for publication in Paris.[24] "KENNEDY AND ALL HANDS YOU HIT SUPER JACK POT AND LAUREL WREATHS ARE IN ORDER," Bunnelle wired the staff in Paris. Reuters had picked up Kennedy's flash nineteen minutes after the AP had put it on the wire, he added, so it was a clear beat as far as he was concerned.[25]

In New York, Kennedy's longer bulletin was coming in slowly, the takes in the queue with other stories on the heavily-trafficked wire. At 9:42 the AP had enough confidence in Kennedy's report to alert members that they could now release their mountain of prepared "Victory in Europe" material. However, fifteen minutes later the Nashville bureau cabled that neither the UP nor INS had yet announced the surrender, bringing Babb and his colleagues in New York up short.[26] If SHAEF had officially announced the surrender, why were the other agencies not flashing the news?

Piecing together the sequence of events, Babb told London that he had held up the original flash until the bulletin with Kennedy's name and the location of the signing had arrived. He asked if the London bureau had verified that the flash had come from Kennedy before it had sent the subsequent bulletin. Fifteen minutes later, Babb contacted London stressing that he needed "QUICKLY" any information it had about the "MEANS KENNEDY USED SCORE HIS BEAT." Bunnelle replied that Kennedy's flash came from Paris by phone from Gudebrod, but that London had not sent it on until Kennedy himself came on the line to verify its authenticity. Since flashes usually did not include an identifying byline, London had not sent one. Bunnelle apologized for the lag in sending the bulletin but explained that this had been "UNAVOIDABLE BECAUSE OF VERY BAD CONNECTION." Bunnelle added that Kennedy wanted "US UN-MENTION USE PHONE." He also wanted to know if the rival agencies had released the story yet.[27]

Babb cabled the Paris office asking for SHAEF's official comment, as well as an accounting of how Kennedy attained the story before the other agencies. He heard nothing back. He also queried London to see if Bunnelle knew how Kennedy had sent the story. Shortly after 11 a.m. (New York time), Bunnelle replied cryptically that he did not have Kennedy's permission to reveal the means used to transmit the story. He had no further details, but he too had requested that the AP office in Paris send him an explanation of the beat. At the same time the AP explained to editors nationwide that Kennedy's report had been sent from Paris to the London office and had been relayed from there to New York. This was true but not particularly informative.[28]

As Babb, Gould, and Bunnelle frantically tried to contact Paris for more details, SHAEF had already suspended the Associated Press there, cutting off its access to cable and telephone lines. In an unprecedented move, the suspension applied not only to the Paris office but also to the AP across the continent, a move taken after the other agencies had cried foul. The INS's bureau chief in London, Joseph Kingsbury-Smith, was the first to alert PRD to Kennedy's story after he received a message about it from his office in New York. At roughly the same time, the United Press wired

Lewis demanding to know why the AP had the surrender story ahead of the UP. Lewis, in turn, fumed to SHAEF's Burroughs Matthews that its supposedly airtight system of communications security had "sprung a leak." Unsure of what had happened but suspecting malfeasance, Ernest Dupuy recommended that General Allen immediately suspend the AP until the leak could be identified. Allen did so at 4:40 p.m. (Paris time), then directed Matthews, Thor Smith, and Colonel Martin Ralph, PRD's communications chief, to investigate. Five minutes later SHAEF issued a statement stressing that it had not made an official announcement regarding the surrender. Tellingly, it did not deny the substance of Kennedy's story.[29]

Matthews went to the copy room, where he found that Kennedy's logged dispatches remained in the outgoing basket. None had moved on the official wire. Meanwhile, Kennedy walked the block to the PRD offices in the American Express Building to protest the suspension. He insisted that he had never breached any confidence. Allen told him that he had assigned officers to investigate the matter and would have nothing more to do with Kennedy until he received their report.[30]

Thereafter Kennedy ran across Matthews on the street outside the Scribe, and he freely admitted sending the story. When Matthews asked how he had transmitted the story Kennedy replied, "I will say the same thing to you that I said to Colonel [George] Warden, that is, it is up to you to find out." Kennedy argued that the story raised no security concern and that neither he nor his agency could submit to political censorship.[31]

Even as Allen suspended the AP, the rest of the press corps at the Scribe was in high dudgeon at having been scooped. Nonetheless, the reporters erupted only after Allen, to Kennedy "by this time an expert at rubbing salt into open wounds," informed them that the embargo still held and would remain in place until the next afternoon. Correspondents could quote Kennedy's story but not add any of their own details or report on the surrender independently. This infuriated the correspondents who in effect were being told they could only amplify Kennedy's scoop, one they charged had been scored by deceit. SHAEF continued its official silence on the matter. "The effect of such a ruling on the already shattered nerves of the correspondents may be imagined," Kennedy drily commented. For Thor Smith, the "pressure and recriminations" piled in "from all sides" as he tried to sort rumor from fact.[32]

Things were scarcely less fraught in Washington on a day that should have been one of joyous relief. Immediately after learning of the Flensburg broadcast, Churchill alerted the White House that he felt great pressure to move up the announcement in London. Roosevelt's long-standing chief of staff, Admiral William D. Leahy, who was serving in the same capacity for President Truman, telephoned Churchill early Monday morning, Washington time. Leahy conveyed Truman's decision not to act without obtaining Stalin's agreement. Churchill responded that the Germans had announced the surrender on the radio just the previous hour. "What is the use of me and the President looking to be the only two people in the world who don't know what is going on?" Churchill fumed. The news was leaking out in both the United States and Britain, he reminded Leahy, and he had concluded that it was "absolutely necessary" to make an official announcement in a matter of hours, at 6 p.m. London time (noon in Washington). Churchill agreed to try to contact Stalin but warned of haphazard communications with Moscow.

Churchill and Leahy talked past each other for some time, Leahy repeating that Truman felt obliged to honor the agreement with Stalin, while Churchill kept insisting that the horse had already left that barn. Leahy agreed to contact Major General John Deane of the military mission in Moscow through a direct teletype line, hoping Deane could get the Russians to acquiesce to an earlier release time. If the Russians agreed by 11:30 that morning, then Washington too would make an official surrender announcement at noon, the moment Churchill would use to make one in London. King George was scheduled to speak three hours later. "It is impossible to stop it now that the German announcement has been on the wire," Churchill reiterated. Given what the news agencies were now reporting, "it is an idiotic position" Churchill railed, referring to waiting for the Russians. "In view of the German announcement, I have got to tell the English people whether it is true or false. I can not agree to delay that."[33]

One can understand Churchill's impatience. People were celebrating in the streets on at least two continents. In New York, thousands gathered tentatively in Times Square and elsewhere. There was initial hesitance because of the recent false alarms and the cautions on the radio that Truman had yet to vouchsafe the news. In Washington, there was bewilderment that the end of the war in Europe had been revealed in such a muddled way, especially after the public statement that there would be no official announcement until one could be coordinated with the British and the Russians. As the AP story broke, the press flocked to the White House, joining hundreds of people gathered at the gates only to be gently shooed away by the police. News desks in papers across the country were soon swamped with phone calls from ordinary citizens checking on the truth of the surrender reports they had heard on the radio.[34]

The British public was more than willing to accept the Kennedy scoop as authentic. It had been at war with Germany for six long years, and Britain had less stake in the continuing war in the Pacific. Thousands had gathered in Piccadilly Circus before noon. "Civilians and service men and women thronged the road and pavements, carrying flags and wearing paper hats," the *Times* reported the next day. "Cheering demonstrators climbed to the roofs of buses" while cars honked out Beethoven's four note victory theme. The crowds cheered Churchill as he left 10 Downing Street, tipping his hat and flashing the V for Victory sign.[35]

When officials in the Pentagon heard Kennedy's flash broadcast on the local radio, they immediately contacted SHAEF Forward for an explanation. In an intermittent teleprinter conference with Reims spanning several hours, Colonel Frank McCarthy, General George Marshall's aide-de-camp tried to clarify what had actually happened and then scrambled to get the official announcement pushed forward to noon. McCarthy first asked if the report on the radio in Washington was an official announcement from Eisenhower. Lieutenant Colonel Walter Scott, a SHAEF staff officer, sent a colleague scuttling down the corridor to Eisenhower's office for an answer. When he returned, Scott assured McCarthy that Eisenhower had not made any such statement. McCarthy replied that the details in the story as broadcast were consistent with those that SHAEF had cabled to the War Department the night before; even if no official announcement had been made, ticker tape was falling in New York. McCarthy conveyed General Marshall's impatience to learn how the leak had occurred, to which Scott could only reply that SHAEF was investigating.[36]

While communicating with Scott, McCarthy also stayed in touch with General Deane. Fulfilling Leahy's promise to Churchill, he directed Deane to contact Russian officials about moving forward the release time. McCarthy alerted Scott that both Truman and Churchill were frantically trying to contact Stalin to urge a victory statement at noon, now only thirty minutes away. Scott also disclosed that SHAEF had determined that Kennedy had leaked the story himself, most likely through a private telephone line, and that the AP was now suspended from transmitting anything, including service messages. With only twenty minutes remaining before Churchill intended to announce in London, Deane alerted McCarthy that the Russians would not agree to the change in timing because they had not yet received confirmation of the signing from their own representative, General Susloparoff.[37]

McCarthy notified Churchill just minutes before noon that, given the Russian position, Truman was committed to withholding the statement until the next day. Churchill asked incredulously if the official position of the US government was that the BBC was behind the Flensburg broadcast and all of the US radio bulletins. McCarthy simply repeated that Truman would not announce until the next morning.[38]

McCarthy relayed the Russian position to SHAEF Forward. He still believed that Churchill very well might announce the surrender without Russian acquiescence, but since it was already a good ten minutes past noon with no word from London, perhaps not. In any case, Truman was committed to the original release time. In a final teletype to Deane, McCarthy indicated that while it was then 12:15, US radio had yet to carry news of a statement from Churchill even though as far as he knew it had been the prime minister's intention to make one.[39] As it turned out, Churchill reluctantly held off on the official announcement until the next day, but only after issuing a statement at 7:40 p.m. (London time) that May 8 would officially be designated as VE Day, in essence telegraphing the news.

As the noon hour approached in the AP's offices in New York, Babb and his colleagues had confidence in Kennedy's reporting, but the silence from SHAEF—and from the other agencies—was nerve-racking. The next few hours would mix frantic activity with utter confusion. Babb cabled Paris about SHAEF's recent statement that it had not yet announced the German surrender nor authorized any story to that effect. "APPRECIATE SOONEST DETAILED REASONS THIS STATEMENT," the AP asked, its tone becoming more insistent with each query.[40]

Just after noon CBS carried a broadcast from Edward R. Murrow in London reporting that Truman and Churchill had been prepared to issue official word of the surrender at noon, but there had been a delay because

Stalin was not yet ready to do the same. At roughly the same time, the AP in New York learned that both the UP and the INS in Paris were reporting the bare fact that filing privileges for the AP in Europe had been suspended. Once again the AP staff in New York cabled Paris. "NEED REPORT QUICKEST," they now demanded, "SURELY AUTHORITIES PERMIT YOU NOTIFY US SITUATION." Bunnelle alerted New York shortly before one o'clock that he had been unable to contact Kennedy. His call to Paris had not been returned, and he suspected that the army was preventing Kennedy from contacting London. A few minutes later he added that since the AP was no longer allowed to call the bureau in Paris, he had asked newspaper friends in London to pass on any information about Kennedy they received. A detailed account of what was going on would have to wait until Kennedy surfaced.[41]

Whatever lingering doubts Babb may have had about Kennedy's story were soon dispelled. Two messages arrived from London at the bottom of the hour. One contained the MOI's bulletin that the next day would be designated as VE Day. The other was a copy of King George's congratulatory message to Eisenhower for his "complete and crushing victory," labeled not to be released in New York before 6:30 p.m. Even so, the White House yet again stated at two o'clock that it would make no surrender announcement until it could be coordinated with the other Allied leaders. At mid-afternoon word went out on the INS wire that the reason for SHAEF's suspension of the AP was indeed Kennedy's dispatch.[42]

As the day wore on (and turned to evening in Paris), the mad scramble continued. Bunnelle wired his superiors in New York that the AP should send a "STRONG DIRECT PROTEST" to SHAEF and the War Department about the drastic action taken in suspending the AP's transmission rights, especially with no claim that military security had been at issue. Bunnelle reminded those in New York that the "LIGHTEST PENALTY" had been imposed on the AP's competitors over the unauthorized broadcasts from Paris at its liberation the previous August even "WHILE OPERATIONS IN FULL BLAST." Bunnelle vowed to relinquish his accreditation credentials if SHAEF attempted to suspend the AP in London.[43]

Without yet hearing directly from Kennedy, Kent Cooper in New York felt he had a strong enough grasp of the facts to make Bunnelle's advised protest to the military. He wrote first to Eisenhower, asking if the reports of the AP suspension were true; if they were, he sought an explanation. If the suspension was the result of the actions of one individual, he demanded to know why the entire AP in Europe was being punished. The credentials of individual reporters had been revoked in the past, but never had an entire news organization been so sanctioned. If only one person was involved, Cooper pressed SHAEF to identify him and supply that person's explanation, "SINCE APPARENTLY EYE AM UNABLE TO COMMUNICATE WITH HIM MYSELF." Cooper followed this with a similar cable to Secretary of War Henry Stimson, adding that the AP had not put Kennedy's story on the wire until an hour after the German government itself had announced its surrender. "IF THE ACCOUNT IS TRUE," Cooper added, "SURELY THE UNITED STATES GOVERNMENT DOES NOT WANT TO PLAY A JOKE ON THE AMERICAN PEOPLE" by withholding information known to the rest of the world.[44]

In further evidence of the rivalry between print and broadcast media, Cooper followed with a cable to President Truman requesting that the White House give all newspapers confidential advance word of the statement so that they could publish it simultaneously with the public announcement itself, allowing "NEWSPAPERS THE OPPORTUNITY TO DISCHARGE THEIR RESPONSIBILITY TO THE PUBLIC EQUAL WITH RADIO." Cooper copied these messages to the AP membership as a confidential note (that is, not for publication), adding that he had told the authorities that the withholding of information should "not be carried to the point of absurdity." He contacted Stephen Early, the longtime White House press secretary and FDR intimate, to apprise him of the AP's messages to Truman and Stimson. Cooper warned that censorship should not be carried to a "RIDICULOUS LEVEL."[45]

Just minutes before Cooper sent his cable to SHAEF (at 2:38 p.m. New York time), Bunnelle wired that he had finally been able to contact Paris "BY SPECIAL MEANS" but so far had only confirmed that Allen had indeed suspended the AP "IN THIS THEATER" and that he would try to acquire more details. He also advised that it would be "INEXPEDIENT DISCLOSE NOW THAT DIRECT CONTACT MADE," given SHAEF's suspension, which seemed to apply not only to dispatches but also to communication of any sort.[46] Bunnelle's reference here to a "special means"

of communication between the AP in Paris and London alludes to yet another clandestine circuit the AP had discovered unbeknownst to SHAEF.

Don Doane, a staffer in London covering the air war, had learned of a
direct teleprinter line outside censorship control between the Eighth Air
Force information bureau in the MOI and the Ninth Air Force public
relations office in the Scribe. The line was used to transmit material for
briefings in Paris about air operations in England. Doane had befriended
the sergeant who operated the line in the MOI. When Bunnelle asked him
if he knew of any way to reach the AP in Paris, Doane approached the
sergeant for help. In return for a bottle of whiskey, the sergeant allowed
Doane, who could operate a teletype, to contact the Scribe. The sergeant
guarded the door while Doane phoned Bunnelle in the AP offices on
Fleet Street more than a mile away and relayed Bunnelle's questions to
Paris.[47]

An unsuspecting sergeant, Eduard Dieball, happened to be on duty in
the Ninth Air Force office that night while the regular crew of enlisted
men was out for a meal (and perhaps to celebrate). When Doane's first
message came through, Dieball responded that he should check back
later since everyone was at dinner. When Doane did so shortly before
nine o'clock, Dieball in Paris was able to go to the AP suite in the Scribe
to fetch Gudebrod down to the air force office. Doane asked Gudebrod if
the AP in fact had been suspended and if so for what reason; Gudebrod
said that no announcement had been made and that he could not at this
point say any more. He did tell Doane that both Kennedy and Morin had
filed "informatives" (service messages) to Cooper explaining the situation, but he suspected that both may have been intercepted by SHAEF.
Doane relayed Bunnelle's rather desperate suggestion that the AP staff
contact a delegation of U.S. senators in Paris at the time for their views
on withholding such news from the public, with said senators to reply
directly to the AP in New York or London. Gudebrod was also able to
relay the service message from Kennedy that he assumed SHAEF had
intercepted:

ASSOCIATED SUSPENDED FROM ALL OPERATIONS IN THIS THE-
ATER ON ORDER PUBLIC RELATIONS AS RESULT MY STORY ON
GERMAN UNCONDITIONAL SURRENDER AT REIMS STOP THIS
STORY CORRECT AND I REGARD OUR JOB AS TELLING PUBLIC

WHAT HAPPENED RATHER THAN PLEASING WHIMS OF SHAEF
PUBLIC RELATIONS OR SUBMITTING TO CENSORSHIP WHEN NO
SECURITY ISSUE INVOLVED STOP ASK IMMEDIATE PROTEST TO
WAR DEPT ON GROUNDS PURELY POLITICAL CENSORSHIP.[48]

The Bunnelle-to-Doane-to-Dieball-to-Gudebrod-to-Kennedy circuit was
precarious, but it worked in this instance. Shortly thereafter the officer in
charge of the air force office in Paris returned from dinner. He knew of the
AP suspension, so when Dieball told him of the AP's use of the teleprinter,
the officer sent a message to London that the AP could not use the circuit
any longer because "TO DO SO JEOPARDIZES WHAT STANDING WE
HAVE WITH SHAEF."[49] With this, Doane grabbed the tape from the teleprinter and left.

Having finally heard from Paris, Bunnelle cabled Cooper that the
facts he had gathered indicated that the AP was the victim of a "HASTY
MILITARY BUREAUCRATIC ACTION WHICH AGAINST ALL PRIN-
CIPLES FREE PRESS." As far as Bunnelle knew, this supremely important
news was being suppressed for illegitimate reasons. Although the suspension also applied to the AP's private telephone at the Scribe and therefore
Kennedy and Morin's service messages most likely had not reached Cooper, Bunnelle wondered if the AP in Paris could still receive messages. He
advised that if he were in Kennedy's shoes, he would much appreciate
hearing from Cooper. Fifteen minutes later, Bunnelle sent Cooper Kennedy's message as received through Gudebrod and added that this had
been received in London "THROUGH SPECIAL COMMUNICATIONS
CHANNEL." It would not be smart to reveal that the London office had
been in direct contact with Paris. That said, Bunnelle could see no reason
why Kennedy's statement could not be published.[50]

When this cable reached New York, Cooper was still digesting Morin's message, which had arrived mid-afternoon. Allen had agreed that
Morin and Kennedy could notify their supervisors in London and New
York of their suspension, but this ruling evidently had not reached the
PRD censors, and word was not sent from the Scribe until after nine that
night. Morin's message simply told the AP that he could supply no more
information about Kennedy's story because Allen had suspended the AP
pending SHAEF's investigation. A second message confirmed that Allen
had modified his order so that it now applied not just to Paris but to the

AP reporters filing from anywhere in "this theater." Morin was also able to send a short message to Bunnelle, presumably warning him to keep quiet about the means used to get the story to London, saying that the AP was suspended for the moment "BUT MUST EMPHASIZE REEMPHASIZE NOTHING SHOULD BE PUBLISHED OR TRANSMITTED FOR ANY REASON ABOUT DETAILS KENNEDY'S GREAT BEAT UNTIL HE PERSONALLY AUTHORIZES."[51]

At this moment Cooper hesitated, despite his earlier strong words to Eisenhower, Stimson, and the AP membership. He first asked if Bunnelle knew whether Kennedy's dispatch had passed censorship in Paris, then asked what Reuters and Exchange Telegraph were reporting. He cautioned that it would be unwise to publish Kennedy's message until the AP had gotten a response from Eisenhower or the White House. In a final wire sent to London late that afternoon to be forwarded to

Figure 4.3. A formal portrait taken in 1944 of the AP's long-serving general manager. Kent Cooper was a self-professed champion of worldwide freedom of the press but an even more ferocious champion of the Associated Press itself. Courtesy AP Images.

Kennedy, Cooper confessed that he had just learned that the three words "SHAEF officially announced" had been added by editors in New York to Kennedy's flash. This was no small matter since SHAEF had used these three words as a club to batter Kennedy, with Allen charging that they made it seem like Eisenhower had violated the intergovernmental agreement.[52]

In Paris and as the afternoon waned, Allen's investigating committee continued their work. Knowing now that there had not been a mistake in the copy room nor any other error in the PRD's handling of Kennedy's material, Colonel Ralph considered what other routes the AP might have used to bypass official channels. He assigned his deputy in PRD's Communications Branch, Major Howard Schwartz, to discover if it was possible to telephone London from the Scribe while eluding censorship control. Just after seven o'clock that night, Schwartz tried to reach London from the Scribe by asking the hotel operator to connect with the Paris military telephone exchange; he then requested that the military operator connect him with the MOI at Senate House. When the MOI operator answered, Schwartz asked for the AP. The operator responded that she was uncertain whom he was asking for, at which point the line was lost. Twenty minutes later, Schwartz tried a different route. He contacted the main UK military exchange, and this time, instead of the MOI, he asked to connect with the private phone of a friend in Shepherd's Bush. Within a minute or two he was talking with his friend. Schwartz had made both calls from a civilian phone and yet had not been challenged by security. Though he had no proof that Kennedy used this means to contact the London office, Schwartz had at the least exposed a glaring flaw in SHAEF's communications security.[53]

After hearing this from the investigation at ten o'clock, Allen placed a rare phone call to the Pentagon and spoke with Colonel Luther Hill, General Alexander Surles's deputy acting in his absence. Secretary of War Stimson's special adviser for public relations, Arthur Page, also participated, a clear sign that the matter was top of mind in Washington. Allen explained that his inquiry revealed that the story had not been sent through official channels but rather most likely through a civilian telephone. He had concluded that the leak was the result of an individual and not the AP as a whole, so he had lifted the theater-wide suspension. Kennedy had admitted that he "deliberately violated all regulations," Allen claimed and also admitted that he had violated the pledge on the plane, claims Kennedy consistently denied. Allen told Hill and Page that the press corps in Paris was exerting intense pressure to release the surrender story, but that Eisenhower was determined to stick to the schedule. In a triumph of understatement, Allen admitted that this had placed the PRD in a "very unfortunate position." The correspondents in the Paris press corps had assured him they would not violate regulations, but Allen warned that the "Kennedy case is a very hot subject over here." Kennedy kept insisting that there was no security issue in the story, and Allen suspected that this would remain the AP's defense. However, Allen maintained that there was little if any sympathy for Kennedy at the Scribe.[54]

The AP suspension was short-lived. Having lifted it everywhere but in Paris by ten o'clock, an hour later Allen lifted it on all staffers in Paris except Kennedy and Gudebrod (as well as Bunnelle in London, whom Allen suspected had abetted the premature release). Relman Morin was then able to send New York a more complete account of the day's events, recounting Kennedy's trip to Reims and stressing that by noon "Paris was aflame" with reports of the surrender, culminating with word of the Flensburg broadcast.

Kennedy went to SHAEF authorities declaring his intention to file (unless they could identify security concerns) only after everyone in the Scribe had learned of the Flensburg broadcast, Morin wrote. As if to prove Kennedy's point, SHAEF censors cut the portion of Morin's cable stressing Kennedy's willingness to hold his copy while elsewhere cutting his assertion that military security was the only acceptable rationale for stops. Morin recited the suspension particulars to New York, noting that SHAEF had even disconnected the telephone lines in the AP's offices at the Scribe. AP reporters had been barred from the briefing room. Morin directly contradicted Allen by saying that many reporters at the Scribe had shaken Kennedy's hand and "CONGRATULATED" him on the "STAND HE HAD TAKEN AND TREMENDOUS BEAT HE HAD SCORED—EVEN AT THEIR EXPENSE."[55]

Once word of the AP's suspension reached its members, support began to trickle into the New York office. The first to react was Josephus Daniels, the editor and publisher of the Raleigh *News & Observer*. Daniels was a progressive Democrat, a former secretary of the Navy and longtime ally of Franklin Roosevelt; his son Jonathan was then serving as President

Truman's press secretary. At three o'clock the elder Daniels had cabled the White House expressing his opposition to the suspension of the AP. By five o'clock, the AP reported that even the United Press's president, Roy Howard, who himself had been so excoriated over the false armistice story years before, urged Truman to intervene on behalf of his rival. "The Associated Press has a well-earned reputation for public-spirited journalistic service," Howard offered, but did not hesitate to add that "it and all its member papers should not be subjected, as was the United Press and its clientele in 1918, to the unfair inferences which are sure to result unless this suspension is immediately withdrawn."[56]

By eight o'clock that night the Associated Press had assembled enough such commentary to put out a digest of the reaction to the AP's suspension. "Criticism of the suspension action," the story concluded, "was coupled in many cases with condemnation of the official blackout on confirmation from Allied sources and with congratulations on Kennedy's exclusive story." One city editor reported that the telephones in his newsroom had been ringing all afternoon as readers protested the suspension. The editors of the *New York Post* had complained to the White House that "the news of the German surrender has been deliberately withheld from the public by high Allied officials," a sentiment echoed by another who also condemned Eisenhower's suspension of the AP as "unwarranted and a transgression of democratic principles." The editor of the Boston *Traveller* termed it "stupid and outrageous." The managing editor of the Salt Lake *Deseret News* sent congratulations to both the agency and Kennedy "for having guts enough to cut through red tape and tell America what's going on."[57]

In London, the public was convinced that the war was over even without an official announcement. Toward six o'clock three Lancaster bombers flew low over London, dropping green and red lights. Shop fronts sprouted the flags of the Allied nations. People crowded into the pubs as barkeeps retrieved whiskey and champagne long stashed away. Large bonfires ringed London, and most public buildings were floodlit for the first time since 1939. Tugs and other small craft raced up and down the Thames, tooting their horns. "VE Day may be tomorrow," the *New York Times* reported, "but London could not wait."[58]

In New York, whatever public skepticism had greeted the unconfirmed news of the surrender in the late morning seemed to disappear once the first editions of the evening paper hit the streets. "Where in Times Square there had been only some hundreds of people," a British observer reported, "now there were thousands in a tumult of joy." Tickertape and confetti showered down from windows, quickly covering the streets. Still, the observer thought that "although the joy was great it had not the violence of spirit of the armistice celebration of 1918." Too many had died, and Japan still fought on. To a reporter in the city, New Yorkers seemed to be reacting to the news in different ways; many celebrated with the enthusiasm of "New Year's Eve and Election Night rolled into one," whereas others were restrained, flocking into churches for a moment of "quiet thanksgiving," realizing that a bitter struggle still remained in the Pacific and perhaps still grieving the loss of the architect of the victory, Franklin Roosevelt, the previous month.[59]

As May 7 wound down, exhaustion set in among officials on two continents. For SHAEF staffers, one word best described the day's events. "Have reached the snafu of snafus!" Ernest Dupuy wrote in his diary late that night, calling Kennedy a "stinker" and alarmed that the correspondents at the Scribe were "clamoring for blood." Thor Smith would write the next night that he had been a "significant part of the greatest journalistic snafu in history," and later referred to the entire episode as the "Surrender Snafu." Harry Butcher wrote in his diary that Kennedy's story had "caused the damndedest snafu I have ever experienced. It's not only snafu but tarfu and fumtu. I've learned the hard way it is much easier to start a war than to stop one."[60]

We do not know how Kennedy spent the night. In *Ed Kennedy's War* he claims that once suspended he could not work but was otherwise unconstrained by SHAEF. He had gone out to join the street celebrations. Given that he had barely slept in two days, presumably midnight found him in bed.[61] Bunnelle wired Kennedy his assurance that New York and not London had added "Allies officially announced" to his dispatch.[62] Based on the record of cable traffic that night, Morin held down the fort in the AP office.

The rest of the press corps in Paris, notwithstanding Morin's comment that correspondents had congratulated Kennedy, ended the day infuriated by their plight—scooped by Kennedy but still prevented from reporting on the surrender. As fireworks exploded over the Seine and while French civilians and Allied troops danced in Parisian streets, the PRD canceled its evening briefing for the first time since D-Day. "Press Headquarters was like a wake," the AP reported, "Correspondents gathered in little knots, talking over news they could not write." Those celebrating outside "had seen the headlines in the afternoon papers and heard enough on their radios to convince them Germany had surrendered even if victory sirens had not wailed."[63]

That night the *New York Times* received a service message from Drew Middleton, one of its correspondents in Paris. He was furious that his surrender story was being held by SHAEF censorship. Middleton had come to the *Times* from the AP the previous year, and would be the paper's preeminent military correspondent for decades. He admired the military and criticized it cautiously, but Middleton explained that he had been caught in the biggest "'snafu' in the history of the war," this after laboring on the story for more than a day. "I am browned off, fed up, burnt up and put out," Middleton fumed. His "story will probably be released tomorrow," he wrote, "which will only be 24 hours late."[64] Middleton was wrong. In the event, officials did not acknowledge the surrender for a full day and a half.

At the Hotel Scribe

When Kennedy awoke the next morning, May 8, he found a cable from Kent Cooper apprising him of the "STAGGERING FILE OF MESSAGES COMMENDING YOU UPON YOUR JOB" that the AP had received.[1] Americans awoke to read in their morning papers editorial criticism of SHAEF both for withholding news of the surrender and for suspending the AP. The AP had been able to get Relman Morin's account of what had occurred in Paris onto the wire in time for the late editions of morning papers. Morin led with the lifting of the general suspension of the AP in Europe, but the story also included Kennedy's statement that "he considered the function of his staff and of himself was to report the news, and that he did not feel bound by any considerations of political censorship." Morin described Kennedy as "one of the world's most experienced war correspondents," and he stressed that Kennedy had not acted furtively but rather had announced his intention to transmit the story for all to hear.[2]

AP coverage that morning continued to summarize the reaction to its suspension. The agency also distributed roundups of editorial comment appearing in morning papers, with most criticism directed at the army rather than the AP. "The most important news story of modern times was mangled yesterday by the worst combination of red tape and of government stupidity that the present generation has ever seen," inveighed the Syracuse *Post-Herald*. The *Philadelphia Record* agreed: "It was a ghastly paradox that, in the hour of triumph for democratic ideals, the public relations office of the United States Army should be guilty of the most undemocratic act." The *New York Post* denounced the army for acting "with an arrogance that is foreign not only to our constitutional system, but to US military tradition. And it invites a rebuke."[3]

Others specifically came to Kennedy's defense. For example, the Oakland (CA) *Tribune* predicted that "when our leaders in authority fully wake up to the fact that this is not their war, but the people's war, we may expect an apology to Mr. Kennedy for his splendid service to the people."[4] After deriding the suspension as "one of the most stupid and far-reaching blunders" perpetrated by military censorship, the *Miami News* termed the army's treatment of Kennedy as "poor reward for what evidently was one of the most enterprising journalistic jobs of [the] era." That afternoon, the Paterson (NJ) *Evening News* called for Kennedy to be awarded the Pulitzer Prize.[5] The litany continued through successive updates of the story; if any editors publicly defended the army's suspension, or criticized Kennedy for his scoop, in the twenty-four hours after the news break, the AP did not note it.

As telegrams of support flooded the AP office in New York and editorials condemning the army continued to chatter off the teleprinter throughout the morning, Cooper felt secure enough to wire Kennedy that he would be happy to send the "most outstanding of the avalanche" of commentary that he had received if military authorities in Paris wanted to know something of public opinion before they decided Kennedy's fate. Cooper wrote a waspish message to Alexander Day Surles in the War Department, hoping the general was considering what amount of the comment the AP would be allowed to send to Paris "WITHIN OUR RE-STRICTED FACILITIES." Cooper could not resist adding that "EACH NEWSPAPER WOULD GLADLY SEND YOU CLIPPING OF FULL

TEXT OF THE EXPRESSIONS IF YOU WANT ME TO ASK THEM ON YOUR BEHALF."[6]

Kennedy would have been as buoyed as Cooper by this support from across the country. Eisenhower did not share their mood. He wrote General Marshall an "eyes only" message in the morning informing him that he had sent a delegation headed by his deputy, Air Marshal Tedder, to Berlin to sign a formal instrument of surrender rather than go himself. He was relieved that the Russians were finally on board, but he confided that "to be perfectly frank, the four days just passed have taken more out of me and my staff" than had the entire campaign since D-Day. Kennedy's actions, in particular, caused him distress: "If it is true, as alleged, that the Head of the A.P. bureau here broke the pledge of secrecy under which he was permitted to witness negotiations and, in addition, used commercial lines out of Paris merely to get a scoop for his company, then he was guilty of something that might have had the most unfortunate repercussions, *involving additional loss of American lives.*"[7]

Correspondents at the Scribe spent much of the morning drafting various letters of protest as they prepared for the showdown they had demanded with General Frank Allen. At that meeting "the Scribe wolf-pack leaped" on an outmatched Allen, who faced the roomful of angry war correspondents on his own, his senior aides elsewhere. Harry Butcher and Ernest Dupuy had flown to Berlin with the press contingent covering the Russian surrender ceremony; Thor Smith was on his way to Reims to work with Eisenhower on a statement regarding the surrender snafu. When the "hog-caller" blasted three times, more than sixty correspondents crowded into the main briefing room at noon. Kennedy was banned, although several other Associated Press staffers were allowed to observe but not to speak at the meeting. Joseph Evans, *Newsweek*'s chief European correspondent, presided, and he presented Allen with the draft of a letter the correspondents intended to send to Eisenhower that afternoon.[8] Evans read the letter in full to the group:

> We, the undersigned Shaef [*sic*] accredited correspondents, have learned with utter astonishment of the decision to lift the ban on the Associated Press in connection with the unauthorized publication of the official news of the unconditional surrender of Germany.

It is our firm conviction that this action is the most outrageously unfair treatment of those news agencies and newspapers whose correspondents have respected the confidence placed in them by Shaef, and who, as a result of so doing, have suffered the most disgraceful, deliberate and unethical double-cross in the history of journalism.

We are advised that Shaef is now taking the position that the Associated Press as an organization was not guilty of any infraction of Shaef regulations. That position, in our opinion, is indefensible. The organization in question published the story and made no effort whatever to retract it when it became evident that its publication was a flagrant violation of Shaef security regulations imposed on all other correspondents concerned.

Furthermore, the Paris bureau of the Associated Press distributed the story to all French newspapers. This involved the activities of more than one representative of that agency.

It is an accepted fact that an organization is responsible for its personnel, especially in the case of men assigned as war correspondents to a theater of military operations, and even more especially in the case of men selected as bureau chiefs.

Each accredited Shaef correspondent who participated in the mission in question was pledged on his honor to secrecy by Brigadier General Allen. Allen made to the correspondents involved a statement to the following effect: "This story is off the record until the respective heads of the allied governments announce the fact to the world. I therefore pledge each and every one of you on your honor not to communicate the result of this conference or the fact of its existence until it is released by PRD Shaef."

The Associated Press cannot escape responsibility for the fact that a man selected as its representative at Shaef, and who was among those present when General Allen imposed his secrecy pledge, deliberately circumvented Shaef censorship in order to file his story for immediate publication in complete defiance of the pledge. Much less can the Associated Press escape responsibility for continuing to publish the story when it was evident that it was unauthorized.

To permit the Associate Press to carry at the time of its authorized release any official news out of the ETO concerning the surrender of Germany is in our opinion, most unjust to those correspondents who have kept faith with you.

If this decision is allowed to stand, it will, in our opinion, completely undermine any sense of responsibility on the part of the correspondents to abide by or respect in the future Shaef PRD rules and regulations.

The fact that the Associated Press correspondent was able to telephone an unauthorized story of this nature to London is in itself glaring evidence of incompetence on the part of that branch of the allied military which is responsible for security in Paris.

That the Associated Press should be permitted to continue to benefit from its defiance of a solemn pledge of secrecy imposed by Shaef on news of such importance to the world is incredible.[9]

This letter is striking for several reasons. First, even if accused of "the most disgraceful, deliberate and unethical double-cross in the history of journalism," Kennedy is not named in the letter, although it alludes to him and his actions; indeed, the correspondents' anger seems directed more toward the AP as a whole than toward Kennedy. Second, they were angrier still at SHAEF for lifting the suspension on the AP, which occurred to the correspondents' "utter astonishment." They twist the knife in further by pointing to the botched security which allowed Kennedy to call London. Third, the correspondents focus on the honor pledge on the plane rather than the violation of the written accreditation agreement all correspondents signed. It is difficult to know what to make of this, but it is an intriguing, indeed puzzling, aspect of the entire controversy. Why the focus on the impromptu pledge on the plane rather than the official written accreditation agreement all correspondents signed, committing them to follow all military rules and regulations, especially censorship controls?

Finally, what the correspondents were asking of Eisenhower and SHAEF, their actual demand, is somewhat buried in the statement but would be clarified at the meeting. The correspondents were not asking that Kennedy be sanctioned; rather, they demanded no less than that the Associated Press be prohibited from reporting on the official surrender once it was announced. More than one observer later would point to this request from the press to officialdom to muzzle itself as an instance so rare as to be bizarre. However, to those who signed the letter, for the military not to sanction the AP would be "outrageously unfair" to those who had honored the embargo. Whatever their intentions, the sharp tone of the letter was unmistakable, even if tempered by the press's respect for Eisenhower.

Evans finished reading the letter, which several correspondents quickly declared excellent. Drew Middleton moved that it be sent to Eisenhower immediately. Before Middleton's motion could be seconded, Edward Angly of the *Chicago Sun* asked General Allen if the letter quoted him correctly since he was the only SHAEF official mentioned by name. All of his comments to them would be off the record, Allen replied, but he confirmed that he had made the statement attributed to him. The INS's James Kilgallen added that while it had been very noisy on the plane to Reims, everyone had been close enough to Allen to hear him. Kilgallen recalled that Kennedy had sat beside him and took notes while Allen spoke.

Another reporter asked Allen if he considered anything in the letter to be false. Allen replied that the only thing he could point to was the statement about SHAEF determining that the AP as an organization was innocent of any infraction. Allen deflected, insisting that the investigation was still ongoing and no conclusions had been reached. The text of the letter was edited to reflect that point, and the final draft stated that any judgment that the AP had not violated regulations was "indefensible," but it did not explicitly attribute that judgment to SHAEF.

Allen and the reporters turned to the lifting of the ban on the AP. Allen explained that it had only applied while PRD investigated Kennedy's unauthorized transmission of the story. It had not been meant as punishment, and any penalties would await the end of the full investigation. The debate turned to whether SHAEF could sanction not only correspondents but also their news organizations as well, with reporters claiming the army had done so in the past, as when an organization was prohibited from using copy by a suspended or disaccredited correspondent. Allen claimed that he did not have the authority to punish entire news organizations for the actions of individual members.

Marshall Yarrow of Reuters interjected that Kennedy had actually boasted at a correspondents' meeting the previous week that he, like "any correspondent worth his salt," had been suspended by the army in the past. Yarrow charged that the AP had adopted a policy of flouting the military's directives. Allen could only respond that the PRD was investigating. Several in the meeting complained that Kennedy's scoop, despite his suspension, was still appearing in papers in the United States. Regardless of the results of the investigation, the Associated Press should be prevented from reporting on the official surrender, what one reporter termed "the last great story from the Theater." Evans reminded the group that their letter to Eisenhower had addressed just that issue. Allen added that although Kennedy's legitimate copy had passed censorship, it was still impounded and would not be released.

A reporter asked if it was true that the AP had its own telephone line to London, to which Allen could only respond that the issue was being examined. Evans asked the group if it was ready to vote on Middleton's motion to send the letter. Albert Glarner of the Exchange Telegraph agency suggested that the letter be held until the PRD's investigation was complete.[10] Mark Watson of the *Baltimore Sun* agreed. "If we are going to shoot somebody," Watson reasoned, "let's see first who we're going to shoot and what we were shooting him for."[11] Drew Middleton challenged the group: "You realize gentlemen you have taken the worst beating of your lives. The question is what are you going to do about it?" With that, Glarner's motion to defer was quickly rejected. Joseph Kingsbury-Smith moved, with a second by Helen Kirkpatrick, that the protest letter be delivered to Eisenhower at once. The motion passed without opposition.

Charles Wertenbaker, still seething about his exclusion from the Reims ceremony, moved a vote of no confidence in the PRD for its mishandling of the entire episode. Drew Middleton, still "browned off" by his exclusion as well, quickly seconded this motion. A reporter again asked Allen about his power to punish the AP. Allen reiterated that as he understood it, he had no authority to sanction entire organizations. When asked who did, he replied the War Department, if anyone. Allen and the frustrated reporters went around in circles on this issue, with Allen insisting that punishments for any censorship violations or other rule-breaking, such as Tully and Irwin's unauthorized trip to Berlin, accrued to the individuals involved and not their organizations. Eventually Wertenbaker's motion was withdrawn for possible later action.[12]

The reporters tacked to the question of communications security with a colonel, unidentified in the transcript but presumably Colonel Martin Ralph of the PRD's Communications Branch, insisting that there were no communications channels from Paris that SHAEF did not control. A reporter then asked in that case how had Kennedy's message gotten out, to a resounding "Hear! Hear!" from the room. Allen could only reply yet again that the inquiry continued, perhaps to be wrapped up later that afternoon. He hoped he could disclose the report to the correspondents once he had submitted it to Eisenhower. The reporters continued to hound Allen about what they clearly saw as inconsistencies in his responses. If Allen did not have the power to punish organizations, why had he been able to suspend the AP throughout Europe the day before? Allen repeated his familiar refrain that the ban had been part of a security investigation, which he had the authority to initiate.

The army transcript of the meeting indicates that at this point "there was a lengthy discussion concerning the accommodation at Reims," accommodation here presumably meaning SHAEF's selection of the press witnesses to the surrender. This remained a bone of contention for those who had been barred from the ceremony, especially Raymond Daniell, Kirkpatrick, and Middleton. Correspondents took issue with SHAEF's statement that the Association of American Correspondents in London

Figure 5.1. Reporters seen in the briefing room at the Hotel Scribe, awaiting Colonel Dupuy in February 1945. There were typically fewer reporters at these conferences over that winter during pauses in the fighting, but the room would have been at least this packed for the confrontation with General Allen on May 8. Courtesy United States Army Heritage and Education Center, Richard H. Merrick Papers, Carlisle, PA.

(AACL) had approved of the composition of the press contingent, an assertion that the AACL had denied in a letter to SHAEF. When pressed, Allen conceded that given the circumstances two days before, an adjustment to the previously agreed arrangement for coverage of a surrender had been required, as close as he came to acknowledging the error.

Another correspondent then returned to the issue of whether the Associated Press would be able to file stories regarding the official announcement scheduled to take place in less than two hours. Allen again conceded that it would, driving the correspondents to cable their letter to Reims straightaway, with a demand that the AP be prohibited from reporting on the upcoming announcement. The letter was signed by fifty-four correspondents. Although the motion to approve it had passed without objection, several in the room did not sign. The exact number who abstained was not recorded. The correspondents then agreed that Douglas Williams of the *Daily Telegraph*, representing the British press, would join Evans in making sure that Eisenhower received the letter and understood its urgency.

Unable to let the issue rest, a reporter asked Allen if he thought a journalist of Kennedy's experience would have acted as he did without his employer's backing. The reporter did not think so; Allen said that he did not know. A motion was made and seconded "that the ban on the AP be extended for twenty-four hours after the announcement of the surrender of Germany." This time the vote was not unanimous as both Larry Rue of the *Chicago Tribune* and John O'Connell of the *Bangor (ME) Daily News* stood in opposition, advocating Glarner's approach.[13] They also opposed, on principle, any action by journalists that would deny millions of readers access to the news. Rue asked if the reporters really wanted to "cut off the news to 1400 newspapers," those served by the Associated Press, many exclusively. O'Connell warned that the reporters who did sign might find themselves with some explaining to do, given that most of their own newspapers had decided to carry the AP story to "give American readers news of the peace without delay." A second motion was made, but no vote taken, urging that were the AP suspended, then other agencies would endeavor to supply news of the official surrender announcement to its member papers without charge.[14]

As the meeting broke up, Allen had even more disturbing off-the-record news for the press. Despite Churchill's declaration that he would speak at three o'clock, the Russians had demanded yet another delay, and so the embargo might be extended. The reporters mulled over the implications of this, peppering Allen with questions. The army transcript contains none of their exchange, but few of the correspondents left the meeting satisfied by Allen's answers. Matters remained as cloudy as the fug of cigarette smoke in the briefing room.

The *New York Times*'s Daniell, one of the least satisfied, dashed off a long account of the previous forty-eight hours, blaming the PRD for "one of the greatest fiascos yet in a long history of blundering bureaucracy." Whereas Daniell reserved some choice words for Kennedy, he lacerated the army for botching coverage of the surrender from start to end. The *Times* made Daniell's story available to the AP "given the widespread controversy over the news policies" of SHAEF, and so it was widely reprinted. Kennedy felt that those who signed the protest letter were just responding to the criticism from their home offices. The best the press corps could do under the circumstances was to blame him, then act as if the scoop had not occurred and that the world was somehow still anxiously awaiting the announcement of war's end. Of the demand for the twenty-four-hour suspension, Kennedy could not resist: "Here was an episode in the long struggle for the freedom of the press never likely to be set on canvass: an elite battalion of knights of the press waging a fight to deny a part of the press the right to report news."[15]

General Allen was less certain than he let on that he lacked the authority to punish entire news organizations for the misdeeds of their employees. He dashed off a message to the War Department asking if this was, in fact, the case. When the surrender was officially and anticlimactically announced at three o'clock that afternoon, Eisenhower had yet to respond to the correspondents' letter, and so the AP retained its filing privileges at SHAEF as elsewhere. Despite Truman's determination to coordinate with the Russians, so frustrating to SHAEF and the press both, Moscow held off issuing its own declaration until 1 a.m. the next day, and so the coveted three-capital simultaneous announcement never actually materialized.[16] Holding to the release time had been all for naught, which only increased the frustration of all at the Scribe.

The Associated Press in New York spent much of the day trying to identify the reporters who had witnessed the surrender; specifically, it wanted to know who of that group had signed the protest letter. At first

New York understood there to have been only seven correspondents in Reims. Once it had received an accurate list of the seventeen in the War Room and matched it against those who had signed the protest letter, the New York office noted that of the fourteen correspondents in Reims (other than Kennedy and the two service reporters), five had not signed. The Paris bureau was to check on whether they had refused to do so or simply had not been at the meeting; if they had refused, had they stated their reasons? James Long on the agency's staff in Paris sent New York a quick summary of the correspondents' meeting he had observed, which prompted Robert Bunnelle in London to inquire if the United Press reporter at the meeting had joined the protest even though Roy Howard had publicly called for the lifting of the suspension.[17] In fact, no less than six United Press correspondents had signed the letter, including Boyd Lewis. As the day progressed and despite the editorial support pouring in, AP officials grew increasingly defensive.

The AP's anxiety stemmed from its inability to learn Kennedy's side of the story. During the night SHAEF had replied to Cooper's request for an explanation of the suspension. Writing for Eisenhower, Allen confirmed that the Associated Press had been suspended during the investigation of the unauthorized story. It had been lifted for all correspondents other than Kennedy, whose accreditation remained suspended due to his "SELF ADMITTED DELIBERATE VIOLATION" of regulations and his breach of confidence in not fulfilling his pledge to secrecy.[18] For whatever reason, this message was held in the War Department until 3:30 that afternoon. Cooper cabled the Paris office, after assuming that the SHAEF statement had already been released there. He asked Kennedy to send his response to the statement quickly.[19] Throughout the day messages ping-ponged across the Atlantic.

Morin replied that the SHAEF statement had not yet been distributed in Paris, and that authorities there did not know if Eisenhower or anyone else had even made one for release. When the War Department finally sent Eisenhower's message to Cooper, he promptly relayed it back to Paris, pointing out that it did not contain the requested response from Kennedy. Early that evening Cooper sent a longer message to Eisenhower acknowledging SHAEF's reply but "RESPECTFULLY AND URGENTLY" asking him to afford Kennedy a means to "STATE HIS CASE PERSONALLY" to his boss. The American people as well as the AP membership deserved

all of the facts and not just the "BRIEF UNILATERAL AND UNDOCU-
MENTED STATEMENT" that Allen had crafted for Eisenhower. Cooper also asked for clear guidance from SHAEF on how military security
figured in the embargo, as well as a general assurance that the military
would get out of the censorship business altogether now that the war
in Europe had ended. "THERE IS GENERAL CONCERN OVER POS-
SIBILITY CONTINUANCE CENSORSHIP OVER POLITICAL MAT-
TERS IN A EUROPE AT PEACE," Cooper wrote. Cooper's pique led him
to note, when he put Eisenhower's statement on the wire, that it came a
full twenty-four hours after Cooper's request for an explanation and also
without Kennedy's version of the story.[20]

Cooper also explored whether he could publish Kennedy's original
story, passed by censors in Reims but still embargoed. When Morin filed
a dispatch that seemed to be based in part on Kennedy's eyewitness account, Cooper asked the Paris bureau if what had been sent was part of
Kennedy's original story and whether his byline could be used. Paris replied that SHAEF remained adamant that Kennedy could not be quoted
on the Reims matter. "All available eyewitness information," however,
had been incorporated in Morin's dispatch. The story was carried na-
tionally on May 9 with a Reims dateline but without a byline. It began
with a statement that the story supplemented the bulletin Kennedy had
issued on Monday and provided the first account of the surrender. "It
is believed this is based on Kennedy's original dispatch," was the AP's
formulation. The story itself varied little from those filed by the other
press eyewitnesses and focused on General Alfred Jodl's speech with its
self-pitying claim that the Germans had suffered more than others in the
war. Kennedy had noted that as Jodl pleaded for mercy for the German
people, a "huge chart tabulating Allied casualties" hung on the wall behind him.[21]

Meanwhile the investigators worked quickly, and by the evening of
May 8 had completed their assignment. Their report recounted the pledge
on the plane, Kennedy's announced intention to break the embargo, his
taunt to Burroughs Matthews about transmitting the story, the AP's premature release of the surrender news, and the ultimate suspension of the
AP. With the help of confidential information from the Ministry of Information, Smith, Ralph, and Matthews had concluded that the AP had
indeed telephoned the story to London, and the report detailed Major

Howard Schwartz's confirmation the previous day that it was possible to do so from Paris without going through censorship or being questioned in any way. The report flagged this as a serious security flaw.

The officers had not been able to establish the time or place from which Morton Gudebrod or Kennedy spoke to London. They had, however, unearthed the second channel, the air force teleprinter, that Bunnelle and Don Doane in London had used to contact Gudebrod while the AP was suspended. The report concluded that Kennedy and others in the AP "deliberately broke two established principles of honest journalism: a) the violation of a confidential news source; and b) the system of holding the release of embargoed news stories, regardless of whether military security is involved or not." They added that SHAEF did indeed believe that military security was involved without explaining how, then recommended that Kennedy, Gudebrod, and Bunnelle be disaccredited immediately and that their case be referred to the inspector general for possible court-martial.[22]

The precise route Kennedy had used to get the story out remained unclear to the investigators. Well before the war ended, Jack Redding, the 12th Army Group PRO, had been concerned about the lack of safeguards to prevent a reporter from circumventing censorship. He had been assured by the Signal Corps that there was no way for a reporter to call through the Paris military switchboard, which controlled all telephone traffic out of the region.[23] However, as Thor Smith later revealed, a new cable connecting Paris and London had been installed just weeks before the surrender, and censorship security had not yet been applied to it. This cable seems to have been the means used for the Associated Press to get the jump on the surrender of forces to Montgomery days earlier, for example. In any case, the PRD investigators had indeed uncovered an embarrassing breach of telephone security, presumably related to the new cable.

Most accounts of the surrender assume this was how Kennedy contacted London. Lewis asserted that there was an unofficial way to reach London by telephone, which sometimes served to connect correspondents with their London bureaus or friends for private talk. Anyone could lift the phone in the Scribe and ask to be connected with the Paris military switchboard; then, in an authoritative voice, they could state that "colonel somebody or other wanted to be connected with London military." The military exchange in London would then connect to the local number. Lewis was certain that Kennedy had reached London in this way and gotten his story through before the line broke.[24]

Just such accounts led one recent historian to write that Kennedy had found it easy to get the story out—he had simply used the phone.[25] Kennedy indeed used the telephone but in a way that had not been so simple. The PRD investigators had discovered a plausible way Kennedy might have reached London, but it turned out not to have been the one he used. The Office of Censorship in Washington informed the War Department on May 12 that it had learned (most likely from the MOI) that the Kennedy story had gone by a telephone line assigned to the *Stars and Stripes* and connecting its offices in the Scribe with those in London. The same line had been the conduit for the AP's scoop of the German surrender to Montgomery the previous week.[26] It was this line that Bunnelle and Kennedy were both at such pains to keep confidential. Alan Gould years after the war revealed that Gudebrod and another AP staffer in Paris, John Colburn, had discovered it.[27] Gould did not go into detail, but much as Doane had located an uncensored teleprinter line, Gudebrod had succeeded simply by befriending army personnel, perhaps even a sympathetic journalist in the *Stars and Stripes* office. In any case, both Dupuy and Bunnelle later confirmed that Kennedy had employed the *Stars and Stripes* channel, which likely was carried on the newly-installed cable. Bunnelle even suggested that *Stars and Stripes* staff routinely used it for private calls to London.[28]

Moreover, it was not quite as straightforward to connect with London as Lewis and others suggested. Codewords, changed daily, were needed to complete a call through the military switchboard. The AP had discovered, in the *Stars and Stripes* connection, a useful tool it clearly wished to hide. This seems the only reason that Austin Bealmear would have urged all to keep it secret after the Montgomery scoop. What is less clear is precisely how the connection worked. Both Gudebrod and Kennedy insisted that they had called from the AP office in the Scribe, in which case the call might have been routed through the *Stars and Stripes* office. Possibly one or both of them made the call from *Stars and Stripes* and dissembled about this in order to protect their coconspirator there. In either case, SHAEF did not investigate the *Stars and Stripes* or its personnel once the leak was discovered, and may not have wanted to advertise such embarrassing security holes even after the war had ended.

At the same time Smith, Ralph, and Matthews were calling for Kennedy's court-martial, others rose to his defense. "HEARTIEST CONGRATULATIONS YOUR WORLDWIDE BEAT," Ray Brock of the North America Newspaper Alliance wrote to Kennedy.[29] "KENNEDY YOURE MAGNIFICENT HEARTIEST CONGRATULATIONS YOU LOUSE," wrote George Lait, Kennedy's old colleague from North Africa.[30] Perhaps the warmest testimonial came from a respected foreign correspondent who had moved from the INS to the AP in 1944, Graham Hovey. As soon as he heard of Kennedy's suspension, Hovey dashed off a column defending the reporter's integrity. He praised Kennedy as "one of the most selfless war correspondents in the business. He is also one of the best." While Kennedy had fought on behalf of US soldiers, on behalf of his staff, and on behalf of "all competitive newsmen," Hovey reminded readers that "to date no one has recorded a battle he waged on behalf of Ed Kennedy." He cited instances of Kennedy's selflessness and his achievements as a journalist, including Kennedy's championing a rival reporter whom he felt had been unfairly suspended in North Africa, Hovey himself. Although Kennedy was usually mild-mannered and soft-spoken, in Hovey's experience Kennedy could be ferocious when he encountered what he considered inappropriate censorship.[31]

Combined with the continuing din of editorial criticism of the surrender embargo and the AP suspension, such stories led George Marshall in Washington to counsel Eisenhower to proceed cautiously. "The press here is almost unanimously taking the line that Kennedy only reported to the people of the United States what was true and what they had a right to know," he wrote SHAEF that night. "In view of the attempt to martyrize him, I suggest you may wish to make a statement."[32] This latter suggestion was not quite as anodyne as it might sound. In effect Marshall told SHAEF to clean up its own mess. This message was made more explicit in another cable that night, this time to Allen, stating that SHAEF, and not the War Department, must make a statement as soon as possible:

PRESS AND RADIO IS FEATURING ASSOCIATED PRESS STORY AS GREAT SCOOP AND MAKING A MARTYR OUT OF KENNEDY AS VICTIM OF UNJUSTIFIED WITHHOLDING OF NEWS BY YOUR

HEADQUARTERS. PRESS GENERALLY IS REFERRING TO THE IN-
CIDENT AS THE GREAT SNAFU OF THE WAR. NOTHING WILL BE
DONE AT THIS END.[33]

Thor Smith's wife Mary was herself a journalist who as chance would
have it worked for the Associated Press in Reno, Nevada. Having access
to what came off the AP's internal wire, she was at first confused by what
she read. If Kennedy had jumped the gun, then shame on him. She did
question, though, why the story had been withheld. She had read the material Cooper had distributed defending the AP, and she was also aware
that while the flash had stated that the surrender had been announced
officially, Kennedy's bulletin did not. By the next day, though, she was
referring to "Ed Kennedy's flagrant violation of [the] confidence placed
in him."[34]

Mary Smith's letters crossed paths with one her husband wrote late
on the night of May 8. He had been ordered to fly to Reims in the
morning to help Eisenhower craft a statement, and he was in no mood
to join the "bedlam going on in the streets of Paris" outside his hotel.
"The world celebrates and I sweat," he confessed, because he had been
"a very significant part of the greatest journalistic snafu in history."
Insisting that the news embargo had been imposed by political leaders,
he protested in frustration tinged with self-pity that "we in the PRD are
victims, over great protest lasting several months, of the greatest hand-
tying exhibition that ever came along the pike." To top it off, PRD had
needed to deal with the AP and Kennedy's "absolute violation of professional journalistic integrity that leaves all of us stupefied." He confessed
that "for the record, I have a four-letter Anglo-Saxon word for Kennedy
and that judgement of him goes for every war correspondent in this theater." While Paris celebrated, a bitter and exhausted Smith confessed,
"I am numb." SHAEF's triumphal moment had been coopted by the
controversy.[35]

Butcher and Dupuy were quite numb as well the next morning, but
by reason of extreme fatigue made worse by hangovers. They had flown
with the press pool to Berlin earlier that day to witness the surrender
spectacular the Russians were staging in the ruins of that city. If the Reims
surrender was restrained and spartan, the Berlin surrender was trium-
phalist and immoderate. The Russians may have had cynical motives for

Figure 5.2. Captain Harry Butcher, Eisenhower's aide, brandishes the two pens used in the surrender ceremony, which he had presented to Eisenhower. Butcher often served as Eisenhower's behind-the-scenes emissary to the press, and had even been loaned out to the Public Relations Division to troubleshoot communications issues after the liberation of Paris in August 1944. Courtesy National Archives (111-SC-261105).

insisting on the delay, but they also legitimately wanted clarity about the war's outcome. With the ambiguities of the armistice in 1918 in mind, the Russians insisted that all three German armed services (army, air force, and navy) sign the surrender, unlike at Reims, so that none could claim they had been betrayed by the others. The ruins of Berlin would also reinforce to Germany its utter defeat in a way which the Compiègne railway car (the site of the armistice in 1918) never had, nor the Ecole Professionelle in Reims ever could. The Soviets also wanted to send the message to their own people and to the world that the Germans had surrendered to them. From the Russian perspective, its people had won the war with only marginal assistance from the Western Allies. To make just this point the Russians desired, and held, a grand-scale ceremony unlike the short and spare event in France.

Hoping to mollify the Russians, the previous day Eisenhower had offered to go to Berlin himself for the surrender. Churchill, among others, convinced him to send his deputy in his place so as not to enhance the Soviet show.[36] The PRD also had to prepare for this second surrender as the Kennedy drama unfolded throughout the day. It dipped back into the ECLIPSE file for plans to cover various end-of-war scenarios.[37] There was surprisingly little blowback from the press when the PRD announced that the Russian-choreographed surrender would be covered by a pool of just ten journalists. The Russians had balked at a larger group, and so the PRD defaulted to a revision of its plan for a pool in the case of an airborne entry into Berlin.[38]

The pool consisted of two agency reporters (one British and one American); two correspondents from daily newspapers (one from each country); a BBC and a US broadcaster, two representatives from service newspapers, and both still and newsreel photographers. This was the plan that had been agreed to by the leaders of the correspondents association in London over the winter. It had done so reluctantly, if Daniell is to be believed, unhappy with the pooling arrangement and much else. The plan again privileged the agencies, but unlike the Reims list did not exclude reporters for individual newspapers. This may well have had to do with the criticism they had received after Reims from Daniell, Kirkpatrick, and others. Lacking dedicated transmission facilities in Berlin, the pool would return to Paris to file.[39]

Both Dupuy and Butcher kept detailed notes of the whirlwind trip to Berlin.[40] Dupuy describes a dawn drive to Orly Airport, where the Press Flying Squad, so-named, joined a delegation large enough to fill four C-47s. The planes took off in perfect weather shortly after eight. The transports landed mid-morning at a grass airfield near Stendal on the Elbe, where they were to be joined by another contingent from 21st Army Group, including Field Marshal Wilhelm Keitel. As they waited, Butcher wandered the airfield and talked with GIs brandishing looted souvenirs. Cameras, watches, and lugers seemed to be the preferred items. Butcher drew a sword inscribed with the name "Eisenhauer" from a pile to present to the general.[41]

After the half-hour flight to Berlin the SHAEF contingent stumbled off the planes at Tempelhof airport into a full-scale reception, complete with military bands, parading troops, and welcoming speeches. Russian photographers documented it all. Keitel and the other Germans were shunted off to another part of the airport while a thirty-car convoy of Allied officials set off around the western periphery of the bombed-out city. The Russians had directed them away from the city center, claiming that it remained too dangerous. Butcher was struck by the Russian women in uniform at seeming every corner, directing traffic or otherwise involved in frontline work. The convoy arrived at the undamaged suburb of Kalshorst where the military's engineering school served as the surrender site. The concrete modernist structure was surrounded by cottages for faculty and staff; Butcher and Dupuy were taken to one where another smartly turned out Russian soldier served them a full meal complete with wine and vodka. After lunch Butcher made it a point to use the powerful German radio receiver in the cottage to hear the official announcements of the Reims surrender from Truman, Churchill, and de Gaulle.

The delegation then assembled at the main building of the engineering school for another event staged for the Russian media, a ceremony replete with much inter-Allied saluting and back-slapping. The press pool then milled around for several hours before being told of a delay—the surrender documents needed to be redrawn to reflect some last-minute changes. When all parties reconvened at eight o'clock, they were informed that the Allies were still negotiating finer points. Much of this dickering took place well within earshot of the reporters circulating through the room. By ten o'clock, the temperature had turned colder and the waiting more tiresome. Finally, and just before tempers flared, all moved to a vast conference hall for the signing itself. If Bedell Smith had thought that the Reims surrender had been lit like a Hollywood set, Butcher observed that "we were now looking at something that was super-Hollywood."[42] At least a hundred cameramen were in the room with klieg lights ablaze. Marshal Georgy Zhukov sat at the center of the head table with Air Marshal Tedder on his right and Generals Carl Spaatz and Jean de Lattre de Tassigny (there as official witnesses) on the left. The Russian political commissar Andrey Vyshinsky sat in civilian clothes to the side of Tedder.[43]

The Russians did not hide the fact that they had staged the entire event to emphasize their preeminence.

Below the head table three others filled the room, one for the Allied press, a center table filled with Allied officers, and a smaller one for the Germans. When Field Marshal Keitel entered gripping his silver baton, the Russian photographers swarmed, and a fight momentarily broke out among the jostling cameramen. Butcher's seat placed him within six feet of the Germans. He thought that Admiral General Hans-Georg von Friedeburg looked morose, with deep black circles under his eyes. Keitel still seemed defiant and could be heard hissing impatiently in the ear of his American translator that the surrender deadline left insufficient time to alert German troops. Dupuy also noted that Keitel and Friedeburg seemed to be arguing over just this point. The Allies remained unmoved. Once all signatures were affixed, Keitel and the Germans abruptly marched out to their waiting cars.

Once the Germans left, the real party began. Banquet tables were brought in and a full service set. The meal itself did not begin until nearly two o'clock in the morning, when the Allies feasted on roast chicken and strawberries soaked in cognac and drank toast after toast. Butcher soon found himself several vodkas for the worse and returned to his cottage to collapse. Dupuy was circumspect in writing to his wife but confessed to feeling a bit wobbly himself. The dinner continued until the SHAEF contingent returned to Tempelhof for a dawn departure. Butcher had to be roused from bed with the end of Brigadier William Turner's walking stick, but he later took comfort knowing that several generals had needed to be carried to their cars.

This time the Allies drove through central Berlin along a route carefully cleared and guarded by the Russians. They were stunned by the extent of the bombing damage. They paused briefly in front of the ruins of the Hotel Adlon (and were warned that it was filled with booby-traps), then passed the Reichstag and stopped at the Reich Chancellery. Dupuy, Butcher, and Turner followed Tex O'Reilly of the *New York Herald Tribune* and the UP's Joe Grigg into the building, one familiar to the reporters from prewar days. They each took a memento from what they presumed to be Hitler's office. Dupuy grabbed an ornate brass inkstand from the desk before scrambling back to Tempelhof for the inevitable departure ceremony.[44] Once in the air and as the reporters began working on their stories, Dupuy and Butcher tried to sleep it off. For them, the war had ended—again.

For the next week, the surrender controversy played out on three fronts—at SHAEF, within the Associated Press, and on the pages of US newspapers. Heeding Marshall's warning that public opinion was initially sympathetic to Kennedy and his directive that SHAEF, having made the mess, should not expect the War Department to fix it, the PRD went to work. Thor Smith spent much of the evening of V-E Day drafting a bill of particulars against Kennedy and the Associated Press. "The proper punishment was a public dis-crediting of the whole thing," he confided to his wife. Smith flew to Reims on the morning of May 9. That afternoon he huddled with Eisenhower and Bedell Smith for better than an hour crafting a statement for General Allen.[45]

In Paris, the press corps continued to seethe. Daniell's diatribe against both Kennedy and PRD had been published in the United States that morning and had been read with approval by the reporters at the Scribe. If Daniell had fulminated against SHAEF's attempt to suppress the surrender news as "one of the greatest fiascos yet in a long history of blundering bureaucracy," he had also indicted both Kennedy and the Associated Press for putting "a premium on dishonesty." Their actions would also put "a brake upon free coverage of historic events in the future." The correspondents in Paris, according to a frustrated Daniell, believed that "the Associated Press behaved very badly and that the only people whose freedom to report the news had been infringed were those who kept their word and followed the rules."[46]

None were more incensed than the bureau chiefs of the rival agencies. The UP's Lewis had written his own eyewitness account stressing that Kennedy had voiced no objection to the pledge on the plane, and he joined the chorus that accused him of a "breach of faith." That same day another UP correspondent wrote to Lewis detailing past occasions when Kennedy had gotten into trouble with authorities "in every other theater, moving on to the next one just before the hammer came down." Among other misdeeds, he accused Kennedy of trying to jump the filing line during the landings in Southern France only to have been stymied by AFHQ officials. INS's European chief, Joseph Kingsbury-Smith, complained to Eisenhower directly that whatever SHAEF's good intentions, the INS and the other agencies "were placed on Tuesday morning in the untenable position of being ridiculed publicly by the Associated Press for having been scooped." The INS was proud of its record in abiding by SHAEF censorship rules and could not stand by while the AP was rewarded for its "flagrant violation" of the same. "The injustice and unfairness of this situation cannot be too strongly emphasized," Kingsbury-Smith groused, convinced that "something more concrete" was required by way of punishment for Kennedy and the AP.[47]

SHAEF was already at such work, however. As Thor Smith and Eisenhower drafted their response, officials in London informed Bunnelle without explanation that he too had been suspended. Bunnelle could only infer that it had to do with the surrender story. The suspension meant very little, Bunnelle assured Cooper, given that he still had access to all civilian communications channels in London. Bunnelle also confirmed to Cooper that, as far as he knew, no one on the London staff had violated any SHAEF regulations.[48]

Cooper continued to be bombarded with messages from the AP's membership while he waited to communicate with Kennedy. Late that morning and with both his London and Paris bureau chiefs suspended, Cooper informed Morin that he thought Kennedy should return to New York as soon as possible to talk to him face-to-face. He intended to appoint Wes Gallagher as acting bureau chief in his stead, "but without any prejudice whatever to Kennedy's case and solely that we may continue normal operations."[49] Shortly thereafter he did indeed hear from Kennedy, although indirectly. In a message received at noon but evidently written the night before, Morin passed on the note that Kennedy had posted on the correspondents' bulletin board in the Scribe:

I saw the representative of the existing German government sign the agreement of unconditional surrender.

I was informed by a representative of SHAEF Public Relations that although no issue of military security was involved, SHAEF Public Relations intended to suppress this news from the public until a later time.

I informed a representative of SHAEF Public Relations that I could not accept this view, since it had been conceded that no military security was involved and that I intended to send the story.

I sent the story.[50]

Kennedy remained adamant that it was "completely incorrect" to say that he had "admitted any breach of confidence" as Eisenhower's statement the previous day had asserted. Kennedy "did what he considered was his duty and is still of that opinion," and he was "deeply grateful" for Cooper's support.[51] Kennedy's statement and Morin's follow-up were put out on the AP wire in time to be included in some evening papers, but most of the coverage that day, especially in the morning papers, centered on Kennedy's suspension and the correspondents' protest meeting.

The editorial opinion that day focused on SHAEF's folly in trying to keep news of the surrender from the people. Many agreed that continuing to withhold the news even after the Flensburg broadcast and Churchill's designation of May 8 as V-E Day was beyond reason. The *Daily Mirror* in New York more tersely derided the news embargo as a "monument to official stupidity."[52] Few if any papers defended the embargo.

Opinion about Kennedy was more mixed. At first noncommittal, many were willing to comment after Eisenhower's statement and the Paris correspondents' protest. Most scoops were measured in minutes, John Pennekamp pointed out in the *Miami Herald*. Kennedy's had held up for more than a day, the kind of beat "that every newspaperman dreams about, hopes for and regards as impossible." Penalizing him for it was more than "silly" given that "NEWS IS NEWS WHEN IT HAPPENS. And Kennedy put it out WHILE IT WAS STILL NEWS." Without resorting to capitalization, the *Parsons (KS) Sun and Republican* made much the same point. News of the surrender "came when it did due to the determination and enterprise of a seasoned Associated Press man who thought less of political censorship than he did of his obligation to get the news to the public at the earliest possible moment." As such, he had left the rest of the SHAEF press corps at the post. "Kennedy was living up to the best traditions of a free press," the paper concluded. "He saw his duty and performed it."[53]

Others disagreed. Predictably the United Press and its owner, the Scripps-Howard newspaper chain, led the way, payback for the Associated Press's schadenfreude a quarter century earlier. An editorial published widely in Scripps Howard papers slammed Kennedy for violating the pledge on the plane and attacked the AP for continuing to tout the scoop even after Eisenhower had suspended the reporter. Others focused on Kennedy's betrayal of a confidence, which the Kansas City *Kansan* called "a misdeed which deserves the condemnation which has been heaped upon the AP and its erring reporter by colleagues and the newspaper business generally." The *Seattle Star* opined that "the newspaper profession cannot exist unless it has the confidence of the people with [whom] it deals," and for that reason it could not "condone Kennedy's broken faith nor the Associated Press' acceptance of and distribution of a story sent under broken faith."[54]

Such commentary shed little new light on either the facts or underlying issues involved, although the *San Antonio Express* did point out that news flashes typically were not published verbatim but rather were meant to alert newsrooms that publishable bulletins would quickly follow. It pointed out that the phrase "SHAEF officially announced," although it appeared in the AP flash, actually did not appear in any of the AP's published stories. Thus SHAEF's use of this as part of its rationale for punishing the AP, arguing that it had embarrassed Eisenhower with the Russians, struck the *Express* as a flimsy pretext.[55] Granted the need for reporters to honor such confidences, akin to protecting sources today, nonetheless the sharp and often ethically dubious practices of many newsrooms in the first half of the twentieth century (for example, in misrepresenting themselves to witnesses while covering crime stories) makes this earnestness about confidences seems quaint, or hypocritical, or both.

Whatever the range of editorial opinion, the correspondents' protest in Paris dominated the front pages on May 8. Much the same would happen the next day when the statement written by Smith and Eisenhower for General Allen made the headlines. Overnight Allen had also received final confirmation from the War Department that SHAEF only had the right to punish individual journalists and not news organizations. "Even when his story is distorted by his home office," Surles informed Allen, "it is the correspondent who is disciplined." Surles agreed with Allen that there was no basis to discipline the Associated Press by restricting its transmission rights from Europe.[56]

Thus Allen felt he was on solid ground when he called a press conference that afternoon to read to the assembled reporters the eight-hundred-word statement drafted in Reims. In it he laid out what were termed the "facts" relevant to the AP's premature release of the surrender story. When Allen had approached the Supreme Commander about press coverage of any surrender meeting with the Germans, Eisenhower had told him that such negotiations, already in process, "were of utmost secrecy." This was required not only because of the difficulty in coordinating actions with the Russians, but also because the Germans were repeatedly trying to make a separate peace with the Western Allies. Eisenhower had assured the Russians that if allowed to conduct surrender negotiations, he would demand an unconditional surrender on all fronts. Given these circumstances which, according to Allen, "clearly involved security and the saving of American lives," Eisenhower had been reluctant to involve the press in any meetings with the Germans. Only when assured that the journalists involved would not release any information until authorized to do so did the Supreme Commander agree to a small group of correspondents at the surrender.

Using language that would cause Allen problems in the days ahead, he claimed that "the story therefore was not one obtained by press representatives in the ordinary course of their activities in this theatre; it was obtained *by the courtesy* of SHAEF headquarters." Allen then detailed the pledge of secrecy on the plane. Kennedy's violation of his pledge, Allen asserted, placed Eisenhower in the position of having broken a commitment to the Russians and potentially caused a rupture in planning for the surrender ceremony in Berlin. This, in turn, threatened to prolong the war. Allen stressed to the correspondents gathered at the Scribe that the War Department definitively had stated that it had no authority to punish an entire news organization, in this or any other circumstance, for the actions of an individual and despite the gravity of the offense. Allen warned that Kennedy's actions called into question "the extent to which the Allied Command can, in any future case, permit pressmen advance access to news of the most secret character on the same basis that has always applied to the past."

Kennedy's action thus had been a "deliberate violation of good faith, against the reputation of the press for reliability, in spite of a solemn promise, and against security definitively involving possible loss of American and Allied lives."[57] Because of sensitive negotiations with the Russians, security remained an issue to the military even after the Germans had surrendered and thus warranted the news embargo.

Thor Smith's assurance to his wife that Allen's statement "was received with tremendous approval by the rest of the press corps (and . . .

off the record . . . by many legitimate APers)" may have overstated the case, but INS's Virgil Pinkley, for one, was well satisfied with it. In an obsequious telegram to Eisenhower, he thanked the general for the statement, which "justly places blame where it belongs," while praising his support of "freedom of the press and speech which you champion so ardently."[58] The *New York Times*'s Gladwyn Hill was less effusive, merely reporting that the room "expressed general satisfaction with General Allen's statement" even if some objected to Allen's assertion that the press witnessed the surrender only "by courtesy of SHAEF headquarters."[59] In any case, the statement had its desired effect in tamping down the rebellion of the SHAEF press corps as well as the criticism of the PRD in the US press.

Kennedy was allowed to distribute a response to Allen's statement, but not in time for it to appear in the evening papers where SHAEF's announcement dominated the headlines. In that response Kennedy took issue with virtually all of Allen's assertions. He insisted that Allen had told him in Reims that there was no question of military security involved in the surrender; indeed, Allen had told him that Eisenhower had preferred the news to be released immediately to save soldiers' lives, only to have his hands tied by political leaders. Allen's claim that the news needed to be embargoed until the Russians were convinced of Germany's surrender was "astonishing" since a Russian general had himself signed the Reims document. Kennedy found equally bewildering Allen's contention that the story had not been obtained by the press in the "ordinary course" of its work. "Certainly General Allen must know that the purpose of correspondents in this theater is to report news," and what could be more newsworthy than the end of the war?

Regarding the release time, Kennedy conceded that Allen had said at one point in Reims that the story could not be published until after it had been announced by the three heads of government. However, at another time Allen had said that SHAEF might announce the surrender even before the correspondents returned to Paris. In fact, Allen had "made many conflicting statements concerning how the news would be released." Kennedy correctly asserted that censorship had passed his copy in Reims; he had enough confidence in SHAEF censors to believe they would not have passed the story if it indeed contained a security concern. Kennedy emphasized that upon learning of the Flensburg broadcast he had informed Lieutenant Colonel Merrick that he regarded the embargo as "purely political censorship," and that he no longer felt bound to observe it. Kennedy had contacted Allen to inform him of this as well, but "had been told by his secretary that he was too busy to speak to me."

If release of the Reims story had threatened delicate negotiations with the Russians over the formal signing in Berlin, as SHAEF had charged, then "the Reims agreement was an empty gesture," and Eisenhower's own action in notifying forces of the surrender also would have threatened those negotiations. Kennedy ended by restating that in his long experience military censorship had gone far beyond protecting security, and that whenever he had encountered such overreach he had resisted it. He had told General Allen, as he had told authorities in the past, that he "took the guarantee that censorship was confined to military security very seriously," and to submit to such political censorship "would mean the end of a free press and of all freedom in the world."[60] The hyperbole here might hint at mounting anxiety behind Kennedy's public *sang froid*.

Kennedy's statement did not directly address the charge that he had violated journalistic ethics in breaking a confidence, and he only indirectly alluded to Allen's assertion that the press had only been present in Reims "courtesy" of SHAEF. However, he directly engaged and attempted to refute the charge that somehow military security had been involved in the story and thus that he had placed lives in danger. Cooper, for one, was relieved to receive Kennedy's statement, and he assured Kennedy that he would transmit it in full to the AP membership.[61]

As the day wound down, AP members looked for a response from Cooper to Allen's statement. Helen Rogers Reid, for one, the vice president (and soon to be publisher) of the *New York Herald Tribune* was an influential voice in US journalism; when she sent Cooper a telegram urging him to speak out, he felt obliged to do so. Cooper stressed that the Associated Press took seriously its obligation to honor any confidences and agreements in its reporting. He emphasized, though, that he would not judge Kennedy's actions until he had talked with him personally. There the matter rested overnight.[62]

The next day, Thursday, May 10, PRD officials and the press corps in Paris attempted to turn the page by focusing on postwar news coverage in Europe. Smith and Dupuy met with the SHAEF correspondents that day and explained that the Russians had yet to agree to allow western reporters to visit facilities in areas under their control, although they had consented to the press accompanying the small force of US, British, and French troops soon to occupy Berlin. The correspondents demanded that this group must not be limited to such a small number as at Reims. Drawing on the ECLIPSE planning, SHAEF officials proposed that a maximum of seventy-five correspondents might be included in the press contingent. Dupuy also announced that Colonel George Warden would brief the correspondents in some detail on postwar censorship plans the next day. Those plans would become their own source of controversy.[63]

When Cooper arrived at the AP offices in New York that morning, he found an overnight cable from Wes Gallagher relaying Kennedy's response to the AP chief's request that he return to New York. Kennedy wanted to do so,

BUT IN VIEW FACT I SUSPENDED AND NO PRIVATE MEANS COMMUNICATIONS EXIST I UNABLE TO PROCEED THIS MOMENT. ALSO THINK IT BETTER REMAIN HERE PENDING OUTCOME INVESTIGATION AND POSSIBLE CHARGES AGAINST ME. IN VIEW ALLENS ACCUSATIONS BELIEVE I AM ENTITLED TO FAIR HEARING WHICH SOFAR NOT BEEN GIVEN. IN ANY CASE WILL FOLLOW ALL YOUR INSTRUCTIONS.[64]

Now aware of SHAEF's public response to Kennedy's story as well as the full range of editorial opinion in the United States, Cooper equivocated. While he wrote Kennedy that Allen's statement and Kennedy's response were both being transmitted to the AP membership, Cooper also informed Kennedy that the AP in New York had not known there was anything untoward in his initial surrender bulletin either in its censorship approval or in its means of transmission. He underscored that the foreign desk had held the story for eight minutes until the bylined bulletin subsequently appeared, even at the risk of being scooped by another agency. There had been "NO REPEAT NO INKLING OF ANYTHING EXTRAORDINARY CONNECTED WITH YOUR DISPATCHES" until SHAEF had denied that it had issued anything official concerning a German surrender.

In what was to become Cooper's primary indictment of Kennedy's action, he chided the reporter for not alerting the AP to how he had moved the story. This and not the need to keep the Paris office running smoothly (as he had previously claimed) now became Cooper's pretext for replacing Kennedy as bureau chief:

MY DISAPPOINTMENT IN YOUR FAILURE PRECAUTIONARILY TO PREFACE YOUR DISPATCH WITH EXPLANATION OF ATTITUDE AND ACTION YOU TOOK WITH AUTHORITIES SO WE COULD DECIDE HERE MATTER OF POLICY AS RESPECTS ITS USE NOW BECOMES BASIS GALLAGHERS DESIGNATION TAKING CHARGE PARIS.[65]

Kennedy would have been none too happy to receive such clear evidence that Cooper was backsliding in his support, and his reply doubled down on the comments he had sent the day before. The story as filed had been based on what he had seen himself and was correct in all respects, Kennedy claimed, thus he had found no reason to qualify them in any way. He remained convinced that no security issue was involved, despite Allen's statement to the contrary. The censorship stop on the story had contravened announced US policy; thus he had acted accordingly. Kennedy ratcheted up the rhetoric of the day before in stating, "BELIEVE ISSUES INVOLVED ARE FUNDAMENTAL TO EXISTENCE FREE PRESS AND AM CONFIDENT WE CAN SHOW THIS AND WILL GET SUPPORT OF WHOLE FREE WORLD." No longer expressing his gratitude, Kennedy was now "COUNTING ON YOUR CONTINUED SUPPORT," repeating that as yet he had not been allowed to rebut the many accusations made against him.[66]

The controversy remained in something of a holding pattern that day awaiting the results of SHAEF's formal investigation. Bunnelle in London continued to search for exculpatory evidence. He learned that within hours of the agreement being signed, the news had been sent in uncoded messages to dozens of military bases and offices throughout the United Kingdom, including those employing civilians. The messages had been classified only as confidential, very low on the security scale.[67] Although Bunnelle did not say so directly, this information provided further indication that it had been SHAEF that had violated the news embargo, the secrecy pledge, and any agreements with the Russians.

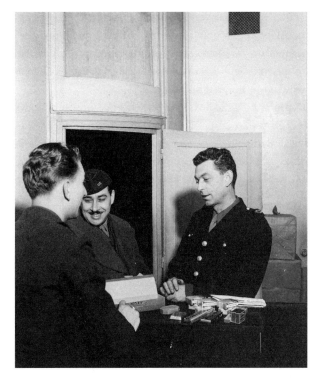

Figure 5.3. Ed Kennedy receives his weekly ration of cigarettes from the PX. This photo was part of an album the Public Relations Division assembled in February 1945 to document its daily operations at the Hotel Scribe. Courtesy National Archives (111-SC-204502).

The bombshell that day came not from London but from Philadelphia. Pressure was mounting on the Associated Press to take a clear position on Kennedy's actions. Cooper continued to hedge, vowing that he would render no judgment until he had spoken with his reporter. A decade later and in defense of his actions, Cooper gave a host of reasons why he felt at the time that he could neither "convict nor acquit" Kennedy. He felt tremendous allegiance to the thousands of AP employees, especially those at some risk overseas. Even though he never wanted to violate military security, Cooper also knew of many cases when security had been invoked to cover up embarrassing facts already known to the enemy. Revealing something of his own self-regard, Cooper worried that Kennedy might have let Cooper's own advocacy of freedom of the press affect his judgment. Finally, he was aware that whatever the criticisms of Kennedy, many in the AP were strongly supportive of him, including one publisher who sent Kennedy a personal check for one thousand dollars. For all these reasons, Cooper publicly remained noncommittal, even as his messages to Kennedy grew more pointed and critical.[68]

Cooper's titular boss did not share his reticence, however, and on May 10 Robert McLean took matters into his own hands. McLean was the publisher of the Philadelphia *Evening Bulletin*, the newspaper he had inherited from his father. He began serving on the AP board of directors in 1924, when he was thirty-three and had become its president in 1938, a position he would hold for twenty years. McLean was a patrician with many ties to the establishment in Washington. He had been contacted by an old friend, Arthur Page, now working for Secretary of War Henry Stimson, who made sure McLean was aware of the War Department's displeasure with Kennedy. He had also heard from several AP directors who disapproved of Kennedy's actions, the AP's nonresponse, or both. After talking it over with Cooper, who by his own account expressed no objection, McLean issued a brief statement on May 10: "The Associated Press profoundly regrets the distribution on Monday of the report of the total surrender in Europe which investigation now clearly discloses was distributed in advance of authorization by Supreme Allied Headquarters. The whole, long honorable record of The Associated Press is based on its high sense of responsibility as to the integrity and authenticity of the news and the observance of obligations voluntarily assumed, as appropriately reaffirmed by the General Manager in his statement of yesterday."[69]

Although couched in generalities and not mentioning Kennedy by name, no one mistook the statement's import. McLean had repudiated Kennedy. Cooper then felt obliged to fall in line, forwarding McLean's statement to Eisenhower while adding his "own personal expression of regret," and hoping the incident would not prejudice SHAEF against Gallagher and his staff going forward.[70] In short, despite his protestations that he would not judge Kennedy until he had talked with him, Cooper on May 10 joined McLean in distancing himself from their Paris bureau chief.

McLean's statement was "welcomed by the army and relieved the tension," Cooper believed.[71] It also appeased those AP members who thought an apology was required. It dampened, if not extinguished, the resentments of the Paris press corps as well as the criticism of opinion writers. For others, McLean's statement would be a stain on the AP's reputation not easily bleached out. May 10 was the day when the agency buckled under to pressure from the government and competitors, the day it sold out one of its most seasoned and loyal employees. For some, it was no less than an act of calculated cowardice.

McLean's words, though, had their desired effect. On Friday morning, any number of papers carried editorials expressing satisfaction that McLean had apologized for Kennedy's transgressions. The *Washington Star* spoke for many when it said that while it knew Kennedy to be a "hard-working, conscientious and honorable newspaperman," his "error was in his failure to observe 'obligations voluntarily assumed.'" In this, "he was wrong." Overall, McLean's statement redirected editorial fire away from the Associated Press and toward military authorities. Even so, in writing that day to his old friend Stephen Early in the White House, Harry Butcher confided that Kennedy's "break of the release date was just about all that I could bear." That said, tension at the Scribe had dissipated after McLean's apology, much to Butcher's great relief.[72]

McLean's statement prompted Kennedy to defend himself yet again, this time to Gladwyn Hill, one of the *New York Times*'s reporters in Paris. On Friday morning the *Times* carried Hill's interview in which Kennedy disputed the central point of McLean's rebuke—that he had violated a confidence with a source. Once he had informed SHAEF of his intention to file the story, Kennedy believed that he had "fulfilled all of the obligations" owed to the military. He rejected the criticism of some that he should have alerted the other correspondents of his intention to break the story, explaining that he had never done so on any other story and did not understand why this one was different. Hill asked Kennedy if he thought he might have a special obligation given the restricted size of the press group in Reims, to which Kennedy responded that it was SHAEF and not he who had made those arrangements. "I didn't try to prevent anybody else from going," he said.[73] For all that, none of the other correspondents in Paris seemed willing to speak up for Kennedy.

Cooper's messages to Kennedy also provided the besieged correspondent little solace. He alerted Kennedy that NBC might approach him to do a broadcast related to his suspension. If so, Cooper urged him to do so "WITH RESTRAINT SINCERITY SIMPLICITY." He warned

Kennedy that while much of the press reporting had been favorable to him, "ANY BROADCAST COULD BE OFFENSIVE" and tilt coverage the other way. Cooper asked Kennedy to send him in advance any scripts he prepared for such a broadcast so Cooper could suggest changes.[74] A second cable asked Wes Gallagher to stress to Kennedy that Cooper was "COUNTING ON HIM UNCONSIDER ACTION ANY KIND THAT WOULD DISTURB RELATIONSHIP WITH ASSOCIATED AND MYSELF." Cooper did not want Kennedy to do anything rash before they had a chance to talk, and he urged Kennedy to "ONKEEP SHIRT."[75] The leash was shortening.

Although the New York office was still having difficulty forming a clear picture of events in Paris, Bunnelle had heard from the bureau there that the PRD's investigation remained ongoing, and that Eisenhower had not yet received a full report. The PRD, though, did promise to supply a public statement on Bunnelle's suspension, about which it had been silent to that point.[76] However, at ten o'clock that night the AP office in Paris learned that Allen had been away from the office all day, and that there would be no further action on the Kennedy and Bunnelle suspensions before the morning.[77]

Allen may have been unavailable because another storm was brewing at the Scribe. It had not gone well when SHAEF's chief censor met with the press as promised to discuss postwar censorship regulations. Colonel Warden outlined what military information would remain censorable as of possible aide to the Japanese, a list which the reporters deemed reasonable. However, the press corps groused about two regulations that had carried over from the previous code. For as long as the war with Japan continued, SHAEF censors would suppress "unauthenticated, inaccurate and false reports, misleading statements and rumors" as well as "reports likely to injure the morale of the Allied forces or the relations between Allied nations."[78] The reporters countered that censors were rarely well placed to judge whether or not a story was accurate, and that the delay while censors investigated destroyed a story's currency. The correspondents "said they considered that their personal reputations and responsibility to readers were sufficient guarantee against their bandying dangerously flimsy reports," according to the *New York Times*.[79] The reporters also objected that "Allied unity" could be used as a pretext to censor any number of legitimate stories from occupied Germany.

Opinion writers stateside also opposed such continuing censorship and often linked it to the Kennedy affair.[80]

A letter that Mary Smith in Reno wrote to her husband at week's end suggests the muddle over Kennedy's surrender story. At that point, she had not received a letter from Thor Smith in more than three weeks.[81] Out of loyalty to her husband, Mary Smith resented that all the "arm chair strategists and prima donna correspondents" at work were second-guessing PRD's performance. Still, "so many things have been so on the top of my list of things I should know." Was it true, for example, that reporters were chased away at Reims while "ten or twenty pretty girls" witnessed the signing? Who had arranged for press coverage of the ceremony? Who had decided that four radio networks would be present but only three newspaper reporters? Still, she admitted that "never in my life have I been so sick of a situation that was brought about because of the failure of an irresponsible correspondent who broke the cardinal principle of journalism—trust."[82]

Thor Smith believed the Allen statement on May 9 had mollified the SHAEF press corps. All that remained of the Kennedy affair was the "final drill of further investigation and final action."[83] After receiving the PRD's initial report, Eisenhower instructed Inspector General Edward C. Betts to review the evidence and recommend for or against court-martial. At the same time, on Saturday the PRD finally took statements from Kennedy and Gudebrod.

Gudebrod recounted how he had given the story to the AP's French desk on the assumption that it had been officially released.[84] Kennedy's succinct three hundred fifty-word statement added little to those he had made previously. He reiterated that Allen and his staff had discussed at Reims various changes in the plan to release news of the surrender, and that Allen had told him that Eisenhower's desire to release the news as soon as possible had been thwarted by political leadership. Once back in Paris, Allen and other SHAEF officials again "made it plain that no military security was involved," Kennedy reiterated. After learning of the Flensburg broadcast and that the news had officially gone out to Allied troops, Kennedy no longer felt bound by military censorship. He then sent the story.[85]

Thor Smith later claimed that Eisenhower had already turned the case over to Betts days before these statements were made. Even if Eisenhower and Bedell Smith remained furious at the release and believed Kennedy's actions fully justified a court-martial, Betts recommended moderation, reminding them that the war in Europe had just been won. Betts argued that the case would be contested by Kennedy and the AP amid much publicity (and some sympathy from the press generally), whatever the evidence. Congress or the civil courts might eventually become involved, and it was difficult to see how that might benefit the army. Court-martial would not even have value as a deterrent given that the war was over, and censorship was soon to be lifted. Betts counseled leniency as the appropriate and politic course.[86]

Allen agreed on May 12. He recommended against court-martial in the cases of Kennedy, Gudebrod, and Bunnelle. He argued that Kennedy and Gudebrod should be disaccredited; both should be ordered out of the theater and returned to the United States. Bunnelle, however, should be cleared of any wrongdoing and his suspension lifted.[87] There matters rested for the remainder of the weekend.

Eisenhower and Bedell Smith did not waste time. On Monday, they approved Allen's recommendations. Allen distributed a statement to the press early that evening, disaccrediting Kennedy for "having deliberately violated the trust reposed in him" by releasing the story through unauthorized channels, and disaccrediting Gudebrod "for taking an active part in the premature release." Both were ordered back to the United States. Bunnelle was reinstated without explanation. The statement noted the Associated Press's apology for distributing the story prior to its authorization. "With this statement," Allen concluded, "this regrettable incident is considered as closed by Supreme Headquarters." Allen wrote personally to Kennedy and Gudebrod, instructing them that they had just three days to put their affairs in order before the return voyage to the United States. Gudebrod was shortly thereafter granted a two-week extension after he contracted pneumonia.[88]

Kennedy issued a brief response after receiving his notice. "My conscience is clear in this matter," he wrote. "I did what I considered my duty and informed SHAEF public relations in advance that I intended to do it. I am fully responsible for the action of Morton Gudebrod in this matter, as he acted under my instructions." When Cooper received this statement in New York he rushed a private message to AP members alerting them that Kennedy's statement "failed to specify that he was not speaking for the Associated Press." Cooper had sent Kennedy a message expressing his displeasure with the bureau chief's failure to state that he had not informed the AP of his intentions. The next day Kennedy, one can presume begrudgingly, added to his statement that the decision to send the story had been his alone. "I sent the fact of the surrender to the Associated Press without explanation of the conditions under which I was sending it," he admitted.[89] Cooper distributed this to all AP members for publication.

Thor Smith spoke for many when writing that night that he was fed up with the entire episode. More than most in PRD, Smith had felt from the beginning that the decision to embargo news of such importance invited disaster. He also did not think much of the PRD's performance throughout, from the hasty selection of the press contingent onward. "I have lived a year in the last two weeks," he wrote his wife, "V-E passed over me like a bad dream." Smith had been responsible not only for investigating Kennedy's premature release but also for dealing with the blowback from the other disgruntled US reporters. "The prima donnas are still screaming, verbally around the Scribe bar . . . and in print," he wrote. Smith could not wait to get home: "I am already sick to death and totally lacking in interest re the many new problems that pop up every day re post-war Europe and our connection with it. Post-war Burlingame [Smith's home] is what I am interested in."[90] If SHAEF thought Allen's statement on May 14 would allow it to put paid to the whole affair, it was sorely mistaken. If anything, Kennedy's punishment only fueled the editorial fires smoldering in the United States.

6

The Debate

SHAEF PRD faced yet another censorship controversy while Ed Kennedy traveled home. Word reached the United States of the plans to continue military censorship as long as SHAEF remained operational. News organizations attacked the legitimacy of such continued information control. The surrender controversy had only stoked fears about the government's excessive control of information. That concern increased when Elmer Davis announced from the Office of War Information that the military had decided to regulate which foreign newspapers and magazines would be imported into Germany. The Allied military governors would decide what information German civilians would receive.[1] Both Eisenhower and Truman quickly overruled Davis, but the press grew suspicious of the government's postwar plans for managing the news.

In Paris reporters grew increasingly restive as the Soviets continued to block US and British reporters from entering the areas of Germany they controlled. It was a sign of Eisenhower's personal affection for Frank Allen as well as his disappointment in Allen's performance at the PRD that after awarding him the Legion of Merit, Eisenhower ordered Allen to take home leave before reassignment. It fell once again on Ernest Dupuy to try to put out the fires in the Scribe briefing room. He had to deal with vocal complaints about censorship, travel restrictions, and a host of lesser issues irking the press. Reporters were also asking questions about the redeployment of troops from Europe to the Pacific, questions to which the PRD as yet had no answers. Finally, Dupuy had to respond to recent stories asserting that Allied authorities were treating high-ranking Nazi prisoners with too much deference, even as reporters complained to him about the high degree of secrecy surrounding the detention of war criminals and the army's refusal to allow interviews with German prisoners of war. All this led to the charge that censorship promised to be as intrusive after the war as during it.

Figure 6.1. Colonel Ernest Dupuy briefing the press at the Hotel Scribe in February 1945. Dupuy's real skill was explaining complex military situations in terms that war correspondents could relay understandably to readers. He was less skilled at the bureaucratic infighting within the army and dealing with competitive rivalries in the media. Courtesy National Archives (111-SC-204496).

Eisenhower tried to address press skepticism over censorship by having Bedell Smith release a statement announcing the effective "end" of such censorship: "In order to clarify the position of this headquarters all correspondents are informed that censorship in this theater is hereby discontinued, except for major troop movements and details connected therewith, and such other matters of high military importance as may require reference to the Supreme Commander." If SHAEF thought this would end the complaints it was mistaken. The reporters' immediate skepticism about what "matters of high military importance" might mean was a measure of how wary correspondents had grown of the baggy language concerning threats to Allied unity in previous censorship regulations. On the last day of May, Dupuy alerted the correspondents in Paris that they still needed to submit copy for censorship, but that while it was impossible to define "matters of high military security" precisely, SHAEF would restrict such stops to major issues such as new or secret weapons. In addition, Dupuy assured reporters that even though SHAEF would not be able to help correspondents who ran into difficulties in Soviet-controlled territory, their dispatches from such trips would be approved for release and SHAEF would take no disciplinary action against them. Dupuy later wrote that this session "relieved the tension among our correspondents to quite a degree," but this may have been wishful thinking on his part.[2]

Thor Smith's letters home give some inkling of how the surrender lingered as an issue even weeks after Kennedy had left Paris. He wrote to his wife Mary several times each week, and by mid-May, he was a man who had reached his limit. While Dupuy dealt with censorship issues, Smith had been tasked with organizing the prospective press contingent to go to Berlin, when and if the Russians gave their blessing. At the moment most in the PRD were "still in a frenzy on our own redeployment," while for their part many reporters were simply "hanging around," he wrote, "hoping to have a Berlin dateline before they go home." Clippings of the editorial reaction to the surrender were just then beginning to reach Paris, and Smith was struck by the number of stories the Associated Press itself had put on the wire "trying to prove to others than themselves that what they did didn't smell."[3]

The next day Mary Smith's letters written as the controversy had unfolded finally reached her husband in Paris. In response to her question about his role in events, Smith confessed that he "was one of the responsible parties in the whole thing. If it was a PRD louse-up, as many and sundry think, then I am the one to blame." After explaining some of the ECLIPSE planning that had been done, and conceding that the last-minute decision to take the smallest group that would not involve pooling had caused problems, Smith took credit for the presence of even that small group of reporters. He remained convinced that little value would have been added by having more press witnesses and that the public had been served well by the group that was there. Mary Smith had asked him about the claim that some twenty girls attended the surrender, which Thor Smith dismissed as a wild accusation. Still, he did explain that after the ceremony, Harry Butcher had escorted "a WAC, a nurse, and a Red Cross girl," the latter presumably Mollie Ford, into the room where the surrender had taken place. Smith admitted that Butcher had made "a mistake."[4]

That same day and not having yet received any letters from him written after the surrender, Mary Smith wrote to her husband once more. She again asked for details of his involvement. She had indirectly heard that he had been one of the officers who had investigated Kennedy, and so she inferred that he could not have been the one who made the arrangements in question.[5] She would be disabused of this when she received the letter he had written that same day with his admission that he had been at the center of the fiasco.

Thor Smith's mood further darkened. "Sunday was my worst day . . . mentally . . . since I've been in the Army, I think," he confessed. "Just one thing piled on another to make me low . . . a nadir. Can't put my finger on it." He was not alone in "starting to think how homesick" he was, especially given there was no longer any war news or other goal to "hype us up." In the weeks since the war had ended, the SHAEF reporters "have gotten more edgy, more demanding." Commentary from the United States on the surrender story continued to filter its way to SHAEF. Smith found an article in *Newsweek* "not too bad," but did not think much of one in *Time* ("highly colored and slanted and unfair"). He was especially upset with Raymond Daniell's highly critical stories about the PRD, telling his wife that they were "not only unfair, but in some major respects definitely untrue and *he knows it*. That disgusts me." Clearly Smith was ready to quit the army. "I just want to be with you, and have time to 'catch up' . . . It's fun to dream."[6]

If PRD officials remained defensive, so too did the Associated Press. Kent Cooper tried to control the damage as he awaited Kennedy's arrival in New York. Cooper mulled over the AP's mistake in assuming Kennedy's flash had been officially sanctioned. On the day after Kennedy was disaccredited, Cooper stressed to the cable desk staff in New York the need to attribute information to its source. "Regardless of how any of us as individuals feel about the San Francisco and Paris instances," Cooper wrote, "we have got to remember that the integrity of The Associated Press is a stake." Cooper feared that the last week's events had placed the AP's reputation for reliability in question (even though Kennedy's account had been scrupulously accurate), so "let's all make this a personal, individual endeavor."[7]

Cooper frequently heard from Robert McLean in the weeks between Kennedy's disaccreditation and his arrival in New York. One can easily detect the tension between the two, as both digested the national commentary and mulled over what to do. McLean objected above all to Kennedy's coopting Eisenhower's judgment regarding security, and he was convinced that many journalists felt the same. Therefore, he urged Cooper to ponder how such thinking as Kennedy's might lead AP staffers to believe "they are carrying a torch for the newspapers and the public." In this regard, Cooper should consider how his own energetic advocacy of freedom of the press might have influenced the staff, including Kennedy. He wondered (and implicitly critiqued) the extent to which after both the San Francisco and Reims episodes, AP dispatches had defensively "showed a tendency to 'bolster' the story, with consequent loss of objectivity." McLean reminded Cooper that whatever he decided in the Kennedy case would influence the behavior of the staff, and at the same time he insisted that the results would be "disastrous" if staffers followed Kennedy in acting unilaterally.[8]

Cooper was stung by McLean's criticism. As he understood it, McLean's "conclusion is that unless something new is disclosed by Kennedy, he should be dismissed summarily." Cooper bridled at the assertion that his own advocacy of press freedoms had led AP staff to act rashly, but he would "find out from Kennedy whether he was in any respect influenced in his actions by my efforts to establish world wide freedom of the press." If Kennedy had been so influenced, Cooper only half-jokingly asked if he would have to renounce freedom of the press to deter AP staffers from following Kennedy's lead. Cooper also complained that McLean's public apology had "constituted a disavowal" of Cooper's own position not to prejudge Kennedy, although he had declared McLean's apology "proper" at the time. Evidently Cooper meant by proper in this context that it was within McLean's authority as president of the AP to do so. Cooper then restated his own conviction that Kennedy's error had been in not notifying New York of his intentions.[9]

McLean responded bluntly that indeed he did "question Kennedy's continued usefulness" to the agency. Still, he saw the wisdom in waiting to act until Cooper and Kennedy had talked. In what Cooper could only have taken as a not-too-thinly-veiled warning, McLean pointed out that if Cooper retained Kennedy, who then committed "another bobble of even minor importance," it might severely damage public confidence in AP's management.[10] Cooper assured McLean that he "thoroughly" understood. He was also "sure that you do not envy me in my responsibilities," Cooper's way of signaling to McLean that he remained in charge of AP operations, including staffing. "I don't shrink from the task before me," he wrote.[11]

This frosty exchange between the two AP leaders conveys the pressure both felt as journalists and AP directors continued to weigh in, and not always with messages of wholehearted support. Even those who expressed sympathy were usually troubled by aspects of the case. The publisher and editor of the *Lubbock (TX) Morning Avalanche*, Charles Guy, objected to McLean's apology, alerting Cooper that it "did not correctly reflect the attitude of a number of Associated Press newspapers— including our own." Guy asked if a poll of AP members had been taken before McLean issued the statement and, if not, suggested it should have been before McLean professed to speak for the AP membership. Those editors, like himself, who had defended Kennedy in print, in Guy's case by arguing that Kennedy had acted in "full keeping with the traditions of a free press," found themselves embarrassed by McLean's public repudiation.[12]

Cooper did not respond directly to Guy but rather forwarded his letter to McLean in Philadelphia. The length of McLean's response reveals how consumed by the issue he and the AP remained even if SHAEF professed to be done with it. He was sorry if his statement had caused Guy any embarrassment, McLean wrote in a two-page, single-spaced letter, but the surrender controversy had required a quick response which had made it impossible to canvass the AP membership. McLean then assembled the various rationales he had been using: that Kennedy had broken his word; that in doing so he had embarrassed the US government and, in particular, Eisenhower; that he had put lives at risk; that he had "taken advantage of" the other correspondents in Paris; and that he had made the entire AP "a party to his action" when he did not notify the agency of what he planned to do. McLean did admit that the military should not have tried to bottle up the story nor have pledged the correspondents to keep it secret after the Flensburg broadcast. He agreed that "censorship has been bungled and the public is tired of being spoon-fed the news." However, in Kennedy's case, "a man had exceeded his authority to the embarrassment of the whole organization." If and when the AP membership was aware of all these factors, McLean predicted they would approve of his statement.[13]

In an affable reply, Guy agreed with McLean's position "if we are going to look at it in a general way." He felt, however, that the German surrender was "the exception which makes the rule," since under the US Constitution censorship was only permissible for security concerns.[14] McLean responded to Guy yet again, this time insisting that Kennedy had interfered with Eisenhower's plan to end the war two or three days sooner by obtaining Russian cooperation. As such, Kennedy had not only betrayed confidence but also privileged his judgment over that of "the leaders of the three greatest nations of the world and the heads of their armies."[15] McLean here did little more than recite SHAEF's analysis of the situation, a line likely obtained through his contacts in the War Department. Thus even before Kennedy had returned to the United States to make his case, McLean, for one, had already made up his mind.

Another letter to McLean, though, may have given him more pause. It came from Melvin Whiteleather, at the time a reporter on assignment in San Francisco for McLean's own newspaper. Whiteleather had been the AP bureau chief in Rome when Kennedy was stationed there in the late 1930s, and he felt compelled to write even though "I'm going to stick my nose into something that is none of my business." When in Rome, Kennedy had impressed him as a "fine fellow personally" and an "excellent craftsman." When Whiteleather heard of the release of the surrender story he had wondered what Kennedy had been thinking. He had two possible explanations. First, Whiteleather wondered if health was not an issue, as with any number of other war correspondents he knew. "Ed had been through the entire war and it has left a distinct mark on him," he judged. When Whiteleather had seen Kennedy recently, "he was a nervous wreck. It was uncomfortable to be in his presence. In other words, he is suffering from what the moderns call 'battle fatigue.'" Whiteleather also wondered if McLean was aware of just how much AP's foreign correspondents felt goaded to beat the competition. Such pressure from New York "has brought a feeling that what was wanted was speed, regardless of whether the facts were straight or not." To Whiteleather's mind, the Connolly episode in San Francisco the month before had been a result of such demands from the home office.[16]

After McLean forwarded this letter to Cooper, Cooper wrote back that if he had known that Kennedy was suffering from "battle fatigue," he would have called him back from Paris immediately. Prompted by Whiteleather's comments, Cooper asked Robert Bunnelle if any Paris staffers had mentioned that Kennedy had been "off balance because of stress or any extenuating or incriminating circumstances." Bunnelle replied that Kennedy had "long been under emotional strain and [was] tired," but he did not know if this had affected Kennedy's judgment. Bunnelle was certain, though, that Kennedy "fully realized what [he was] doing and that he personally was convinced it the right thing at time."[17]

Another letter Cooper received might also have prompted some reflection. It came from an old friend, Benjamin McKelway, a veteran editor on the staff of the *Washington Star*. McKelway served as the president of the American Society of Newspaper Editors in the late 1940s, and he succeeded McLean as president of the AP in 1957. He had been one of a group of eighteen editors invited to Europe in April to witness the horrors of the concentration camps discovered by the advancing Allied armies.[18] During that trip he had spent time in the AP office at the Scribe. McKelway had appreciated Kennedy's work throughout the war, and his "admiration for him and his staff increased as I watched them at work." Kennedy seemed indefatigable: "He was working after midnight every time I saw him and he was on the job early in the morning. He felt his responsibility very keenly." Thus "the accumulated nervous strain of the past weeks and months" might have clouded his judgment over the surrender story. McKelway could imagine Kennedy's conundrum on

May 7: "There he was, with the biggest story of all time, knowing that it might break at any second from any one of dozens of sources—the same sort of leaks have occurred before."

McKelway felt that "after the battle on other phases of political censorship that he had been waging as an honest newspaperman, I suppose this last straw was a bit too much." SHAEF had certainly not been able to defend its decision to "hold the lid down" on the surrender news, and Kennedy had been "deeply disturbed over a condition that he felt was basically wrong." In any case, McKelway could never believe that Kennedy had broken the confidence "for self-aggrandizement" as some were charging. He believed that Kennedy had been punished enough already and hoped that Cooper would leave it at that. Whatever the current climate, McKelway was certain that over time journalists "will have more respect than hostility toward Ed Kennedy and what he did." Even if it had caused the AP some embarrassment at the time, "he taught a lesson that won't be forgotten."[19]

Cooper professed to be "deeply touched" by what McKelway had written. Although others had also thought that Kennedy was suffering from "battle fatigue," no one had said anything to him about it at the time. If they had done so, Cooper suggested, he would have ordered Kennedy home to "restore his equilibrium." Instead, several journalists who had met Kennedy in Paris in the late spring had praised Kennedy as "tops of all the newspapermen," and they had been impressed by the loyalty he elicited from the AP staff in Paris. To Cooper it was "heartbreaking" that Kennedy was coming home under such a cloud. Nonetheless, he hinted to McKelway of Kennedy's impending fate at the AP when he wrote that he knew McKelway would not envy him "the administration of my responsibilities," an echo of his line to McLean.[20] It might pain him, Cooper was suggesting, but Kennedy would have to go.

If Whiteleather and McKelway both seemed to counsel leniency for Kennedy, others who contacted the AP were far less sympathetic. The *New York Times* and its publisher, Arthur Hays Sulzberger, an influential voice on the AP board, proved among Kennedy's most dogged critics throughout May. The extent to which this stemmed from the *Times*'s anger at being excluded from the Lucky Seventeen is difficult to measure. Certainly Daniell's outrage, as expressed in his diatribe the day after the surrender, was shared in the editorial offices of the paper and by its publisher. Sulzberger wrote to General Marshall directly complaining that individual newspapers were not being assigned places at such events. Given its prominence and the size of its syndication service, he proposed (with some cheek) that as the war continued in the Pacific, the *Times* join the three news agencies in the core pool.[21] Marshall did not take the bait, and explained the obvious—protests would inevitably follow if the War Department allowed the *Times* to cover such stories but denied places to other major dailies.[22]

Daniell had also claimed that Kennedy had told him weeks before of his intention to challenge censorship. This only added to Sulzberger's doubts about the AP bureau chief. Moreover, Sulzberger had received a report on May 8 from his managing editor, Edwin James, highly critical of the AP for its handling of the premature surrender story from San Francisco. A former war correspondent and columnist on international affairs, James had been in San Francisco for the United Nations conference and criticized the AP for running the Connolly story before checking it with officials in Washington.[23] With all this as context, the *Times* published a scathing editorial on May 10 referring to Daniell's article and charging that Kennedy "took advantage of his associates and gravely misserved his employers." Kennedy's defense that no security concern was involved was "entirely inadequate" since it conflicted with Eisenhower's reading of the situation. "We regret the incident," the *Times* concluded, "as one which has done grave disservice to the newspaper profession."[24]

A personal memorandum Sulzberger wrote at the time reveals his true feelings about Kennedy himself. The publisher had always believed that there might come a moment during the war when "we would differ so much with the wisdom of a policy laid down by our high command that we would have to assume the responsibility of breaking censorship in order to tell the people what was happening." It would be a fraught decision but one that every self-respecting journalist had to be prepared to make. "But what Kennedy did was entirely different," Sulzberger wrote, "he was merely trying to score a beat."[25] What led to this conclusion about Kennedy's motives is difficult to say since Sulzberger had never met Kennedy, but Daniell's opinion may have held sway.

Sulzberger would not budge from this stance in the weeks to come, even when some of his own reporters came to Kennedy's defense. Frank Kluckhohn, for one, had noted Kennedy's statement that a PRO had told him of Eisenhower's desire to have news of the surrender released as soon as possible. Kluckhohn recalled that "exactly the same thing" happened to him in North Africa when Eisenhower had commanded AFHQ. In a second cable written after Sulzberger had referred him to that day's editorial, Kluckhohn emphasized that he was not debating the issue of breaking a release date, which he condemned, but he merely asked if the *Times* was justifying SHAEF's holding up the surrender news for two days. He stressed that "Cyrus [Sulzberger] and I think Kennedy one of the best."[26]

Others who wrote to Cooper and McLean were more troubled by the perceived failings of the AP leadership than Kennedy's. Nelson Poynter, the publisher of the *St. Petersburg Times* and something of a gadfly, praised McLean for his apology but also urged him to appoint a board committee to look into the San Francisco and Reims errors. He suspected that poor checking of sources by editors in New York had embarrassed the agency as much as Kennedy had. He was even more worried that the AP's response, presumably Cooper's public statements, had to date "been colored and slanted to defend what I consider two gigantic mistakes."[27]

McLean agreed that a report to the AP membership about the handling of both stories would be needed at some point (but by implication, not at that moment). He promised to send Poynter's telegram to the entire AP board, proposing that any such investigation should originate with it. There is no record of any such AP board investigating committee convening. The next week Sulzberger emphasized to McLean that he was less bothered by the initial mistakes in handling the San Francisco and Reims surrender stories than he was by "the manner in which the AP, in my judgement at least, attempted to bolster its stories rather than tell objectively that which had occurred." He wondered if McLean agreed, an unsubtle criticism of Cooper's defensive response to the uproar over both stories. McLean replied tersely that he did.[28]

By the end of the month and as his reckoning with Kennedy approached, Cooper felt the pressure. He may have managed the AP's operations for a quarter century, but his own exchanges with Sulzberger indicate anxiety over his future. Sulzberger had written to him on May 24 referencing the letters he had sent to McLean. Cooper replied that McLean had promised to send him everything he received about the Kennedy affair "so that I could better chart my own course," but that

McLean had not sent along Sulzberger's letters nor any of his replies. In what can only be read as a question about his fate at the AP, he asked: "I am in the position of having been dissected by adverse comment and affectionately and feelingly sewed up by favorable comment. Though the body is still in one piece it is curious to know: Who is to administer the coup de grace?"[29]

Sulzberger replied that he did not know why Cooper should wish for a coup de grace since the board also shared responsibility for the problems.[30] Cooper's next letter was a long and forceful defense of his actions while conceding that both the San Francisco and Reims reports had been "wrong." Regarding the erroneous surrender story from the United Nations conference, Cooper assigned blame to Paul Miller, the AP reporter in charge of coverage there, who "very foolishly went all out to make the story stand up." Miller had accepted responsibility for the blunder, Cooper disclosed, and done so in writing for his personnel file.

Regarding the Reims matter, he agreed that Kennedy's response should have been sent out with Allen's statement.[31] After reading that response, though, Cooper supported McLean's decision to apologize publicly. He insisted that he would have done so himself (although years later Cooper would cite a number of reasons why he had not), but that he thought it had been more appropriate for McLean to "speak for the membership." Sulzberger should appreciate "the tremendous shock" the whole episode had been to "every employee of The Associated Press, including myself." His responsibility was to try to bolster morale in the agency in the wake of this shock, as well as to assure that its channels of communication with the government and the army remained open. Moreover, Cooper hoped Sulzberger would not blame the other members of the Paris staff who had carried on brilliantly after Kennedy's "unwarranted action" that had "made them outcasts in the newspaper colony and coldly treated by the military in Paris." Cooper could only "marvel that we came out so well." The entire Associated Press "owes a very great deal to those employees who suffered isolation and abuse for something that another did." As far as the AP was concerned, "the clouds are beginning to lift," but Cooper had no objection to an investigation.[32]

There matters rested until Kennedy's ship docked in New York. Press commentary on the surrender fiasco abated but did not end. A *New Yorker* article by A. J. Liebling in mid-May, for one, garnered much attention. Liebling himself was an experienced war correspondent who had suffered his own run-ins with SHAEF. Liebling was also a notable media critic; his occasional column in the *New Yorker*, "The Wayward Press," often railed against the extent to which US newspapers were the playthings of their wealthy owners. Freedom of the press, Liebling famously observed, only belonged to those with the money to own one. He was also an unlikely champion of an Associated Press reporter, given his long-standing criticism of the news agencies as peddlers of a bland, corporate journalism.

Liebling's piece, "The A.P. Surrender," was hardly a dispassionate analysis of the fiasco. Rather, it was characteristic Liebling: polemical, hyperbolic, and bitingly funny, but at heart a knowing analysis of the news industry. Liebling called Kennedy "one of my favorite reporters," and praised him as the only member of the Paris press corps with the courage to defy military bureaucrats. His article, though, was less a defense of Kennedy himself than an attack on what he charged was the unseemly collusion between army public relations and the major news organizations. In essence, Liebling took the occasion to settle old scores over the ways PROs and the national agencies had conspired, in his mind, against smaller news organizations, throwing roadblocks in his way because the *New Yorker* was a weekly magazine with relatively few readers.

Liebling also found distasteful what many in the press seemed to accept, what he referred to as combination reporting, when a group of rival correspondents covering the same event cooperated on a story, for example, by agreeing to abide by a prearranged release time. However, the "old-fashioned 'combination' was an agreement freely reached among reporters," Liebling pointed out, "and not a pledge imposed upon the whole group by somebody outside it." That the large news organizations willingly agreed to such combinations imposed by SHAEF "in return for favors that independent journalists didn't get" had led "to the kind of official contempt for the press that the Reims arrangements indicated, with the accompanying view that the opportunity to report history was what SHAEF calls a 'SHAEF privilege,' like a Shubert pass." The Associated Press itself had been in the forefront of establishing this "form of organized subservience," Liebling added.

As Liebling would have it, the news agencies and the few large metropolitan papers that maintained foreign bureaus had done their utmost to exclude other news organizations from war coverage. They were willing to accede to the military's position that since there would never be sufficient facilities at the front to accommodate all of the reporters who wanted to go there, some procedure for selection was needed. The military had turned to the Association of American Correspondents in London to help make such selection, Liebling argued, out of convenience but also on the mistaken notion that the AACL represented all US reporters covering the army in Europe, however much the AACL might be dominated by representatives of the larger news organizations and the four national radio networks.

Although Liebling shared Daniell's outrage that no newspaper reporters were included in the surrender party, he found the latter's anger hypocritical since Daniell, as the president of the AACL in 1942, had "been the chief promoter of the limitations scheme." He had done so after the Dieppe raid, which Quentin Reynolds had covered for *Collier's* but without the sanction of the AACL; after that, Daniell had persuaded the army that "magazine men should be excluded." Liebling quipped that in essence the AACL had "simply transferred to Europe the tendency of American district reporters to play ball with the police lieutenant on the desk."

This was the background to General Allen's "rather spluttery rage" at the correspondents' protest meeting, and Allen seemed to Liebling like "a keeper at the Zoo who has been butted in the behind by his favorite gazelle." Nonetheless, the episode brought to light how military security had been used as an excuse for censorship imposed for a host of illegitimate "political, personal or merely capricious reasons." Liebling heaped the most scorn on what he called "the prodigious amount of pure poodle-faking" on the part of army public relations officers, themselves largely "Hollywood press agents or Chicago rewrite men in civilian life," whom he derided as uniformed "dress-extras." Liebling cited specific cases of officialdom's incompetence throughout the war, which had reached "a high point in *opera-buffa* absurdity" in London prior to D-Day when the military's many public relations units "spent most of their time getting in each other's way." Liebling had a particular bone to pick here as he had been excluded from participating in the D-Day landings. He had turned to a friend in navy public relations to obtain a place on a ship stationed off the Normandy coast on June 6, from where he produced one of the more memorable dispatches of the war.

The correspondents from the news agencies had "adapted themselves well to this squalid milieu and flourished in it," Liebling claimed. Their cooperation with military public relations ("they agreed with everything the dress extras said") allowed them to elbow out reporters like himself. Liebling warned that "the habit of saying yes to people you don't respect is hard to break, which is one reason I think well of Edward Kennedy for breaking it. Also, I think that if any severe punishments is inflicted on the first journalist to disobey an unreasonable order, an era of conformity will set in that will end even the pretense of freedom of the press in any area where there is a brigadier general to agree with."[33] Liebling's broadside was heard in Washington and registered in Paris as well. Janet Flanner, who had returned to continue her "Letter from Paris" for the magazine, cabled the *New Yorker*'s editor William Shawn to alert him that General Allen had seen Liebling's piece and that the four *New Yorker* staffers in Paris had all been summoned to the PRD so that "OUR HEADS CAN BE CUT OFF IN CONVENIENT QUARTET."[34]

On May 18, eleven days after sending the surrender story, Kennedy boarded the *General Gordon*, a troopship returning to New York with fourteen hundred liberated prisoners of war, mostly air force officers. He later would question the legality of the army's order expelling him from France, arguing that his passport and French visa remained valid. Nevertheless, Kennedy understood that he had exhausted his usefulness as a reporter in Paris, and so he decided not to fight the expulsion order.[35] Kennedy intended to get to New York quickly, but he had arrived at le Havre to find thousands of troops also waiting for passage home. He enlisted the help of a public relations officer, Ellis Brandt, who had worked for the United Press before the war, to get him direct passage to New York as soon as possible. Brandt then found him a place on the *General Gordon*. Once Kennedy was aboard Brandt learned that the ship was part of a slow convoy that would stop in the Caribbean before heading to New York. The PRO had tried to get on the ship to rescue Kennedy, but the gangplank had already been lifted.[36]

Kennedy's antagonists in the PRD spun the story differently. According to Thor Smith, Kennedy had arrived in le Havre, looked over the craft on which he was supposed to sail, then spotted a "larger and fancier looking ship." Kennedy pressured Brandt to get him on the better vessel. Brandt discovered that it was bound for the Caribbean only after it had sailed.

Figure 6.2. Staff join Ed Kennedy in the AP office in the Hotel Scribe on the night before the Paris bureau chief returned to the United States. Courtesy AP Images.

"The old slicker out-slicked himself once again," Smith gleefully joked to his wife.[37] Writing later about the episode, Smith added that when those in Paris learned of this, "there were many belly laughs from his still-injured competitors."[38]

Kennedy professed to have had a relaxing and enjoyable crossing, even if the ship was slow and crowded. He enjoyed the tales told by the former prisoners of war, and "for one being sent home in disgrace, I was the recipient of quite a few courtesies." The ship's captain even invited him to lunch one day, then kept Kennedy in conversation all afternoon and urged him to stay for dinner. "I was finding life in the doghouse which General Allen and my fellow correspondents had built for me rather enjoyable," he joked.[39] The *General Gordon* finally reached New York on June 4, after seventeen days at sea. By Kennedy's account the convoy was redirected to Trinidad while in the mid-Atlantic and had not been routed there from the beginning. Either way, Kennedy claimed to have enjoyed the warm weather holiday before the expected frosty reception awaiting him in the AP offices in New York.

By the time Kennedy boarded the ship in le Havre, hundreds of newspapers and dozens of radio commentators had weighed in on the Kennedy affair. The first of the War Department's promised surveys of press and public opinion arrived at Supreme Headquarters with the unwelcome news that despite SHAEF's strong statement and McLean's apology, the editorial comment regarding the controversy was generally unfavorable to SHAEF. The Bureau of Public Relations also admitted that letters to the editor and to the War Department "CONTINUE TO DISAPPROVE ARMY HANDLING ENTIRE EPISODE."[40]

When Kennedy himself read the comments that had accrued at the AP offices in New York, he estimated that 80 percent were supportive.[41] That the Associated Press, McLean's *Evening Bulletin*, Kennedy, the War Department, and the Office of War Information all kept clipping files related to the surrender episode indicates just how much interest there was in gauging such opinion. Each attempted to capture the range of editorial comments. Taken together, they reveal that support for Kennedy was not as one-sided as he believed. They also provided a colloquy of sorts on just how a free press should cover a total war.[42]

Patterns emerge from a careful reading of some 250 of these editorials and columns. Commentary understandably clustered around May 10 and 11, prompted by the correspondents' protest in Paris and Allen's response. The flow of opinion ebbed after Kennedy was disaccredited on May 14. As noted, initial support for Kennedy faded after Allen's statement and faded more with McLean's apology. Overall, significantly more editorials directly criticized Kennedy than supported him (103 vs. 64). However, SHAEF's handling of the situation and government censorship generally received even more criticism (112). Tellingly only a few editorial writers (7) defended the decision to withhold the news of the surrender. Both praise and censure of Kennedy were most often coupled with criticism of that decision, criticism typically laid at SHAEF's doorstep. Finally, though difficult to measure with precision just how the reaction to the Kennedy episode tracked with the political orientation of specific newspapers, those hostile to Roosevelt and his policies appear to have been more supportive of Kennedy and to see him acting to oppose the overreach of the Democratic administration.

A fair portion of editorial comments (48) focused on lauding Kennedy without much explicit comment on other matters. This clustered before Allen's statement and McLean's apology. Defenses of Kennedy ranged from qualified to full-throated. Several characterized Kennedy as an experienced journalist, merely doing his job. "Kennedy is no fly-by-night news reporter," one paper pointed out, while another claimed that he had seen "more of the war against Germany than any other reporter." Others remarked on Kennedy's "courage in pulling the scoop of the century," as one paper noted. The *Winfield (KS) Courier* wrote that he had "acted in all good faith and for the best interests of the American people" and that "because Kennedy had the courage the story reached America almost as soon as it reached Sweden, Germany and France," alluding to a complaint that others made overtly—that news was often unnecessarily slow to reach the US public.[43]

Most who praised him stressed Kennedy's service to the public and belief in the people's right to know. He had been "evidently schooled in the fundamental right of a newspaper to 'learn and publish the truth,'" according to one editorial writer, and "if he had not performed this miracle of reporting we might not yet know of this historic event." Another agreed: "Mr. Kennedy remembered that the first duty of any reporter is to the newspaper reader. No obligation he had was greater than that." Several made the point, as one paper observed, that "news is not just where you find it. It is of utmost importance when you find it." His understanding of this key point motivated Kennedy to act when he did, many felt. Another writer exclaimed that "Edward Kennedy has joined the ranks of journalistic immortals."[44]

For all such support, a greater number of editorials (71) criticized Kennedy without referring to SHAEF and its role in the surrender story. Critics attacked Kennedy variously for violating the release time, betraying his pledge to the military, ignoring his obligation to the other reporters in Paris, jeopardizing the safety of troops in the field, and substituting his judgment for that of the Supreme Commander. Many waited until Allen and Kennedy had released their respective statements before rendering a verdict on Kennedy's actions; of those, most found Kennedy's explanation lacking. Many influential papers, such as the *New York Times*, the *New York Herald Tribune*, and the Louisville *Courier-Journal*, took issue with Kennedy's action but did so sorrowfully. If the press needed to be vigilant against encroachment on its freedoms, the *Courier-Journal* argued, it must do so honorably and "with a constant realization of its responsibility." Kennedy failed on these grounds, and the paper could not endorse his actions.[45]

Others were harsher. The *Charlotte News* intoned that the only fitting consequence of McLean's apology was "the sack for Kennedy, straight-away and publicly and implacably." One writer went even further, refer-ring to Kennedy as a "Quisling" and his actions "a smear of the press from within." To yet another Kennedy was no less than "a disgrace to his profession." May 7 "was and will be remembered," one writer fore-cast, "as one of the worst days for newspaper people the world has ever produced."[46]

Nonetheless, almost half (112) of the editorials ignored Kennedy entirely to criticize and even excoriate official censorship practice and SHAEF's fumbling of the surrender story. The words "folly," "blunder," and more frequently "fiasco" pepper these editorials as they attacked officials not for their actions toward Kennedy, but rather for seeking to keep news of the surrender to themselves. If there was a dominant note sounded in these editorials, this was it. "The American people were entitled to know," as one writer put it simply, a belief that echoed throughout the editorial pages. The *New York Herald Tribune* observed that there was "something sublimely ridiculous in the spectacle of the Allied governments seeking to pen the fluid chaos of Germany's collapse into a neat little package labelled 'V-E Day.'" On May 8 papers were equally scathing about SHAEF's suspension of the entire AP the day before. The *Norfolk Virginian-Pilot* could only sigh over the "assininity" of continuing to hold the surrender news even after the Flensburg broadcast; to suspend the AP after Kennedy's scoop was noth-ing less than an "act of violence against a whole newsgathering agency." It brought upon itself "a condemnation it richly deserved."[47]

A significant number of editorials (22) commended Kennedy and lam-basted officialdom in equal measure, with SHAEF the favorite target. "Asaninity [*sic*] of United States army censorship on the Western Front never was more glaringly demonstrated than by [the] effort to withhold news of the unconditional surrender of Germany from the American peo-ple after the Germans, themselves, had broadcast it to the world," wrote one editorialist. "Happily, and justifiably, one American correspondent refused to be bound by official stupidity."[48]

Yet another slice of opinion (31) condemned both Kennedy for his misdeeds and officials for their mishandling of the whole episode. "We confess we have no journalistic pride in Mr. Kennedy's overzealousness," one paper conceded, but it viewed "the situation as generally messy with military authorities hardly spared the accusation of bunglesome handling of the biggest news event in modern history." This view was shared by others, including the *Augusta (GA) Chronicle*, which could only conclude that "aside from Kennedy's breach of ethics, and the unauthorized news story, the whole matter of the German surrender, from the point of announcing it to the world, was badly bungled. Fiasco is the word for it."[49]

A few editorials focused on aspects of the case that threatened to be lost amid this rhetorical torrent. An editorial writer for the *Cleveland News*, for one, challenged the widespread assertion that Kennedy had broken a cardinal rule of journalism by violating a confidence. In an argument that Kennedy himself would not make until he had returned to the United States, the *News* reminded its readers that such obligations were reciprocal; reporters routinely agreed to hold news, but "it is understood that the person exacting the pledge [in this case, Allen] undertakes not to permit release of the news through any other source. Once the news is out, it is no longer 'confidential.'" After the Flensburg broadcast and other ways that the news had leaked out from SHAEF "the 'confidence' was broken"; the Allied public had the same right to the information as the Germans, and the reporters who had witnessed the surrender thus had every right to try to get the story out. "Mr. Kennedy seems to have been the only correspondent who shared this view," the *News* concluded, and "because of that he finds all but two [Rue and O'Connell in Paris] of his competing newsmen giving testimony against him. But the fact is that it was SHAEF which double-crossed the correspondents, and not Mr. Kennedy. He simply refused to take it. They did."[50]

Such editorial opinion, then, contained equal measures of sober analysis, emotional venting, and score settling. Opinion writers, though, did reach beyond affixing blame for an acknowledged fiasco. They used the episode as a pretext to address concerns about a range of issues of the day—about journalistic ethics for one, about how censorship and government information policy generally had been handled during the war for another, and about the country's changing relationship with Russia, for a third. In this sense, such commentary looked back at government information policy throughout the New Deal and the war even as it looked forward, anticipating the burgeoning ideological conflict between the Soviet Union and the West.

Regarding ethics, there was widespread agreement that Kennedy had erred in violating what was taken to be a confidence, the pledge on the plane. Even his harshest critics admitted that Kennedy had reported truthfully. All agreed the story was momentous. For many journalists, neither circumstance excused the fact that, as one paper put it, Kennedy had "violated the most basic rule of the newspaper world which is never to violate a confidence." Indeed, some waxed rhapsodic over such confidences. "No article in the code of ethical journalism is more sacred than the keeping of a pledge of confidence once given," claimed one editor. "It has about it the sanctity of the confessional, and all newspapermen who have pride in their profession look upon it as a sort of unwritten and unspoken Hippocratic Oath," the writer continued, figuring the reporter as both priest and doctor. Others cast the keeping of a confidence in genteel Victorian terms. "Maintaining release dates is a matter of honor, the word of a gentleman" one editorial writer intoned, conjuring up a world many reporters in the 1940s would not recognize.[51] As portrayed in these editorials, then, honoring such confidences was not so much *a* feature of journalistic ethics as *the* feature of journalistic ethics. Few mentioned that such confidences were two-way streets.

There was also widespread and predictable wariness of censorship, even in wartime; more surprising may have been the widespread insistence that the only reason for censorship was to keep crucial information from the enemy. In that sense, as the *Hartford Courant* put it succinctly, "the justification for censorship ends when the shooting stops." Others chided officials by reminding them that "news does not belong to the government." One editorialist spoke for many when he observed that "no one objects to censorship which involved security of lives, but there has been entirely too much senseless censorship during this war which had no apparent aim other than to display misplaced authority."[52]

Some saw the hold on the surrender story as part of a war-long pattern of questionable censorship decisions invoking military security. One writer asserted that "it is no secret now that much information which the American people have a right to know has been kept from them on some

rather idiotic exaggerations of the military security clause." This was galling because "the people are not children and neither are they dummies.
They can take the bad news with the good." Another took direct aim at
SHAEF in asserting that "ever since the Normandy invasion there has
been so much ineptness and stupidity shown in the conduct of the censors
in Paris that all newspaper men familiar with it have become disgusted."
Kennedy was the wrong target for criticism because "it is the censor in
Paris who deserves censure and not the correspondent who did his duty
as he saw it."[53]

Such commentary followed fairly predictable lines, but two other
threads are more surprising. For one, the surrender fiasco surfaced long-
standing resentments among papers that had long opposed the information policies of the Democratic administration. Such papers, including the
Chicago Tribune and the Philadelphia *Evening Bulletin*, connected the
decision to withhold the surrender news to what it believed to be the Roosevelt administration's heavy-handed manipulation of the press from the
very beginning of the New Deal. The charge was that the administration
had applied slick public relations messaging to all information emanating
from Washington. As McLean's *Evening Bulletin* intoned in mid-May:
"Following the economic debacle of 1932 a whole crop of new ideas in
government sprang up in Washington. To exhibit these to the citizenry in
what was deemed to be the right light, hosts of 'public relations' special-
ists were employed by the departments and bureaus of the Government.
It was the function of these press agents to pass out information favorable to the designs of their superiors. . . . This peacetime phenomenon is
important chiefly as indicative of the state of mind of officialdom before
our entry into war."[54] The *Columbus (OH) Dispatch* shared this view.
The decision of SHAEF to send Kennedy home "in what they hope will be
disgrace" was connected to the "paternalism" of the New Deal which had
metastasized during the war into control of "practically everything they
[Americans] do, from what they read to what they eat."[55] At least some
editorial opinion, then, linked military censorship with government by
press release, by "off-the-record" conferences, and by other techniques of
information management that had been used, and had in some cases been
pioneered by, the Roosevelt administration.[56]

The second line of attack was to note that the US government had kept
such a tight lid on war news that often the public learned of important

events from British, Russian, or even enemy news sources. This was an especially bitter pill for the US press. *PM*'s columnist Tom O'Reilly, for one, wrote that "the Yanks took many a bad beating on news during that European engagement. Things that everybody knew and were keeping secret had a habit of breaking in Parliament or Moscow." O'Reilly also suspected that if Kennedy had not acted, the surrender story would likely have "leaked out somehow and probably through London." *New York Post* columnists Charles Van Devander and William O. Player Jr. echoed this sentiment in giving Kennedy "full credit here for the fact that for once in this war the American press wasn't 'scooped' on a big story by Reuters, TASS, the Soviet radio or the British Ministry of Information." To the columnists, "one of the minor scandals of this war has been the way the American press has been 'bottled up,' time after time, while the British newspapers and the British and Soviet official news agencies have broken big stories of world interest."[57]

Devander and Player, and the *Post* of that era, were liberal in outlook and supporters of Roosevelt, whereas papers less enamored of the president were even more critical. "President Roosevelt liked to throttle the press," the *Kennebec (ME) Journal* charged, complaining that even if there were occasions when information needed to be withheld, "many other instances of the press gag were entirely without right or reason." In particular, when the Big Three met, "the press was restricted to the coverage of background material or color. And after the conferences were over and the people uninformed, various British news gathering agencies invariably broke the story."[58]

Others were even more specific. SHAEF had held to the "infantile assumption" even after the Flensburg broadcast that "they owed no responsibility to the American public to release immediately an official version of what the world already knew." This reminded the *Norfolk Virginian-Pilot* of Roosevelt's meeting with Churchill in Cairo in 1943, which was reported by the British news agency Reuters a week before the US government announced it. Moreover when the two leaders had traveled on to meet Stalin in Tehran, this had been announced by Soviet radio days before the United States officially confirmed it. More than one editorial writer found it doubly galling that not only had the US government agreed to withhold information from the US public at war's end, but it also had done so at the bidding of the Soviet Union. Writing in the *Wheeling (WV)*

News-Register, Austin V. Wood asked, "Since when must we await Mr. Stalin's 'green light' before we are told the truth?"[59]

Thus the surrender story seemingly broke a logjam of resentment at what was seen as excessive news management during the war, resentment often stated in populist terms. One newspaper needed both boldface and capital letters to make the point: "This word, this announcement of peace, was not the business of the President of the United States, nor of Mr. Churchill or Premier Stalin. **IT WAS NOT THEIRS TO WITHHOLD.**" The *Clovis (NM) News Journal* connected these two strains of thought in arguing that "it was the right of the American people and of the other people of the world to know that Germany had surrendered" and then pointing out that as of May 9, "Stalin has still not announced to the Russian people that Germany has surrendered. If that is the way they want things in Russia, it is all right, but it isn't the way we want them in America." The *Portland Oregonian* asked its readers to bear in mind that even days after the Flensburg broadcast, Kennedy's scoop, and its rebroadcast across the world, the Russian people still did not know that the Germans had surrendered. The pledge on the plane, in their view, was akin to such dictatorial thinking, "in reality it represented an effort on the part of the United States army to conform to the Russian brand of censorship."[60] All of this editorial comment points to the way the surrender episode had brought to a head long-standing frustration over what was perceived to be excessive government control of information on the one hand and was also implicated in the impending conflict with the Soviet Union. In this sense, the Kennedy affair may have anticipated the Cold War just as the hot one ended.

7

THE AFTERMATH

As the tugboats shouldered the USS *General Gordon* up to Pier 88 on Manhattan's westside, Kent Cooper was sufficiently concerned about what Kennedy might say upon arriving that he sent an AP executive, Thomas Hagenbuch, crosstown to mind him. A gaggle of reporters awaited Kennedy on the dock. While Hagenbuch scrambled for a taxi, Kennedy, still in his correspondent's uniform, held an impromptu conference. Kennedy stood by his statements in Paris. He denied again that he had breached any confidence or had endangered military security and then begged off from saying much more. When pressed, he denied that there had ever been a "personal row" with General Allen, whom he praised pointedly as a good combat officer.

Kennedy insisted he had never been interested in obtaining a scoop, but only wanted to inform the US public of the surrender he had witnessed. "I consider myself absolutely in the clear and did what I thought was my duty," he responded when asked by a reporter from *PM* if he would do the same thing again under the same circumstances. "The war was over.

There was no military security involved and the people had a right to know." The AP's own lead for the story crucially had Kennedy, when asked if he had any second thoughts, replying, "I've said it before. I would do it again. The war was over. There was no military security involved and the people had a right to know." The AP's reporter was the only one on the dock to include in his story "I would do it again" as a direct quotation from Kennedy, words that Cooper and McLean would soon add to their bill of particulars against the reporter. Kennedy recalled later that he had been asked if he would do it again and had replied, "since I already stated that I believed myself to have acted rightly, that conclusion might be logically drawn."[1]

Deflecting questions about his future at the news agency, Kennedy told the reporters that he had been working intensely for years and hoped most of all for a vacation. With that he crossed town, headed for Cooper's office in Rockefeller Center. "Our meeting was cordial," Kennedy recalled, at least until a secretary brought in the AP's just-written account of his interview on Pier 88. The "I would do it again" quotation clearly displeased Cooper. Kennedy told him that Robert McLean had so thoroughly repudiated his reporting from Paris that he had no choice but to resign. Cooper advised him not to be hasty, but rather to use his substantial accumulated leave while waiting for things to die down.[2]

Over the next days, Kennedy sifted through the editorials and letters sent to the AP weighing in on the surrender controversy. He also met with *Editor & Publisher*'s Dwight Bentel for an extended interview. He recounted the entire episode to Bendel "with the decisiveness of a man who is convinced he is right." Of the pledge on the plane, Kennedy asserted that this was solely a pledge between each correspondent and Allen; at no time had the correspondents made a pledge to each other. Moreover, Kennedy revealed that he had expressed no reservations in making the pledge at the time because "I naturally assumed the release would be a reasonable one and I had not the slightest idea, at the time, that the story would not be cleared in the normal way." He had shared the frustration of the other correspondents with the army's mishandling of the release.

Asked about his assertion in the recent AP wire story that he would do it again, Kennedy said that he had merely been asked directly whether he still believed he had been right. "I wasn't bellowing defiance," he insisted, but in hindsight he should have sent the story "with the flat statement that it was not passed by SHAEF censors so that the Associated Press would have known exactly what it was." This was the only public second-guessing Kennedy ever allowed himself. Besides, as Kennedy must have known, if he had indeed alerted the AP in this way, the story almost certainly would have been stopped by censors in London. Bentel disclosed in a sidebar that the Associated Press stated that Kennedy's current status was "inactive" and that the agency refused further comment. Kennedy left New York on a brief vacation shortly thereafter.[3]

Cooper drafted a lengthy memo to the board of directors after he met with Kennedy. Marked as strictly confidential, the memo and its even lengthier attachments were Cooper's attempt to present to the board "a complete log" of the events surrounding the publication of Kennedy's surrender story. Cooper devoted the bulk of it (and one of the appendices) to upbraiding the War Department and SHAEF. At no point did Cooper admit any responsibility, nor that anyone within the AP other than Kennedy might have made a mistake. The military itself bore most of the blame. Moreover, Cooper's memo never explicitly stated what decision, if any, he had made about Kennedy's future with the Associated Press, even as Cooper made frequent mention of how heavily that question weighed on him.

Cooper began by reminding the board that Kennedy had "nobly, courageously and for a long time at the risk of his life" served the entire membership "with unstinting loyalty, and in the best newspaper traditions." He believed "no one has been held or is at present held in higher esteem by newspaper men that know him, than Kennedy," this notwithstanding the correspondents' protest in Paris. In recounting the events in France on May 7, he insisted that Kennedy "was not, during all that time, sneaking around to see if he could scoop everybody." Most of the other correspondents in Paris had agreed that SHAEF's delay in releasing the news of the end of the war was "a crazy thing to do." The reporters in Paris had not objected "because they were punch drunk from public relations office regimentation or because they didn't give a damn."

Cooper acknowledged that AP members were not of one mind about Kennedy's future with the agency, and that whatever Cooper decided to do would meet with some objection. "There is no precedent in American newspaperdom for such a situation," a situation initiated by what Cooper characterized as "autocratic military authority."[4] Cooper appended to his memo a second document in which he expanded on the myriad failings of the War Department and SHAEF, starting with the decision to withhold release of the news from Reims. To Cooper, the War Department had only itself to blame for the surrender fiasco.[5]

In the end, Cooper came not to praise Kennedy but to bury him. Cooper composed (but had not yet sent) a letter for Kennedy, which he also attached to the board memo. He again lauded the reporter for his war work. He acknowledged that Kennedy had acted in good faith throughout and again blamed the War Department for bungling the surrender. He found it cruelly ironic that Kennedy's report had saved the army from the greater criticism that it would have faced for withholding the news if Kennedy had not acted.

For all that, the AP policy held that agreements about news releases needed to be "scrupulously observed," and that no employee had the right to disregard a pledge of confidence to a source when the source believed it still applied. "Even if the employee feels a situation has arisen that nullifies the pledge he must never proceed regardless," Cooper proclaimed. If said employee felt frustrated in such a situation, he could contact New York for guidance. "In this instance you failed to give the same warning to The Associated Press that you gave the military authorities, namely, that you were going to transmit the story for immediate publication." Given this fact, Cooper "noted with regret" that Kennedy had stated he would "do it again." There followed the only sentence which directly referred to Kennedy's future in the more than forty pages of material that Cooper sent to the board: "Obviously, neither having observed nor being willing to be bound by The Associated Press' requirement of inexorably observing the conditions of the release of news *makes it impossible for you to continue in the service of the Associated Press.*" He provided one caveat—if the board were ever to decide that Kennedy's case was an allowable exception to the principle he had articulated, he would gladly relent. With these circumlocutions, Cooper had it both ways; he signaled to Kennedy that he was fired without declaratively stating as much.[6]

Board members understood Cooper's intent amid the welter of words— that Kennedy could not continue at the AP. Most but by no means all of the board agreed, and several of those did so with reluctance. Frank B. Noyes was the publisher of the *Washington Star* and an influential voice as a former president of the AP. Noyes was not among the reluctant.

Figure 7.1. Pictured at the annual meeting of the Associated Press in April 1943, are (left to right) Robert McLean, president of the Associated Press; Kent Cooper, AP general manager; W.J. Haley, managing director of the Manchester Guardian; and Frank B. Noyes, the publisher of the Washington *Star* and a past president of the AP. McLean and Cooper never enjoyed the closest relationship, and it was further strained by the surrender controversy. Noyes supported McLean's public rebuke of Kennedy and Cooper's decision to fire him. Courtesy AP Images.

He cabled Cooper at once, "ENTIRELY AGREE THAT KENNEDY'S SEPARATION FROM SERVICE IS NECESSARY." McLean, Arthur Sulzberger, and Stuart Perry of the *Adrian (MI)Telegram*, concurred. McLean feared that if such actions as Kennedy's were condoned by the press, "the military would be tempted to set up its own [press] corps" or "to require military status of correspondents," seemingly unaware that in effect it did so already. Although the *Telegram* was a small paper, Perry was a respected member of the board's executive committee. "I think your decision to separate Kennedy from the AP service is not only correct but inescapable," he wrote to Cooper." Others' support was less full-throated. J. R. Knowland, the longtime editor and publisher of the *Oakland Tribune*, wrote to Cooper that he did not "see how you could have taken any other action." Still he had "great sympathy" for Kennedy and confessed that the *Tribune* had been one of the papers that had used his story.[7]

Paul Bellamy, the editor of the Cleveland *Plain Dealer*, similarly wrote that he had wrestled with the matter for long hours. As much as he regretted it, he was "compelled to say that under the rules of the game you had to do what you did." Bellamy also warned Cooper that Kennedy's dismissal would "raise hell in the membership" as there was "a strong body of opinion there which defends Kennedy up to the hilt." There was "something fundamentally cruel to me in the net result, logical and necessary" though it might be. Thus he hoped there might be some path forward that would discourage such practices but not sacrifice Kennedy. Beyond that Bellamy thought that publishers "have been damned blameworthy" in not standing up more forcefully against censorship. Newspapers "have sent gallant individuals like Kennedy up against that barricade, raised hell with them if they got scooped, raised hell with them if they did not get the news and done little or nothing to bring about a change in the attitude of the high command."[8]

Another board member, Roy Roberts of the *Kansas City Star*, seemed just as conflicted about Cooper's argument. On the one hand, as Roberts understood it, Cooper was sacking Kennedy because he had been unrepentantly insisting he would "do it again." Roberts asked, though, if this were really true, after Kennedy's statement to *Editor & Publisher* that he wished he had informed the AP office. Not doing so, Roberts believed, was Kennedy's "chief error," but one he had now stated he regretted. "I think we are losing a hell of a good man," Roberts lamented. Admitting that the *Star* had been among those papers which had published the surrender dispatch even after knowing it was under a cloud, Roberts "wince[d] at making him the goat."[9]

Houston Harte of the San Angelo (TX) *Standard-Times*, the AP's first vice president, made much the same point if in more colorful language. "The members accepted the booty—accepted it knowing it was 'hot merchandise,'" Harte reminded Cooper, "Is there no honor among those who willingly—and I might add avidly—divided the loot?" While Harte agreed with Cooper's points about holding to confidences and release times in the abstract, "when you get down to Kennedy the man, your European manager, your employee with a long record of good conduct to his credit, you give him the ax upon a purely auxiliary complaint." George Booth, the publisher of the *Worcester Telegram*, agreed that Kennedy deserved a better fate than firing. "I don't believe we want to be in the position of stoning him to death," he wrote.[10]

Cooper continued to defend his thinking to board members throughout June and did not waiver in his determination that Kennedy must go.[11] Still he could not bring himself to make a clean and public break with the reporter. As a result the next few months were taken up with the question of his status at the news agency. Cooper did not send Kennedy the letter he had written with the one sentence alluding to his dismissal. They met several more times in June—Kennedy betrayed no overt hostility toward Cooper but portrayed him as something of a ditherer—and at one point Kennedy insisted that if his boss was not going to back him up he should fire him, but Cooper demurred. To the outside world, the AP continued to say only that the reporter was officially "inactive," whatever that meant.

Kennedy was less charitable about McLean, whom he met in Philadelphia at the publisher's request. McLean had inherited the *Evening Bulletin* from his father and although the paper was highly profitable, to Kennedy's mind McLean had done little to improve it. Kennedy thought the *Bulletin*, like McLean, "exudes a prim respectability and a high degree of mercantile flavor." McLean urged Kennedy to "purge" himself by admitting his mistakes. If he did so McLean thought Kennedy could continue at the AP or if not there, then perhaps even at the *Bulletin* of all places. Kennedy insisted that he had done nothing for which he had to apologize. When conversation turned to foreign affairs, Kennedy later could not resist the dig that McLean had "impressed me as a man who got most of his ideas out of *Reader's Digest*." Evidently McLean did little to alter Kennedy's belief that the publisher had sold him out, even as Kennedy had done nothing to convince McLean that he had repented.[12]

When Kennedy returned to New York, Cooper echoed McLean's suggestion that he "purge" himself. Cooper also advised Kennedy to take one of several job offers he had received from outside the Associated Press, including one from the New York *Daily News* to join its Washington bureau. If he did so, they both could save face by announcing that Kennedy had left for a better job elsewhere.[13] Cooper did not mention to Kennedy that Paul Miller, the AP's Washington bureau chief now out of the doghouse after the Connolly flap in San Francisco, had wanted Kennedy reassigned to the capital.[14] Kennedy was even approached to host a nightly radio program, one in which he could take advantage of his notoriety as the reporter other reporters did not like. "You don't know what a future there is in radio for an unethical newspaperman," was the curious recruiting pitch.[15] While the AP deflected queries from the press about his status, Kennedy continued to lie low through the summer's dog days.

For years to come, the question of whether the Associated Press fired Kennedy or he resigned remained unanswered. In August, and having used up his accrued leave, Kennedy wearied of his status in limbo. He submitted his letter of resignation, but an AP executive had "thrust the letter back into my hands and told me to take another vacation."[16] Kennedy then tapped his savings to take up residence mid-town in the Bedford Hotel, spending his time catching up on his reading, going to shows on Broadway, and, according to some newspaper accounts, working on a book about the surrender.

Kennedy alleged that in October the Associated Press deposited some five thousand dollars in his bank account, and that thereafter he received no more paychecks. He assumed this was severance pay, but the AP would neither confirm this nor that he had been fired. Cooper did report to the AP board when it met on October 5 that "Kennedy had been told he should make another connection and that Kennedy's services would be terminated at the close of October 31." The initial idea was for Kennedy to be given three months to find another job, but Cooper insisted Kennedy leave sooner.[17] Kennedy makes no reference to having been informed of the board's action.

A note dated October 19 states that "effective Sept. 30, 1945, the services of Edward Kennedy, foreign staff, are terminated" and directs that a severance check be cut. On November 9, Kennedy also received a note from the AP's auditor asking him to sign a form so that the AP could reimburse him for his own contributions to a life insurance policy. The note began, "in connection with your resignation," which is curious because Kennedy had retained the letter he had intended to submit in August once Cooper's deputy had refused to accept it. Regardless, if the waters were muddy the current was clear; by the fall, the AP and Kennedy had parted ways.[18]

Press interest in the Kennedy case ebbed after May 1945, but it did not evaporate entirely. Rumors abounded. The *Detroit News* reported in November that Kennedy had joined the staff of a leading newspaper,

McLean's Philadelphia *Evening Bulletin* no less. Columnist Danton Walker of the New York *Daily News* stated definitively that Kennedy had quit the AP for a radio job paying $25,000 a year, and that he would also write a syndicated column. The surrender story was even featured as a five-page, nineteen-panel comic in *Picture News*, journalist Emile Gavreau's curious and short-lived effort to present the news to an adult audience in graphic panels.[19]

Kennedy later claimed that he was determined not to take another newspaper job until he had cleared his name. To that end he spent much of his time in the next year on that effort. Kennedy hoped to do so by proving that SHAEF had released the surrender story before he had done so. Kennedy made little progress when he contacted the War Department, but Representative Albert Gore Sr. (D-TN), who had taken an interest in the case, had better luck. In September the Federal Communications Commission verified that the Flensburg broadcast had taken place well before Kennedy's story hit the AP wire.[20] However, Gore could not discover if that broadcast had been sanctioned by army officials.

Kennedy then approached a friend from the war, John (Tex) McCrary, an air force public relations officer popular with reporters in the Mediterranean. He was then editing the *American Mercury* and remained well-connected in Washington. McCrary agreed to look into the Flensburg broadcast. According to Kennedy, McCrary had his air force sources contact Bedell Smith who admitted that SHAEF not only had allowed the broadcast but, in fact, had ordered it: "I believe that this announcement was made on 7 May. The so-called Doenitz Government had not at this time been taken into custody and this announcement was made pursuant to orders from Supreme Headquarters that the German troops were to be informed by every possible means of the surrender and directed to cease resistance."[21] Kennedy was convinced that Bedell Smith's comments provided definite proof that SHAEF itself had broken the release agreement.

Albert Gore was not alone in Congress in criticizing the military for botching the German surrender. Some had been tireless in oversight of the armed services throughout the war; others were upset at what they perceived as excessive deference to the Soviets.[22] Kennedy's effort to clear himself also had come to the attention of Senator Sheridan Downey (D-CA), and so Kennedy sent him Bedell Smith's memo and asked the senator to look into his disaccreditation. Eisenhower, who had replaced George

Marshall as army chief of staff, reviewed the new information supplied by Downey. Acknowledging that it included facts unknown to him in 1945, Eisenhower decided to restore Kennedy's credentials in case he should choose to cover the army again. He did so, however, without rescinding the original SHAEF order sanctioning Kennedy.[23]

In July 1946 Downey announced Eisenhower's action to the press. He entered into the *Congressional Record* Bedell Smith's admission about the Flensburg broadcast. He also entered Kennedy's statement that he had sent the story only after learning of that broadcast, which he took to be an official release. Finally, Downey introduced a letter from the War Department admitting that Kennedy's dispatch had appeared almost two hours after the German announcement.[24]

Downey's statement occasioned a new round of press commentary more than a year after the surrender. For example, *Newsweek* wrote sympathetically about Kennedy's case. After reminding its readers that "no other news story of the entire second world war caused as much furor," *Newsweek* revealed that "the scoop brought little except grief for Kennedy." Although Eisenhower had reinstated Kennedy's accreditation, that gesture had not restored his old job. *Newsweek* recounted how correspondents in Paris, "goaded by their home offices, had roundly condemned" Kennedy the previous May. Similarly, Downey's statement spurred Herb Graffis, a columnist for the *Chicago Times*, to praise Kennedy, swearing that he had never met a harder working or more effective reporter. Kennedy was now "out of work for taking seriously the idea that freedom of expression was one of the freedoms [the] war was fought for." Graffis lambasted his press colleagues for not taking up Kennedy's cause as they had others who had been "pushed around by the Army brass."[25]

Messages arrived at the AP seeking clarification of Kennedy's status. Cooper answered that he would say nothing about Kennedy's situation. "Isn't AP's 'no comment' [an] example of just what [the] AP rails against in the rest of the world," one member asked Cooper. To which Cooper could only reply, "I saw no reason, and I still see no reason, for the Associated Press to make any comment. I hope that you have got confidence enough in me to believe that this is the right thing to say." The reason for Cooper's continued silence on Kennedy's status seemed to be part of a conscious strategy to deal with the matter quietly, as he explained to

Robert McLean: "I brought about the termination of his [Kennedy's] services as inconspicuously as I could."[26]

Convinced that he had been exonerated by Eisenhower, Kennedy felt free to restart his career. Thomas M. Storke, a Democratic politician and publisher of the *Santa Barbara (CA) News-Press*, had long admired Kennedy as a journalist and sympathized with his situation. That autumn he began to sound out journalists he knew about possibly hiring Kennedy, and he wrote to Cooper for a reference. Perhaps thinking it might rid him of Kennedy's presence in New York, Cooper sent a warm and fulsome letter speaking highly of Kennedy's character and the quality of his work. Storke wrote back, commenting that a similar query to a journalist friend in Washington had yielded the response that Kennedy was universally despised there.[27] In any case, in October Storke announced that he had hired Kennedy to be the managing editor of the *News-Press*. This position was a decided come-down for the former Paris bureau chief of the world's largest news agency, as the *News-Press* was an obscure daily in a sleepy (if scenic) California community. That said, Brooklyn-born Kennedy had never been to the American west and was anxious for the change of scene.

In 1946 Kennedy had also married journalist Lyn Crost, a fellow Brooklynite ten years his junior whom he had met in Paris the previous year. While reporting for the *Honolulu Star-Bulletin* Crost had won praise for her coverage of the 442nd Combat Regimental Team, the Japanese-American unit soon to become one of the most decorated of the war.[28] Kennedy's marriage may also have played a role in his decision to make a new life for himself in the west, as Crost had many west coast connections.

As Kennedy settled down in California and started a family, the Reims controversy resurfaced from time to time. On occasion he resurfaced it himself. In June 1947, for example, Kennedy accepted an invitation to address the annual convention of the Texas Press Association. He promised to present for the first time his full version of the surrender episode. At the meeting he called the whole affair "ancient history," but then noted that there was renewed interest in it as the Cold War intensified. Kennedy's account accorded with much he had said to that point and with what he would write thereafter, but he reminded the audience of newspaper editors that he had been in the position of any one of them who held a story only to discover that it had been released, deliberately or inadvertently. "It is the universal practice in such cases to consider the story released to all, after first going through the formality of informing the person who had imposed the release. This is precisely what I decided to do."[29] After the event, the Dallas bureau chief reported to Cooper that "Ed Kennedy makes a good talk on this story. According to his account he was 100 percent right all the way, and apparently was the only person who made no errors."[30]

There matters seemed to rest for the better part of a year. Then in April 1948 Arthur Capper, the crusty Republican senator from Kansas and himself the owner of several home state newspapers, sponsored a bill to award medals to the sixteen reporters who had "kept the faith" over the Reims surrender. Capper publicized his resolutions in a florid article he wrote for the Hearst newspapers' Sunday supplement, *American Weekly*, and which he entered verbatim into the *Congressional Record*:

> From their battle-battered typewriters the century's biggest news mocked and challenged them. Here was the scoop they had lived for all their news-paper lives. Here was the story the whole war-weary world waited to hear. But they chose not to breathe a word of it.
>
> It was physically easy for these correspondents to reach a telephone or telegraph instrument and disclose the momentous happening which they had seen or heard, but it was morally and ethically impossible for them to do anything of the kind.[31]

Why did these reporters deserve commendation for not reporting such a story, what seems something more a dereliction of journalistic duty than worthy of a medal? It was the pledge "imposed on them" by General Allen not to divulge the story until granted permission to do so by the authorities. The reporters' achievement was to have obeyed the military, Capper made clear; in stifling their instinct to beat the competition, they had "met the test gloriously," and thereby proved Eisenhower's trust in the press well-placed.[32]

Capper's encomium was marred by its factual inaccuracies—the reporters did not have easy access to telephone or telegraph facilities, for one thing. Moreover, his list of Reims reporters included two who had not attended the surrender ceremony (Drew Middleton of the *New York Times* and John O'Reilly of the *New York Herald Tribune*) and omitted two who had (Sidor Litvin of TASS and Price Day, the *Baltimore Sun* reporter representing the Exchange Telegraph agency). Capper introduced a second resolution more generally praising news organizations, including the AP, by name, "to make certain that the Associated Press would not be stigmatized by lack of mention of any AP representative among the 16 who had 'kept the faith.'"[33] Capper unmistakably meant both bill and resolution as a direct rebuke of Kennedy, whom he did not mention by name.

All of this was a bit too much for the rebuked. When he read Capper's article in the *American Weekly* and learned of the resolutions, Kennedy objected. As in 1945, action was again being taken "without hearing from all sides concerned," namely, his. Kennedy emphasized that the intervening three years had only strengthened his case and that "fairness would require that you either assure a hearing on the measure or that the bill be withdrawn."[34] Kennedy argued that it also would be unfair to publicize the bill only to kill it in committee, although that seems to be what happened.

Upset over Capper's stunt and to further the case he had been building since May 1945, Kennedy published an account of the controversy in the *Atlantic Monthly* under the now defiant title, "I'd Do It Again." Charles Morton, an *Atlantic* editor, touted Kennedy's article as "rugged stuff" and as presenting "a set of facts pretty well mangled by his opposition and the Army oafs in charge of the nightmarish press arrangements on that occasion." The piece had convinced Morton, for one, that "Kennedy was acting on sound professional grounds" given that "the story was out, irrevocably made public, and technically a dead duck when Kennedy let go of his bulletin."[35]

In "I'd Do It Again," Kennedy walked readers through the sequence of events from his witnessing of the surrender and release of the story, to the furor it caused, to his disaccreditation and Eisenhower's subsequent restoration of his credentials. He presented few new facts, but his criticism of the PRD was sharper than it had been in 1945. He described the pledge on the plane, for one thing, as less a solemn formality than a "rambling talk" by Allen; similarly, the entire press corps in Paris had learned of the impending Reims trip because of amateurish "leaks in Allen's Public Relations staff."

Kennedy admitted that he had accepted the pledge on the plane and had made it "in good faith, intending to honor it." Moreover, in his mind Kennedy did honor it since his pledge had been "not to break the news until it had been released by Supreme Headquarters." SHAEF had done just that in authorizing the Flensburg broadcast. After that, SHAEF's insistence on withholding the story was "admittedly political censorship in clear-cut violation of the cardinal point of US censorship—as enumerated from the White House down—that it would be limited to matters of genuine military security. I made up my mind. I have never regretted my decision." Kennedy told his tale more in sorrow than in anger, even as he described the PRD as inept and the press corps as hysterical after the story broke.

As he had in Texas the year before, Kennedy now framed the surrender story in postwar terms. The Western Allies' willingness to delay the release date, he ventured, stemmed from the US government's position that the victory would be worthless if it led to a new conflict with the Soviet Union "and that almost any price was worth paying to avoid such a development." The Soviet's insistence on a second surrender in Berlin he now saw as "Moscow's first post-war move against the Western powers, a propaganda trick preliminary to the ideological offensive and territorial expansion which started immediately after the surrender was signed." Kennedy was not surprised that the Soviet press never informed the Russian people of the Reims surrender; he was shocked by the US acquiescence to the Russian attempt "to falsify history."[36] In this sense, Kennedy (as had many of the editorialists at the time) saw the jockeying over the surrender as an opening gambit in what would become the Cold War.

Former members of the PRD were less than pleased that the surrender controversy had reappeared in such a fashion. Thor Smith, for one, now an executive with the San Francisco *Call-Bulletin*, asked if the *Atlantic* was interested in *both* sides of the story. "As long as men live who participated in that Reims fiasco," Smith admitted, "the controversy will continue to rage."[37] When the *Atlantic* agreed to consider an article if Smith supplied details that contradicted Kennedy's account, Smith enlisted the aid of Roy Pawley, Burroughs Matthews, and Ernest Dupuy. "I think it time that the record was cleared," Smith pronounced.[38]

All three sent Smith recollections, documents, and encouragement. Pawley, who had returned to the *Daily Telegraph*, wrote from London making two points not often emphasized. He rejected the very premise that Kennedy had achieved a scoop, which to his understanding "was securing of a story and publishing it against competition, not in spilling a story which everyone has." Kennedy had done nothing to obtain the story himself. "In other words," Pawley joked, "Kennedy scooped a handout."

Pawley stressed that in addition to violating his verbal pledge on the plane, Kennedy had violated his written accreditation agreement, a more serious offense. "All correspondents were under military orders," Pawley noted, "accordingly there could be no question that Kennedy, who had accepted military discipline as a condition of service, broke orders."[39] Curiously, military officials did not make this point often or forcefully, instead concentrating on Kennedy's breaking of his word to Allen. Pawley seems to be the only one who raised it, while others focused on the ethical lapse in violating a confidence. At a minimum, Pawley's point calls into some question the notion that, as "quasi-staff" officers in Eisenhower's formulation, the army had accepted war correspondents into the fold. The very fact that flouting censorship regulations seemed to count less than the pledge on the plane suggests that army officials would not apply strict military discipline to Kennedy. It reminds us that although correspondents were uniformed and granted the equivalent rank of captain (largely so that they would be treated as officers if captured), they were not addressed by rank nor saluted. At heart, the army conceived of correspondents as civilians in uniform, akin to military chaplains, and not as soldiers.

Thor Smith assembled his piece, which he titled "Surrender Snafu," and sent it to Morton at the *Atlantic.* While he thought little of Kennedy himself, portraying him as "acting like a fugitive from justice" after his story broke, he also intimated that many in Paris had suspected Kennedy was being made the "whipping boy" for others in the AP who had "condoned, and even abetted" the premature release of the story. Morton, however, decided that Smith had contributed little that was new, and certainly not enough to warrant another article. He offered to publish a letter from Smith rebutting Kennedy's article if he so wished.[40] Such a letter never appeared.

In 1949, Kennedy moved up the California coast to take over as associate editor and publisher of the *Monterey Peninsula Herald,* a modest daily that served an area that was very much a backwater in the days before it became a tourist mecca. Even from peaceful Monterrey, Kennedy found it difficult to put the Reims matter behind him. So did others. Robert McLean, for one, had looked into Kennedy's file yet again as late as 1952, but he did not change his mind about the reporter he had disavowed in

1945.[41] Although he had said nothing to the press about his treatment by the AP, it so gnawed at Kennedy that when Kent Cooper published a book in 1956 with a chapter defending his actions a decade earlier, Kennedy could not resist calling out his former boss. Despite Cooper's self-image as a guardian of press freedom, Kennedy told the North American Newspaper Alliance that he had buckled under pressure in the case of the German surrender story. Kennedy charged that "Mr. Cooper equivocated for a long time and then furtively lined up with elements which had taken a stand against the right of the people to know, without delay, that the war in Europe was over." Cooper "finds the censorship in the case intolerable, my action in not tolerating it perfidious, and his own performance irreproachable."[42] So much for burying the hatchet.

One senses just how the surrender story had become an idée fixe for Kennedy in a far-fetched proposition he put to Cooper. "I suggest a method by which our divergent views of the case might be fairly appraised and the facts determined," he wrote to his longtime boss. "That would be by a jury of three or five fair and disinterested persons which could go into the entire case, hear all sides and make a judgment. I believe it would be a worthwhile undertaking, since the case goes to the roots of press freedom."[43]

Even three years later Kennedy was having a hard time letting go of his sense of grievance. The UP reporter Joseph Grigg, who had been one of the pool reporters covering the Berlin surrender in 1945, wrote an anniversary remembrance that got under Kennedy's skin even as he ran it in the *Herald*. To Kennedy's mind, Grigg downplayed the importance of the Reims surrender in preference for the one he had attended the next day, which the UP reporter had termed "the historic scene of Nazi Germany's total surrender." In an editorial Kennedy outlined his account of the surrender story, presenting the decision to withhold news of the Reims surrender as one of the Soviet Union's greatest propaganda coups. He also claimed that the United Press, as the Associated Press's chief rival, "suffered most in the incident" and hence it had deliberately twisted the story. The UP, which had merged with INS just the year before to form United Press International (UPI), "owes it to its reputation as a reliable news service to correct the article," admonished Kennedy, an article that was "a distortion of facts and a falsification of history."[44]

When the West Coast editor of *Editor & Publisher* learned of Kennedy's editorial, he forwarded it to Thor Smith, at that point working for Hearst's *American Weekly*. Smith, in turn, sent it to Boyd Lewis, asking if he might want to collaborate on a definitive account of the surrender story since "Kennedy has now turned his guns on the UPI as being the culprit."[45] While Lewis thanked Smith for sending him "Ed Kennedy's weird editorial blast," he considered the whole episode water long under the bridge. "The only guy who is still ulcerous is Kennedy," a result of his "guilty conscience," in Lewis's opinion. Kennedy's attitude was "a reflection of his neuroticism, which seemed acute just before the war's end." Lewis professed no interest in rehashing the events of May 1945. "Leave the suffering to the guy who deserves it most," he advised. Despite his stated desire to put the episode behind him, Lewis still felt compelled to revisit the story twice more in print, on the twentieth and thirtieth anniversaries of the German surrender.[46] Kennedy, for his part, never published another word about it.

8

Media-Military Relations
in the Good War

Behind his desk at the *Monterey Peninsula Herald* Ed Kennedy displayed a framed copy of his surrender story on the front page of the *New York Times*. One can only imagine the mix of emotions Kennedy felt when he glanced at it. The story was "one of the greatest news-beats in history," according to the journalism historian Frank Luther Mott, the signal achievement of Kennedy's professional life.[1] Yet it was also a reminder of the promising career that the story had cut short. Whatever ambivalence Kennedy might have felt, he likely would not have displayed the story so prominently if he had serious reservations about his actions on May 7, 1945. Even so, while his daughter remembers him displaying the *Times* front page proudly, she also recalls that in the last years of her father's life "there was something in his past that bothered him. Sometimes he sat at the kitchen table late at night and drank heavily, muttering softly to himself words that I could not catch."[2]

Whatever his regrets or personal demons, Kennedy's previous work as a war correspondent indicates that his actions in May 1945 were not a lapse in judgment by an overworked or shamelessly competitive reporter, as many charged; rather, they were consistent with Kennedy's beliefs and past actions. In 1945 he was as knowledgeable and competent as any US reporter overseas. He had locked horns with military authorities wherever he reported: in Egypt, in Greece, in Algiers, in southern France, and in Paris. He had always survived such scrapes with his credentials and reputation intact. This in itself may account for the evident sangfroid with which Kennedy faced irate SHAEF officials in Paris in 1945. Kennedy had reason for such confidence. His superiors at the AP had consistently praised his work, rewarded him well for it, and in the past had backed him up, as they had with his unauthorized sally to Paris the previous summer. They stood behind Kennedy right up to the moment Robert McLean issued his statement of apology and all but cut him loose.

Granted the news agencies competed ferociously to cover the war, and Kennedy himself relished that competition. Before the surrender story, Kennedy had scored many other scoops, several of which had irritated the AP's rivals. He was neither surprised nor shocked by the Paris press corps' outrage upon learning of his beat. His shock was rather at the lack of support from the Associated Press. Finally, even though several observers found Kennedy tired and edgy leading up to the German surrender, there is little evidence that Kennedy was any more worn down by years of work and worry than others in the press corps or the SHAEF officials in Paris. The weight of evidence, then, does not indicate that Kennedy was driven by reckless zeal or that fatigue had seriously clouded his judgment.

There is, however, ample evidence that encounters with public relations officers and censors from Egypt to Reims had left Kennedy frustrated and wary. He had often expressed his low opinion of the military's public relations operations, which had grown like Topsy during the war. So too had Kennedy's impatience with the army's officiousness such as had ensnared him twice in Provence. Tristram Tupper, George Marshall's brother-in-law, represented to Kennedy the worst sort of PRO, one whose unavailability he mocked and whose actions he scorned. Such officers became more difficult to dismiss or deride as patience wore thin near war's end.

Kennedy had also been chastened during the Patton slapping incident. Although not overtly defensive about his decision to bury the story, in retrospect Kennedy considered it to have been a mistake. His justification to Kent Cooper—that Eisenhower had told him personally that losing Patton

Figure 8.1. The family copy of the front page of the *New York Times* with Kennedy's bylined surrender story. It is now in the possession of his daughter, Julia Kennedy Cochran, herself a journalist. Courtesy AP Images.

would jeopardize the Allied war effort—no longer seemed as compelling as it once had. Kennedy distrusted and disliked such self-censorship, and thereafter he was especially sensitive to the military's attempts to shape or suppress news. The lesson of the Patton episode for him had not been that senior officers should respect enlisted men, nor even that reporters should resist such self-censorship, but rather that his superiors in New York would call him on the carpet for any reticence to report such stories.

More than anything, Kennedy wanted in 1945 to hold Eisenhower to his oft-repeated pledge not to engage in political censorship. Kennedy was more vocal than others on the subject. Another reporter who had also been on the Anzio beachhead found that Kennedy had "a sort of obsession against censorship," although adding "and well he might."[3] On several occasions Eisenhower, first as the Allied commander in North Africa and then as the Supreme Commander in Northwestern Europe, reassured correspondents that censorship would only concern security matters. After being stung by the news blackout he had imposed after the deal with Darlan in Algeria, Eisenhower had reiterated several times his intention to avoid such political censorship thereafter.

Eisenhower had stressed this yet again in an interview with the United Press just weeks before the German surrender, declaring that he imposed censorship "only as demanded by the requirements of military security" and not to withhold news that might demoralize the public or embarrass the army.[4] Although it was not always center stage in the editorial debate surroundings his actions, in Kennedy's mind he determined to break the Reims story because of his opposition to political censorship. Other reporters were as energetic in voicing complaints about excessive or capricious censorship for security, but few had made resisting political censorship such a priority throughout their careers.

Kennedy's first taste of such censorship had occurred in Spain. Having returned to Paris in 1937 after his reporting assignment in Spain and no longer concerned that the Spanish police were reading his mail, he described the control he had encountered to AP officials in New York. "It is such a relief to be freed from the oppressive censorship of Spain, especially in Valencia, that it is a pleasure to write freely," he wrote Cooper. To John Evans he confided that "the Valencia assignment was difficult due to bad conditions and oppressive censorship, which extended to distorting stories and adding words here and there, as well as deleting information.

There were times when I thought the cable desk must have believed me insane." Kennedy later recalled that in Valencia "at times, I was bluntly told that I could write either the Loyalist point of view or write nothing." Faced with such ultimatums, Kennedy often chose to write nothing. In Spain, Kennedy first heard a rationale for such censorship that he never found convincing—"that in a struggle for freedom, it is often necessary to suppress freedom as a part of the battle."[5] Although granting that there were legitimate security reasons to withhold some information, from Spain onward Kennedy would remain wary of what he deemed to be over-reaching political censorship of the type he first encountered in Valencia.

While in the Near East in 1941 he had encountered such censorship that occasionally descended into farce at virtually every stop. In Syria, for example, all mention of French resistance to the British forces was forbidden. Censors would not allow use of the word "prisoner" to refer to any captured French soldiers, substituting for it "non-combatant." This led one correspondent's dispatch to read as censored: "I asked the non-combatants why they had fought so fiercely."[6]

The frustration of the press corps in Cairo with the entire censorship regime boiled over in late 1941. Correspondents demanded a meeting with British authorities to air their grievances over general bureaucratic mismanagement, arbitrary censorship for security, and widespread political censorship. They deputized Kennedy to present these complaints at a meeting with officials from the British embassy and armed forces. Kennedy maintained that since censors would get into trouble only for failing to delete sensitive information, never for deleting too much, "when in doubt, take it out" became the censors' mantra. Moreover, censors had taken to acting "almost like school masters—even correcting the literary style of the correspondents' messages." In all, the journalists in Cairo believed "that the censorship in Egypt was the worst in the world, being more difficult to deal with even than those of Moscow, Berlin and Tokio [*sic*]."[7]

While acknowledging these concerns, the chief British censor remained unmoved, and the meeting hardly mollified Kennedy. Ralph Ingersoll, the publisher and editor of the progressive daily newspaper *PM*, had stopped in Cairo on his way back from an extensive reporting trip to Russia.[8] When he asked Kennedy for his assessment of news coverage from the area, Kennedy responded with a detailed five-page analysis of the situation. British public relations officers in the field were well-meaning, Kennedy believed, but not particularly knowledgeable about the press. Censorship in Cairo, though, "has been unduly oppressive, tyrannical and capricious at times, extremely unintelligent and even dishonest on some occasions." US and British reporters had protested repeatedly to little effect. Kennedy reserved his harshest criticism for the widespread political censorship, which "tends to be blind and more arbitrary." Buck-passing dominated. Censors were reluctant to approve any story with political material and tended to pass it up the chain of command. "It is not unusual for a dispatch to go through the hands of six or eight censors," Kennedy revealed; in fact, one of his stories had passed through sixteen different censors and after six months had yet to be either approved or rejected.

At one censor's office on the Sharia Eloui, "several square yards of the wall [are] covered with 'Stops'—subjects which may not be mentioned in dispatches. Many of them have nothing to do with military information which might be of value to the enemy. They are simply attempts to compel correspondents to write along certain lines." All this led Kennedy to conclude, only half facetiously, that "certain people among the British here seem to lie awake nights thinking of new forms of censorship. They are censorship mad." Political censorship was so extreme that Kennedy wondered whether all US correspondents should leave the theater and let their newspapers rely solely on British communiqués. Readers could then judge them as such and not as independent reporting.[9]

Kennedy did not reach Algiers until after Eisenhower had lifted the political censorship imposed after the Darlan deal, but he would certainly have known about it; and while he was bureau chief in Algiers, he frequently tangled with AFHQ over censorship issues, particularly those with a political dimension. A conflict in 1943 over stories about Yugoslavia especially rankled. The British claimed the Balkans to be within their sphere of influence. They were deeply suspicious of the Yugoslav partisan leader Josip Broz (Tito), and also claimed the right to censor all news from the region. British officials in Cairo, who had been given Allied jurisdiction over Yugoslavian matters, were determined to prevent correspondents from traveling to the Balkans to report on the Tito-backed partisans fighting the Germans, given that the British supported a rival partisan faction. After the British stymied his efforts to meet Tito through normal channels, the AP's Dan De Luce managed to reach Yugoslavia from Italy aboard a small fishing boat and obtained a rare interview with the partisan leader. His was the first direct reporting from Yugoslavia in the more than two years that the Germans had occupied the country. De Luce returned to Italy with five valuable stories.

Kennedy submitted the first four stories to US censors at AFHQ where they were passed and were featured in US newspapers. The fifth, which attempted to gauge popular support for the rival partisan leaders, Algiers referred to Cairo, where British censors spiked it. Kennedy in Algiers alerted Cooper in New York, who protested to the War Department in Washington, claiming both political censorship and illegitimate British interference with the US press.[10] When De Luce won a Pulitzer Prize for his reporting from Yugoslavia, Kennedy reminded New York that the published dispatches had told only half the story; the rest had been suppressed by censorship. In fact, De Luce had also "CARRIED OUT A CEASELESS FIGHT FOR FREEDOM OF THE PRESS SOMETIMES IN THE FACE OF MACHINATIONS OF CROOKED BUREAUCRACY MORE ENERVATING THAN ANY ENEMY FIRE."[11]

In the wake of the Patton furor in November 1943, Kennedy had confronted AFHQ authorities over a host of censorship concerns. Even if Kennedy had withdrawn his impulsive request for Congress to investigate AFHQ's censorship, its chief PRO Joseph Phillips had not forgotten the episode and had pushed Kennedy to supply his list of complaints. When Kennedy did so, Phillips believed that Kennedy's bill of particulars had to be judged against what Phillips claimed was the AP's long-standing conflicts with military censorship in Algiers. In consulting his files, Phillips found that AP reporters "make far more complaints with far less real basis that any other group." He attributed this to the AP's "aggressive staff" that was "so filled with the competitive spirit that it is unwilling to make allowances for delays and mistakes." Presumably, AP staffers were competing against the other news agencies, while the delays and mistakes were the army's.

Phillips had even studied recent AP copy and found "a considerable number of instances in which the Associated Press had obviously been pressing to get ahead of the release line [time] or to play up an operation out of proportion." Phillips had worked up the information into a chart, but Kennedy had remained unconvinced that it was in the best interest of both the AP and the war effort, in Phillips's words, "to stick with the guidances rather than to play every story to it's [*sic*] utmost." Phillips's message was that the AP should fall in line with the army's view of any particular subject. Kennedy had resisted that notion, but he was willing to admit to Phillips that he might have been too rough at times on AFHQ's censors, who were mostly inexperienced junior officers. He promised that in the future he would bring any specific complaints to Phillips himself, a concession which seemed to lower the temperature.[12]

It did not take long for those complaints to surface. The AP protested when the army held up Relman (Pat) Morin's account of the German attack on three clearly marked US hospital ships near the Italian coast. Morin's story was not cleared by AFHQ until twelve hours after CBS had broadcast news of the bombing. Kennedy could only cable New York that censorship was now "ECLIPSING ALL PAST RECORDS FOR CHAOS STUPIDITY INEFFICIENCY." After Jumbo Wilson replaced Eisenhower at AFHQ, Paul Miller in Washington reminded New York of his "unenviable censorship record in Cairo which apparently now will be our misfortune to suffer at Algiers." Miller took some comfort in the fact that whatever the faults of US military censorship, "as bad as it is, still [it] is better than some."[13]

In early 1944, British authorities in Cairo again stymied efforts to report on the partisans fighting the Germans in Yugoslavia. Cairo had promised that it would permit two reporters to travel to the Balkans, but it had not done so. In May, the AP's Joseph Morton located a work-around. Morton found a way to get a list of questions to Tito via Yugoslav officials in Italy, then he wrote a comprehensive story based on Tito's responses. Army censors in Italy refused to pass it. This was "PURELY POLITICAL CENSORSHIP," Kennedy charged, and as he wrote New York constituted a "CENSORSHIP SCANDAL TEN TIMES MORE IMPORTANT THAN SUPPRESSION PATTON INCIDENT." If allowed to stand, it would lead to "PERMANENT ALLIED POLITICAL CENSORSHIP IN EUROPE AND END OF ALL FREEDOM IN REPORTING POLITICAL NEWS FROM HERE." The reason for Allied intransigence, Kennedy later wrote, was that "British officials were infuriated that we had pierced the wall of censorship they had built around Tito" and had done so without violating any regulations.[14]

Cooper cabled General Wilson asking him to intervene in the matter, given the assurances both British and US officials had made about political censorship in the past. If the story could not be passed, Cooper wanted a specific explanation of why. General Tupper, soon to be Kennedy's nemesis in southern France, defended the handling of the Tito story to Alexander Surles in Washington. According to Tupper, Kennedy had stated that by agreement with Tito, if anything in his remarks was censored by the Allies, then nothing could be used. Tupper found that there was considerable censorable information in the interview, including the strength of forces in Yugoslavia, the locations of warships, and Tito's criticisms of other leaders. "Censors inform me that military and political matters touched upon in [the] article are inseparable," Tupper explained.[15]

Surles alerted Tupper that the AP was "beginning to spread [the] political censorship charge." Given that the AP was now willing to accept cuts regarding operations or military strength, he urged Tupper to make a clearer distinction between the security and political portions of the Tito story. He advised Tupper that diplomacy might be compromised if the press charged that the "military is suppressing a declaration by Tito." A week later Surles contacted AFHQ again with news that the AP was publishing a "bitter attack" on Wilson's censorship practices as a result of the Tito story, charging that he had violated the Allied policy against political censorship.[16]

Secretary of State Cordell Hull reinforced Surles's message that diplomacy might be damaged, especially after a story authorized by Tito had reached New York from Moscow. Hull was convinced that "political censorship in Algiers will do more damage than the stories they might kill, especially when such stories can get here through channels which Algiers cannot control." Hull told AFHQ in no uncertain terms that the State Department, the Office of Censorship and both the War and Navy departments all agreed that there should be no more censorship of strictly political matters. It seems clear that neither Surles nor Hull were eager to deal with the blowback in Washington from questionable decisions regarding political censorship made in the field. Military officials in Europe and North Africa did not have to read the daily newspaper editorials or respond to politicians challenging such censorship. AFHQ countered that the attacks on its practices were not based on fact and were "eminently unfair." The Tito interview was so laced with sensitive military information that it had to be stopped. In the end though, Kennedy's continued pressure and Washington's intervention had their desired effect. The Tito story was eventually passed and published.[17]

Kennedy's difficulties with AFHQ censorship authorities did not end there. In May, the chief censor of AFHQ's Information and Censorship Section, Lieutenant Colonel Victor Scott-Bailey, had drawn up a list of the difficulties the INC had encountered with the Associated Press and Kennedy. "The AP staff have always behaved in an aggressive and uncooperative manner with Censorship since November 1942," the date of the original TORCH landings, Scott-Bailey informed the incoming INC chief, Brigadier General Arthur McChrystal. Scott-Bailey then raised the matter of Kennedy's offhand demand for a Congressional inquiry after AFHQ's mishandling of the Patton slapping incident, which INC had not forgotten. He attached a series of Kennedy's "offensive" service messages to New York, including one in which Kennedy had informed Cooper that "censorship this theater is so rotten it stinks to high heaven," and that he stood on his right to publish that criticism. Scott-Bailey accused Kennedy of recommending to staff that they disregard censorship regulations. He also condemned Kennedy's "inaccurate and malicious comments" about censorship's handling of De Luce's stories the previous fall. Scott-Bailey did not propose any specific action against Kennedy but rather seemed to be documenting a case against him. Although AFHQ felt it had every right to disaccredit Kennedy, in the end it had judged that to do so would be "inadvisable," fearing the commotion it would cause. Surles in Washington could only agree.[18]

For Kennedy, principle and pragmatism aligned in the surrender story. Kennedy's personal dislike of the army's public relations bureaucracy dovetailed nicely with his professional distaste for political censorship. As Paris bureau chief, he knew of a way, a legitimate way in his mind, to beat the competition to a story he would willingly defy authorities to report. After the Flensburg broadcast, by which SHAEF itself had made the news public, it was untenable for the army to argue that the news needed to be kept under wraps for security reasons. As even Thor Smith and other SHAEF officials warned their superiors at the time, it was a far-fetched notion, bordering on lunacy, to imagine the thirty-six-hour embargo on release of the German surrender would hold when much of the world was already celebrating the event. Kennedy sent his flash only after confirmation of the German broadcast, and only after announcing to SHAEF officials his intention to do so. He reasoned that military censorship was no longer legitimate since the war had ended. As Ben McKelway had written to Cooper, "after the battle on other phases of political censorship that he has been waging as an honest newspaperman, I suppose this last straw was a bit too much."[19] Kennedy felt no further obligation to submit such news to SHAEF censors even if SHAEF begged to differ. Kennedy's encounters with political censorship stretching back to Spain through the Balkans, North Africa, and Italy make his decision to break the surrender story hardly surprising. Indeed, it seems almost inevitable.

If Kennedy's actions on May 7 are explicable, so too are those of the other actors in this drama. There is some questionable decision-making but little perfidy to be discovered in the episode. The picture that emerges is one of people exhausted and impatient at the end of a long war, reflexively acting according to their respective institutional imperatives. SHAEF had no real desire to withhold news of the German surrender; indeed, it feared that doing so might prolong the fighting and unnecessarily cost lives. Eisenhower and the staff at SHAEF may have been genuinely wary of censorship in this instance, but they were obeying orders emanating from leaders in Washington. The overheated reaction of the press corps in Paris may have had less to do with its resentment of Kennedy for beating them on the story than with long-festering grievances against military public relations generally and SHAEF PRD in particular. One can only imagine the frustration correspondents in Paris must have felt when prevented by SHAEF from reporting the "greatest story of the war" even as celebrations broke out across Paris and elsewhere.

The Associated Press, in the persons of Cooper and McLean, would have been understandably cautious about such a release after its misreporting from San Francisco had just caused such embarrassment. Moreover, the AP would have been open to charges of hypocrisy if it did not disapprove Kennedy's actions, if only because of its own criticism of the unauthorized Paris broadcasts eight months earlier. Although McLean's hasty repudiation of Kennedy remains the most questionable act in the entire affair, he too did so only after officials in Washington urged on him that Kennedy's actions had recklessly endangered troops in the field. Indeed, the terrific heat generated by Kennedy's scoop may have been the consequence of all believing their actions were justified because within the limits of their institutional fields of vision, they were.

Years later another intriguing theory emerged for why the official release was delayed for so long. It provides an alternative explanation for the vehemence with which Allen and others at SHAEF reacted to Kennedy's scoop. Robert Murphy, the career diplomat who had served as Eisenhower's chief civil affairs adviser from North Africa to Germany, wrote in his memoir that "what had happened was that [Bedell] Smith, harassed by a thousand complex matters of highest importance, had suffered a rare lapse of memory." In his haste, Murphy asserted, Smith had given the Germans the wrong document to sign, a previous draft of the one that the Russians had just approved. The delay was imposed to allow the Allies to claim that the Reims event had merely been preparatory to the Berlin surrender where the Germans signed the approved document.[20]

In 1970, Kennedy's ex-wife sorted through some of his papers, perhaps for the first time since his death seven years earlier. She left a note among his files pointing to Murphy's account as raising the possibility that SHAEF's delay in releasing news of the surrender was not actually at the behest of the Russians, but rather the act of US officials too embarrassed to admit their mistake. Though tempting to think that Allen's heated reaction to Kennedy's release, banning all AP communications from Europe, makes more sense if he were also limiting the damage from SHAEF's blunder, there is no evidence other than Murphy's conjecture to support this view. The record indicates that the last-minute changes in the surrender documents had more to do with adding a French signatory than with any bureaucratic incompetence.[21] Murphy had also tangled with Bedell Smith on more than one occasion during the war, and his pointing the finger at Eisenhower's stern chief-of-staff might have been a form of payback.

Throughout the war, then, Kennedy clashed repeatedly with inexperienced or timid censors over specific security stops. He had found British officials to be particularly unhelpful, if only because the British were more willing to deploy political censorship in the service of foreign policy, as in Yugoslavia and the Near East. Whenever Kennedy caught the whiff of political censorship, though, he opposed it. And before Reims, it had often been in the air.

Overall, the scattered historical record once assembled makes visible what lies beneath Kennedy's brief mention in journalism history. It tells us much about the war's biggest scoop, which in turn prompted the stooshie over the war's most tangled media story. If that record illuminates Kennedy's motives and actions, it also helps sort through the tangle of ethical issues for journalism at the heart of the case. For all the editorial fulminating about brass hats, censorship, Kennedy's presumption, and SHAEF's alleged kowtowing to the Russians, much of the comment on the surrender story focused on the charge that Kennedy had violated fundamental journalistic ethics. The debate over the ethics of his action is also what has kept the Kennedy story in media textbooks ever since. If Kennedy's scoop was unethical as fifty-four of his colleagues charged in Paris, what made it so? What first principles did he violate?

Since the 1950s, the Society of Professional Journalists (SPJ) has articulated four basic ethical commandments: to seek and report the truth, to minimize harm, to act independently, and to be transparent and accountable. Enhanced by additional commentary and position papers, these four principles "form the foundation of ethical journalism" for the SPJ.[22] It is difficult to see how Kennedy's actions violated any of them.

No one questioned whether Kennedy's story was factually true; he reported what he had seen in Reims accurately. The only error in the flash bulletin as released was that SHAEF had officially announced the surrender, but this was added by editors in New York. The admonition to "minimize harm," which largely concerns harm to individuals through loss of privacy and such, conceivably might apply in this situation as one charge against Kennedy was that he had endangered troops. However, the assertions of several, including Butcher, that Eisenhower himself wanted to announce the surrender immediately for reasons of troop safety but had been overruled by his superiors, indicate that even the SHAEF commander believed the greater threat lay in withholding news of the surrender.

The code's guidance to "act independently" urged journalists to avoid conflicts of interest and advertisers' suasion, but the accusation against Kennedy was that he had acted too independently. Kennedy did inform SHAEF, the governing authority, of his intention to release the story. Beyond this, Kennedy might have told London that his story was unauthorized if he had not abruptly lost the telephone connection that day. Kennedy also seemed to abide by the final principle that journalists should be accountable and transparent, in that from the start he took full responsibility for his action and consistently gave the same explanation for doing what he did. Kennedy's story never changed. Kennedy's work on the whole seems to embody these principles rather than to flout them, and it was such considerations that weighed heavily for Tom Curley, the AP's president when he publicly apologized in 2012 for the agency's treatment of Kennedy in 1945. For Curley, Kennedy "did everything just right."[23]

Yet the furor in 1945 was fierce; the condemnation of Kennedy's ethical lapses was severe even as there was some confusion about the precise nature of those lapses. At the time, the charge was that the public's right to know, its right to the news (and Kennedy's ethical duty to report it) did not trump his obligation to hold to agreements made with sources, including agreements over release times. The constant chorus in 1945 was that Kennedy had committed an egregious violation of a confidence or a breach of promise. Indeed one striking feature of the debate during the Kennedy affair was the application of a genteel rhetoric (confidences, oaths, sacred pledges, honor, and such) to the competitive and at times cutthroat business of daily journalism. There was some dispute, though, about whose confidence Kennedy had violated, and what promise he had breached.

What most critics meant when they charged Kennedy with betraying or violating a confidence had to do, most broadly, with revealing information he had been told confidentially and which he had agreed to hold until that source permitted its release. When journalists today speak of confidentiality, or protecting confidential sources, they are most concerned with not revealing a source's identity rather than with not revealing the information itself. Identity was clearly not the issue in 1945. In Kennedy's case, the issue was releasing information before the source, in this case, SHAEF, had given its permission. As Kennedy admitted, abiding such release times for security reasons had been standard practice for reporters throughout the war, a practice he had always honored.

Kennedy's inexcusable sin had been violating "the pledge on the plane," which was taken to be a commitment to General Allen not to release the story until authorized to do so. For the press, contravening the pledge on the plane also compromised the very bargain essential to reporting the war: the military would share sensitive information with reporters before it could be made public; reporters would not transmit the same without permission. In this sense, Kennedy had threatened the media's access to information and officialdom. This was the confidence, the promise to keep the information confidential until authorized to release it, that

Kennedy had supposedly breached. Even those who had initially supported Kennedy and criticized the official handling of the surrender story often changed their opinion once Eisenhower's statement, through Allen, came out accusing Kennedy of a "self-admitted deliberate breach of confidence," a statement then reinforced by McLean's apology.[24]

However, Kennedy and his defenders argued that such agreements between a reporter and a source involved reciprocal responsibilities. Both parties agreed to withhold information until a specified time. If the news leaked or was otherwise made public, such agreements no longer obtained, the confidence no longer held. In the case of the German surrender, SHAEF itself had broken the agreement when it sanctioned the Flensburg broadcast, and thereafter Kennedy was no longer ethically bound to abide by his commitment to hold the news.

To those who found Kennedy's actions justified, he was simply reporting a truth already made public and known to the Germans. In the event, Allied control of the story had grown shakier by the hour. At noon on May 8, the Allied press in Paris seemed to be the only group in Europe not able to report it. Official release at SHAEF was scheduled for three o'clock that afternoon, but the army warned there might be yet another delay, even after the Flensburg broadcast, even as workers were staging Downing Street for Churchill's victory speech, and even as Parisians and New Yorkers were dancing in the street. In this light Kennedy's decision seems neither ill-conceived nor consciously heroic but rather an obvious one. His obligation as a journalist to the public reduced his honor-based pledge on the plane, which had already been violated by SHAEF, to a nicety.

There was yet another form of confidence that a few critics found at play in the case. They charged that Kennedy had broken his word not to military authorities but to the rest of the press corps. They asserted that Kennedy was ethically bound to alert the rest of the reporters to his intention before transmitting the surrender story. In this telling, Kennedy's pledge was not to the military but to his peers in the Paris press corps. Kennedy himself referred to such as "pack reporting, a system sometimes employed by lazy and unenterprising newspapermen under which no member of the combination sends his office a story without first informing the others." A. J. Liebling had charged that the military had all but imposed what had been an informal arrangement among newspaper reporters, what he called "combination" reporting, onto the entire accredited press corps, aided and abetted by the Association of American Correspondents in London. There were those at the time who believed that Kennedy had violated this second type of confidence, as did Maureen McKernan who wrote to the AP that her many years of experience as a reporter in New York told her that if Kennedy had not informed the other reporters who had been on the plane of what he was going to do, then he had committed a serious breach of ethics.[25]

It fell to the ultraconservative columnist Fulton Lewis to distinguish between the two types of confidences, "those agreed to by lazy reporters and those of censorship." Kennedy was too good a reporter to consider the first, and since no issue of military security was involved, to Lewis's mind, the second did not apply either. "SHAEF's game is one of the oldest in the racket, as you well know," Lewis wrote to Cooper. "If you are afraid some news is going to leak out and you can't control it, you call the reporters in, put them under secrecy, tell them the story and thereby bottle them up for your own protection." In the charge that Kennedy had violated a pledge made to other reporters, then, the surrender saga unearths a journalistic practice, such combination reporting, rarely mentioned in journalism histories but apparently widespread and well-known at the time.[26] Regardless, Kennedy by all evidence did not feel his pledge on the plane had been given to the other reporters.

One fundamental ethical conundrum remains. Did Kennedy adequately weigh legitimate security concerns against the public's right to information? Journalists agreed that ordinarily the military was justified in suppressing news that might risk lives or in other ways help the enemy. Reporters were more than happy to withhold information about troop movements, about the precise times and locations of attacks and the like, even when they knew the facts well in advance. Journalists also agreed that they could only assess the military situation if they had access not only to the battlefield but also to the knowledge and thinking of military leaders. Leaders would reveal what they knew to the press only if they trusted reporters to keep it to themselves. This was the bargain Eisenhower frequently championed: he would speak to reporters frankly and they would know the greater part of what he knew; in return, they would keep any sensitive information confidential. Balanced against these imperatives, though, was the journalist's fundamental purpose— the SPJ first principle—to seek the truth and report it in service of the public's right to know, itself at the heart of the First Amendment's guarantee of freedom of the press. Kennedy considered all of these factors and determined that, in the case of the German surrender, since hostilities had ended the public's right to know could be honored without compromising security. If his action might not be greeted warmly by military authorities and might jeopardize reporters' access, then Kennedy could live with that after a war's worth of sparring with those officials. Still this essential ethical quandary—how to balance both security needs and access to sources against the journalist's duty to report and the public's right to know would confound reporters in the field throughout World War II and in every conflict thereafter.

If the full story of the Kennedy affair illuminates but does not fully resolve such ethical conundrums, it speaks more definitively to the nature of the relationship between the media and the military at the time. Indeed, it forces us to reexamine much of what we think we know about that relationship. Andy Rooney's assertion that reporters and the military were "all on the same side" during the war without "the usual confrontation between authority and the press" conveys what has become the conventional wisdom (even in journalistic circles) on the subject.[27] It echoes in the testimony before Congress of Rooney's colleague Walter Cronkite in the wake of the Gulf War, a moment when the media and the military authorities in both Saudi Arabia and Washington were at loggerheads. "With an arrogance foreign to the democratic system, the U.S. military in Saudi Arabia is trampling on the American people's right to know," Cronkite lectured the panel.

One of a handful of star witnesses, Cronkite had covered the European theater for the United Press. He advised the military "to pattern its public relations after its handling of the press in World War II, a war we won and which left few questions about the press-military relationship." Even the censors had been "civilians called to wartime duty," often lawyers "as concerned with the public's right to know as the military's right to certain secrets." These censors were "open to appeal" when reporters "thought their stories were being held up for political reasons." Cronkite even recalled that "we frequently won those arguments."[28] The military—and the press—could do far worse, he suggested, than to revert to the system that had served all so well during the Second World War.

It goes without saying that the Second World War still exists as a powerful landmark in US cultural memory, suffused with emotional heft and symbolic meaning. Historians exploring the ways that it is remembered often use the trope of the "Good War," evoking the title of Studs Terkel's oral history. Terkel's is a clear-eyed and sober view of the war, one that does not sand away its rough edges. However, his title has come to represent a highly varnished view of that event. Michael Adams examines the creation of the Good War trope itself, the belief that "in this mythic time of the Good War, everyone was united; there were no racial or gender tensions, no class conflicts. Things worked better, from kitchen gadgets to public schools. Families were well-adjusted; kids read a lot and respected their elders; parents didn't divorce." The media's relationship with the military was yet another aspect of US culture that "worked better" during the Second World War. Ironically, memorializing the war, the public memory of it, often seems based as much on forgetting as remembering. As Kenneth Rose points out, we tend to think of the Second World War "not as it was but as it should have been."[29]

Such Good War nostalgia permeates most accounts of the relationship between the press and the military in the Second World War, accounts that stress their singular cooperation when judged against subsequent conflicts. This was especially true of Vietnam, the "bad" war that gave rise to so many Good War comparisons. Neil Hickey, for one, a veteran reporter writing in 2002 about the ongoing war in Afghanistan, stressed that "in wartime, the press and the military are rarely on cozy, familial terms"; such good feeling, in fact, "hasn't happened since World War II." By the 1990s, coauthors Frank Aukofer and William P. Lawrence, one a journalist and the other a professional soldier, concluded that "the war represented the high-water mark of military-media relations," in large part because "combat correspondents were accepted by the armed forces as comrades fighting for the same cause." Michael Sweeney, the historian who has looked most carefully at US war reporting and the government's information management in the Second World War, reached much the same conclusion that during that war "the press, military and government acted in relative harmony despite the functioning of the largest federal bureaucracies of censorship and propaganda in American history." Even Phillip Knightley, who holds a jaundiced view of the quality of reporting during the Second World War, blames such poor journalism on correspondents who were too close to military officials rather than too distant.[30] Essential amity, so all would have it, characterized the relationship between the media and the military at the time.

Yet reconstructing the controversy over Kennedy's story and all that led up to it provides us with a strikingly different and far more complex picture. Friction between military officials and the press occurred often; it was not a rarity. Such friction had less to do with reporters' questioning war aims than with the logistics of access, with communications failures, and more rarely and heatedly with censorship the press considered political in nature. It reveals a military often ill-equipped to accommodate independent reporting. National rivalries, for example, which Eisenhower had some success in keeping in check among the Allied armies, often surfaced in the reporting of the war.

Kennedy was hardly alone among US reporters in observing the tension between military officers and the correspondents in their charge. Barely a reporter's memoir exists without remarks, some offhand and others more pointed, disparaging military public relations officials. Few were as direct as Liebling, who pilloried PROs as uniformed "dress-extras." CBS correspondent Eric Sevareid found that army officials considered the press to be "unco-operative and quite unmanageable." Some PROs, Sevareid believed, resented the fact that correspondents could use the war to advance their careers and make money; for their part, combat correspondents often suffered in dangerous and miserable conditions, resenting the "cozy, routine life" led by PROs safely behind the front lines.[31] In sum, Kennedy and others in the press corps frequently considered army officials as obstacles to good reporting rather than as helpmates. By May 1945 Kennedy had wearied of military officiousness and obstinance, and he had devised workarounds when he could, as with the *Stars and Stripes* telephone line to London.

For their part, army officials often revealed an equal disdain for reporters. Even one of the PROs most respected by correspondents, Barney Oldfield, could not resist the jibe that while "no profession is without its myopia," among the press "it is usually found in advanced stages." James Quirk was another PRO valued by correspondents, yet in his letters to his wife he derided those whom he called "visiting firemen," correspondents who flew over from England for visits to 12th Army Group Headquarters before quickly returning to London's comforts. Quirk mocked one unnamed reporter in particular who gave speeches in the United States about his dramatic experiences in Normandy when Quirk knew full well the reporter had never been to the front. Ernest Dupuy's disparagement of the press ranged from calling Merrill "Red" Mueller of NBC "a stinkeroo on all counts," to charging that the *Chicago Tribune*'s Larry Rue was "always griping," and had hired a secretary in London to turn "his maudlin ravings into news stories." He reserved his harshest criticism, though, for BBC personnel in general whom he deemed the worst of "all the damned dirty sons of bitches" for their frequent violations of security.[32]

Thor Smith was less splenetic than Dupuy, but he was similarly worn down by constant squabbles with the press. "The headaches in the job are starting to boil up," Smith admitted in late July 1944. Once it was clear that the D-Day landings had firmly established the Allies in France and tension relaxed somewhat, he found that the press's "competitive scramble" returned, "with all its attendant bitching and squawking." Red Mueller particularly seemed to irritate army staffers. Besides Dupuy, he also annoyed Smith in the days before Paris was liberated by boasting incessantly of his intimate knowledge of the city. Smith described Mueller as "a cocky, conceited little guy" who thought "the whole PR set-up stinks, and tells everyone in no uncertain terms."[33]

For fear of overcorrecting here, one must acknowledge that, especially as the war progressed, military public relations and the press often did fashion a sustainable working relationship. After all of the miscues in North Africa and problems in Italy, SHAEF, for its part, went out of its way to include the press in planning for the Normandy invasion. From the liberation of Paris in August 1944 until the end of the war eight months later, PROs proved more nimble at meeting the requirements of correspondents in the field, from faster transmission of copy to more consistent censorship guidance. Veteran correspondents were increasingly trusted to leave press camps for the front lines without conducting officers. Many correspondents came to appreciate the efforts of the most effective PROs. In particular, Tex McCrary and Jay Vessels in the Mediterranean, and Oldfield and Quirk in Northwestern Europe, were praised by reporters for their ingenuity and effectiveness. As Cronkite did before Congress, others voiced satisfaction with the reasonableness of most censorship decisions; by war's end, many remarked that censors were able to work with a light touch because reporters by then self-censored, knowing well what subjects were prohibited.

What is more, there were PROs at SHAEF like Burroughs Matthews, Roy Pawley, and Barry Bingham, the naval PRO attached to PRD, who were veteran journalists themselves and who inherently respected the press even as they might clash with individual reporters. Many correspondents, PROs, and censors, then, built viable and sustainable working relationships that kept a river of information flowing to the Allied publics, however vague and sanitized of the actual horrors of war. There is some measure of truth, then, to the notion that the media and the military cooperated during the war, if for no other reason than all were committed to defeating an enemy that all considered evil. The cause was just.

Yet the surrender story surfaced a surprising and persistent tension in the war most historians downplay.[34] The point is merely that to figure the media-military relationship in this way, as marked by a "cooperative working relationship" and to point to it as a model to emulate, is to overlook what the Kennedy affair reveals, incidents large and small of the media and the military at loggerheads. Throughout the war, Eisenhower also succeeded in holding together the British and US officers on his staff, even in the face of pronounced national antagonisms. The extent of those rivalries is another reality, one often lost in Good War generalizations. Not only were the two main Allied armies rivals, the two press corps were deeply suspicious of each other. Add in the Canadians and the national frictions only increased. While believing in the Allied cause, for example, BBC radio newsmen, according to one British historian, "were fierce partisans of the British and Empire war effort against the similarly partisan American publicity machine."[35] Eisenhower was iron-willed about breeches in Allied amity, but he could not prevent them all and PRD dealt with its share.

The surrender saga also calls into question another bromide about the war—that it was well-reported. Historian Joseph Mathews, writing in 1957, discovered that in the wake of World War II "the overwhelming sentiment of those who publicly voiced opinions was in agreement: the war was accurately and fully reported, 'the best reported war in history.'"[36] The sense of the Second World War as the "best reported" (in terms of its quantity, accuracy, and timeliness) war in history was often repeated even during the war itself, as did Cooper, for example, in making the claim and using the very phrase in communications with Eisenhower. However, Ed Kennedy was not alone in charging that excessive censorship for security—but even more dangerously political censorship—often prevented journalists from accurately and fully informing the US public about the progress of the war. Political censorship, in particular, flew in the face of democratic values. The issue was not a trifle.

During the Second World War the Western democracies believed they had a winning weapon to wield in the propaganda war against fascism— the truth. Both the American Office of War Information and the British Ministry of Information would base their domestic propaganda efforts on what the OWI's Archibald MacLeish championed as a "strategy of truth" aimed at deflecting the distaste in democracies for government-managed information.[37] Even outward-facing propaganda would rely as much as possible on fact rather than mimic Goebbels' commitment to the big lie. The head of the Political Warfare Executive insisted that British propaganda would only be effective if it was accurate. A reputation for truth and consistency, he believed, would pay off in the end with domestic and international audiences, both of which were skeptical about government-sourced war news.[38]

That other pillar of wartime information management, censorship, was grounded in a similar impulse. In establishing the Office of Censorship just days after the attack at Pearl Harbor, President Roosevelt reassured the country that censorship would extend only to matters of military security.[39] In Britain, Defence Regulation No. 3 prohibited British subjects from "publishing information which might be useful to an enemy." However, Britain's chief censor through much of the war insisted that the regulation only pertained to military matters.[40] Both governments declared that they would not apply political, or what the British termed policy, censorship. Only facts and never opinion would be regulated. Beyond this, political censorship came to include reporting of the political situations of countries in the war zone, as well as news that might prove embarrassing to the governments prosecuting the war (and thus depress morale).

Yet even as authorities denied the existence of formal political censorship, a loophole in the censorship regimes in both countries allowed for it. In Britain, a decision by the Government in March 1942, just months after the United States entered the war, modified Defence Regulation No. 3 to give press censors additional powers to ban from messages leaving the UK "any word or passage which was likely to create disharmony among the Allied Nations."[41] General Eisenhower, for all his assurances that military security was the only justification for censorship, allowed one significant exception: nothing that might damage Allied unity would pass through AFHQ and later SHAEF censorship. As early as January 1943, Eisenhower's aide Robert Murphy had assured no less than the Combined Chiefs of Staff that just two restrictions were placed on press dispatches from North Africa: those that reported operational military information and those that suggested Anglo-American disunity.[42]

Eisenhower himself made the same point in a meeting with US reporters in the run-up to the Normandy landings: the only information he considered out of bounds was that involving military security or that criticized an ally.[43] Allied unity was the stated rationale for the ban on reporting about the political strife in French North Africa as well as the pretext for adhering to Russian desires in May 1945. Allied unity indeed became the rationale most often used to enforce political censorship when it occurred throughout the war, a feature of information policy that would bedevil media-military relations. While professing to censor only for military security, Allied authorities invoked morale and unity as a pretext to suppress information either known to the enemy or of no value to it, but still of some importance to Allied political calculations. In certain circumstances, then, the strategy of truth proved insufficient and was pushed to the side.

Rather than confirming the belief that the media and military cooperated amicably during the Second World War and thereby provided the benchmark by which all subsequent conflict reporting has been measured, a careful reading of surviving records suggests a markedly different tale. Rather than cooperation, the experience of press relations and information management during the war in Europe was inflected with every sort of competitive friction. Reporters tangled with army public relations and censorship officers. News organizations tangled with each other. Branches of the armed forces worked at cross purposes. Policy makers in the Roosevelt administration feuded with military leaders in the field over how to deal with the fourth estate. In sum, Andy Rooney's sense of everyone pulling in the same direction seems a bit of misremembering, as the Irish say.

Thus the controversy over Kennedy's surrender story leads us to question the premise at the heart of the master narrative of US war reporting—that the media and the military cooperated during the Second World War. Every subsequent conflict, large and small, has sparked renewed debate and prompted a flood of white papers, case studies, and books on that relationship. In this expanding literature, a main narrative thread emerges, a consensus view of the history of US war reporting. It conceives the Second World War as a baseline for the next seventy-five years and posits that the Vietnam War marked a profound deterioration of the military's relations with the press corps, a low point that still resonates for both press and military.

Indeed from whatever vantage point, the Second World War is seen as a largely harmonious moment in the otherwise fraught history of media-military relations, relations marked more often than not by contention and seemingly litigated anew after every conflict. For instance, after the Gulf War, a sociologist and a military affairs reporter, Charles Moskos and Thomas Ricks, respectively, were commissioned to examine the history of those relations. When they did, they described much of this same landscape: "The conventional treatment of the media and the military is to posit a halcyon relationship that characterized World War II." Thereafter the Vietnam War proved the decisive turning point. Military historian Douglas Porch, for another, writing after the attacks on 9/11, made much the same argument: a "general consensus" existed among academics, the military, and the press that during the Second World War "a cooperative working relationship" had existed, which "collapsed in the 1960s" and had never been rebuilt.[44]

The coverage of war changed abruptly in Vietnam. That conflict, beginning in the early 1960s and ending with the fall of Saigon in 1975, remains the pivotal event in the metanarrative of US war reporting. In Vietnam the press were initially unrestricted in where they could go and what they could write; they had relatively free access and faced limited censorship. When those reporters indicated that the army's optimistic communiqués from Saigon did not accord with the more sobering reality they witnessed in the field, the accusation arose that negative reporting from Vietnam turned US public opinion against the war. Despite studies that indicate the media followed rather than led public opinion on Vietnam, resentments persisted for both press and military. "World War II marked the end of amicable military-media relations," another historian concludes.

"In future conflicts, especially during the Vietnam War, the military and journalists often took opposing views of the conflict."[45]

The debate over the press's role in turning the country against the war in Vietnam continues. Television brought combat into US households for the first time, and, so the argument ran, left the country with little stomach for further involvement. Porch stresses that the impact of Vietnam on press relations was "profound." From that point forward, the press tended to regard the conditions of Vietnam (that is, free access and minimal censorship) as the norm, not an anomaly. The military saw it as proof of the need to keep the press at arm's length and to view it as an adversary, "liberal in political outlook," and "invariably hostile to military values and missions." The admonition among army staff became: "Real men don't talk to the press."[46]

If Vietnam left the media and the military mutually resentful and suspicious, every conflict thereafter seemed to spark new frictions. Every scheme to deal with the media formulated by the Department of Defense seemed to be a response to the shortcomings of the previous plan. The initial Pentagon response after Vietnam was simply to keep the press at bay during actual operations. Thus in 1983 the media were not allowed to accompany the forces that invaded Grenada. When news organizations protested, reporters were then permitted limited access to the island, but only with military minders. Grenada provoked an uproar in the press and led the Pentagon to establish press pools well before any anticipated action. The military operation in Panama in 1990 was the first time the pool system was put to a real test and it proved a disaster. Panama showed that habits lingered from Southeast Asia as Secretary of Defense Dick Cheney, still influenced by the Vietnam debacle, distrusted the press and did not authorize the official pool to travel with troops to Panama. As a consequence, nonpool reporters who made their way to the country on their own actually beat pool reporters to what stories existed after combat ended in a matter of days.[47]

The Gulf War the very next year prompted yet another change in strategy. Briefings in Saudi Arabia were combined with controlled media pools with limited access to combat units. The Gulf War was, according to Jason DeParle who covered it, the "first major conflict where the policy was to confine reporters to escorted pools that sharply curtailed when and how they could talk to troops."[48] In this new system, a select group of correspondents accompanied troops, then shared their reports with the rest of press corps back in Riyadh. Main oversight of the media again occurred in the office of Secretary of Defense Cheney, who had been faulted for excessive secrecy during the action in Panama. Operational decisions devolved to field commanders, many of whom had been left deeply suspicious of reporters by Vietnam. The ability to restrict access to battle areas also allowed military authorities to bend reporting their way, and television allowed the military to speak directly to the public through briefings unmediated by journalists.[49] As DeParle analyzes it, "the decision to confine reporting to official pools represented a departure not only from Vietnam, but also from World War II, where reporters had generally been given wide access to combat action and to commanders, with their dispatches reviewed by military censors for security violations."

Daniel Hallin argues that in the wake of the Gulf War, military attitudes shifted yet again, "returning to something like the Second World War view that the media are a useful part of the war effort."[50] A group of officials led by Pete Williams, then the Pentagon's chief spokesperson and now a correspondent for NBC, devised a new system allowing media to be embedded with specific military units. During the Iraq War in 2003, controversy shortly followed when the practice occurred on a large scale. Though embedding solved the issue of access, it was no panacea. Critics, including many in the press, questioned whether a journalist who was reliant on a small unit for their personal safety could objectively report on its actions.[51] Moreover, embeds needed to abide by certain censorship restrictions and to agree to use only military communications channels. In this way they were subject to some level of control. In sum, none of these postwar systems recalled the halcyon days of the Second World War for either the press or the military.

The Kennedy affair disrupts just this narrative. The press's road to the German surrender reveals that their dealings with the military often had been fractious and confrontational, and it conflicts with the sense of that relationship as cooperative, even close. Two possible conclusions can be drawn from this. For some, like the army public relations officer who after the war wrote a master's thesis on the controversy, Kennedy's reporting of the German surrender, and not Vietnam, marked a watershed, the point at which military officials no longer felt they could trust reporters.[52] Conversely, documentary evidence from the war reveals that the storm over the surrender story occurred after a war's worth of sporadic tension between reporters and their military handlers, and that the depiction of that relationship as amicable needs some significant qualification. In this sense, the surrender episode also instructs on the sheer messiness of the past, on the hazards of reducing murky history into clear narratives.

During the Second World War, then, Ed Kennedy routinely—and other journalists with varying frequency—clashed with military officials over matters small and large. They did so partly compelled by competitive pressures. The press most complained to AFHQ and subsequently to SHAEF about shortcomings in logistics and communications, especially communications, matters central to this competition. Journalists were frequently suspicious that rival organizations had gained some advantage unfairly. The news agencies competed aggressively, as did the broadcast networks. So too did the major dailies with syndicates, the *Times* and the *Herald Tribune* in New York, and the *Tribune* and the *Daily News* in Chicago, and news magazines, from *Time-Life* to *Collier's* to the *New Yorker*. Magazine journalists, in particular, argued that the military's system for determining press pools, as with its press flying squad, privileged some groups of reporters over others.

More important, Kennedy constantly had to hold his ground with army officials—from junior censors to actual policy makers—over the limits of military security and prerogative. So too did the veteran press corps following Eisenhower through the war. That contested space most often centered on political censorship. Reporters could endorse US war aims, support the troops, *and* hold authorities to account. Or so the press corps believed. The relationship of the media and the military in the Second World War, shorn of Good War nostalgia, then, looks more and not less, like that in future conflicts than most accounts would have us believe.

Edward Kennedy was hit by a car while walking in Monterey on a dreary early winter night in 1963. Initially expected to recover from his injuries, Kennedy died at age fifty-eight in the hospital several days later. As it turned out and according to the coroner's report, the accident had so weakened him that he succumbed to an undiagnosed late-stage throat cancer. Kennedy had not seen a doctor in years. Still, one can imagine that Kennedy, a heavy smoker, must have known something was seriously wrong.[53]

Kennedy in California might melodramatically evoke Napoleon on Elba, exiled from the centers of journalistic action where he had thrived, his finger no longer on the pulse of great events. Kennedy's retreat to the west might also suggest Dick Diver's tragic withdrawal into obscurity at the end of F. Scott Fitzgerald's *Tender Is the Night*. For all that, Big Sur country is spectacularly beautiful and after the war attracted all sorts of interesting people. Perhaps that provides reason enough to believe Kennedy when he spoke of his contentment there. Perhaps Kennedy felt that he could never equal the intensity and importance of reporting the war in the postwar world of civilian, corporatized journalism, and so was happy to escape it.

Kennedy always insisted that he had not been soured by his fate after breaking the news of the German surrender. "I regret to destroy a myth that I came to a bad end as a result of the story," he wrote, "but the fact is that the whole affair, while altering the course of my life, did not bring me one minute of grief. . . . I tried not to become embittered or imagine myself a martyr. I think I succeeded."[54] Written in the years just after the war, one wonders if such equanimity persisted.

One also wonders if a more accurate measure of the price Kennedy paid for his action is contained in a letter he wrote to Cooper in 1944. This was as Kennedy was taking over in Paris, supervising the AP's reporting from Northwestern Europe. As the end of the war came into sight, Cooper queried the AP's overseas staff about their postwar ambitions. Kennedy expressed only one wish—to return to the Paris bureau as its permanent chief. "That has been my goal since I started work for the A.P. twelve years ago," he confessed. He had learned during the war how to run a bureau, and Kennedy was convinced that France would play a pivotal role in postwar Europe. "I have also worked hard myself," Kennedy added, and "[the Paris] bureau has always been my pride." Although ambitious, Kennedy was not a self-promoting careerist. In this case, though, he did not hide his light under a basket. "If you can see your way clear to give me the Paris bureau, I shall deeply appreciate it, consider it a full reward for the work I have done throughout the war and do my best to make the A.P. coverage from Paris the very best."[55] It was to be a reward withheld, an ambition unfulfilled.

NOTES

Introduction

1. Quoted in Smith to Eisenhower, May 9, 1945, RG 331, Entry 6, Box 10, National Archives and Records Administration, College Park, MD (henceforth NARA).

2. Drew Middleton et al. to Eisenhower, May 8, 1945, RG 331, Entry 85A, Box 44, NARA.

3. "Complete Text of SHAEF Official Transcript of Meeting of Accredited Allied War Correspondents," May 8, 1945, AP 21.39 Edward Kennedy Papers (henceforth EKP), Box 3, Folder 23, Associated Press Corporate Archives, New York, NY (henceforth APCA).

4. Ray Moseley, *Reporting War: How Foreign Correspondents Risked Capture, Torture and Death to Cover World War II* (New Haven: Yale University Press, 2017), 319.

5. "WWII Correspondent, Fired for Big Scoop on Surrender, Gets Posthumous Apology from the AP," *Washington Post*, May 7, 2012; Nu Yang, "Journalists Campaign to Award Posthumous Pulitzer to Edward Kennedy," *Editor & Publisher*, November 9, 2012, 8; "Ed Kennedy's War," *AP Corporate Archives* 4, no. 2 (July 2012): 2.

6. Edward Kennedy, "I'd Do It Again," *Atlantic Monthly* 182, no. 2 (August 1948): 36–41; Julia Kennedy Cochran, ed., *Ed Kennedy's War: V-E Day, Censorship, & the Associated Press* (Baton Rouge: Louisiana State University Press, 2012).

7. Andy Rooney, interview with author, September 22, 2008, New York, New York.

8. Douglas Porch, "'No Bad Stories': The American Media-Military Relationship," *Naval War College Review* 50, no. 1 (Winter 2002): 85.

9. Charles C. Moskos and Thomas E. Ricks, *Reporting War When There Is No War: The Media and the Military in Peace and Humanitarian Operations* (Chicago: Robert R. McCormick Tribune Foundation, 1996), 8.

10. For notice of a compliant press, see, among others, Phillip Knightly, *The First Casualty* (New York: Harcourt Brace Jovanovich, 1975), 275ff.; Mary Mander, *Pen and Sword: American War Correspondents, 1898–1975* (Urbana: University of Illinois Press, 2010), 88–90; and Michael S. Sweeney, *Secrets of Victory: The Office of Censorship and the American Press and Radio in World War II* (Chapel Hill: University of North Carolina Press, 2001), 213–17.

11. Steven Casey, *The War Beat, Europe: The American Media at War against Nazi Germany* (New York: Oxford University Press, 2017) and *The War Beat, Pacific: The American Media at War against Japan* (New York: Oxford University Press, 2021). See also Nicholas Sarantakes, "Warriors of Word and Sword: The Battle of Okinawa, Media Coverage, and Truman's Reevaluation of Strategy in the Pacific," *Journal of American-East Asian Relations* 22 (2016): 343–67.

1. Reporting the War in Europe

1. For more on the history of the Scribe, see Ronald Weber, *Dateline-Liberated Paris: The Hotel Scribe and the Invasion of the Press* (Lanham, MD: Rowman & Littlefield, 2019).

2. A. J. Liebling, "Letter from Paris," *New Yorker*, September 9, 1944, 44.

3. John Redding, "Manuscript for Publicity Book—Paris," John M. Redding Papers, Box 7, Harry S. Truman Presidential Library, Independence, MO (henceforth TL); James Quirk to Elizabeth Quirk, August 25 and 26, 1944, both James T. Quirk Papers, Box 1, TL.

4. Stanley Cloud and Lynne Olson, *The Murrow Boys* (Boston: Houghton-Mifflin, 1996), 214–16.

5. Ernest Dupuy, "Behind the Elephants: SHAEF Public Relations from the Pentagon to Berlin," 163–70, R. Ernest Dupuy Papers, Reel 1, Wisconsin Historical Society, Madison, WI (henceforth WHS). Dupuy's manuscript will henceforth be cited as "Behind the Elephants."

6. John MacVane, *On the Air in World War II* (New York: William Morrow, 1979), 279–80; "Report of the Investigation of Ernest Hemingway," December 21, 1944, RG 338, Entry 50483, Box 2, NARA.

7. Dupuy to Chief of Staff, SHAEF, September 4, 1944, RG 331, Entry 1, Box 4. NARA; MacVane, *On the Air*, 294; Col. E.C. Roenecke to Manning, LeSueur, et al., [September 1944], RG 331, Entry 1, Box 4. NARA; Dupuy, "Behind the Elephants," 174.

8. Cooper, "Informative Note to Members," September 1, 1944, Robert McLean Papers, Box 24, Folder 343, APCA.

9. Cooper, "Informative Note to Members," September 22, 1944, Robert McLean Papers, Box 24, Folder 343, APCA.

10. Dupuy, "Behind the Elephants," 393; Thor Smith to Dupuy, March 15, 1946, Thor Smith Papers, Box 3, EL.

11. Smith to Dupuy, March 15, 1946.

12. Maj. Kenneth C. McCreedy, *Planning the Peace: Operation Eclipse and the Occupation of Germany* (Fort Leavenworth, KS: School of Advanced Military Studies, 1994–95), 4–10. Their plans, first under the codename RANKIN and then after the successful Normandy invasion as TALISMAN, envisioned several possible scenarios, only one of which was the simultaneous and unconditional surrender of all German forces as called for by the Allied leaders at the Casablanca conference in January 1943.

13. Neville to Dupuy, September 3, 1944, RG 331, Entry 82, Box 4, NARA.

14. Redding to Fitzgerald, September 12, 1944, RG 331, Entry 82, Box 4, NARA.

15. Thor Smith to Mary B. Smith, May 18, 1945, Thor Smith Papers, Box 3, EL.

16. War Department Bureau of Public Relations, "Outline of a Plan for the Handling of Newspaper Correspondents, Radio Commentators and Newsreel Men in Time of Emergency," June 4, 1941, RG 165, Entry 499, Box 3, NARA.

17. Dupuy, "Behind the Elephants," 52.

18. There was no equivalent organization of British correspondents. When needing input from the British press, SHAEF relied on the Newspaper and Periodical Emergency Council, a group of influential editors and publishers that the British government consulted over wartime information policy. The council was often referred to as the Will Committee after its director, William Will, a well-known and respected newspaper executive.

19. A. J. Liebling, "The A.P. Surrender," *New Yorker*, May 19, 1945, 57–58; Don Whitehead to Raymond Sokolow, [n.d.], A. J. Liebling Collection #4613, Box 40, Division of Rare and Manuscript Collections, Cornell University Library, Ithaca, NY; Quentin Reynolds, *By Quentin Reynolds* (New York: McGraw-Hill, 1963), 276.

20. "Public Relations Plan—Initial Occupation of Berlin," October 5, 1944, RG 331, Entry 82, Box 4, NARA.

21. Bradley to Bedell Smith, September 25, 1944, RG 331, Entry 1, Box 5, NARA; "Draft Notes on Meeting Held on October 21, 1944 to Discuss Plans for Coverage of Armistice," RG 331, Entry 82, Box 12, NARA; and Neville to Heald, November 23, 1944, RG 331, Entry 82, Box 12, NARA. TALISMAN had been renamed ECLIPSE after a security breach at the end of October 1944. Thereafter, all planning for the occupation of Germany occurred under that codename (McCreedy, *Planning the Peace*, 12).

22. Graham to PRD, SHAEF Rear, January 20, 1945, RG 331, Entry 82, Box 4, NARA.

23. Graham to Asst. Chief of Staff, G-3, January 24, 1945; Scott-Bailey to Butcher, February 8, 1945; and "Operation ECLIPSE- Notes for Meeting- Feb 6, 1945"; all RG 331, Entry 82, Box 4, NARA.

24. Allen to Chief of Staff, March 26, 1945, RG 331, Entry 1, Box 5, NARA.

25. "Operation 'Jackplane' Amended Copy," April 30, 1945, Thor Smith Papers, Box 6, EL. Curiously, there is no record of Jackplane in the SHAEF PRD files nor elsewhere at the National Archives. Smith's copy of the plan seems to be the only one to survive.

26. *Ed Kennedy's War*, 3,4. Kennedy's full biography would be difficult to write since little information about his personal life exists. He was not someone who divulged much to others. There is no family cache of letters or other documents. His memoir of the war devotes less than three pages to his life before starting to work as a foreign correspondent when he was thirty. While that memoir, published in 2012, and the AP archives provide details of his professional life once he joined the news agency, there are only two sources for information about Kennedy's early career before that time—Julia Kennedy Cochran's short prologue to her father's memoir and a two-page biographical letter Kennedy himself wrote at the behest of his employer shortly after joining the Associated Press—and even those sources conflict in some significant details.

27. For more on the history of the Associated Press, see Jonathan Silberstein-Loeb, *The International Distribution of News: The Associated Press, Press Association, and Reuters, 1848–1947* (New York: Cambridge University Press, 2014); Richard A. Schwarzlose, *The Nation's Newbrokers*, vol. 2, *The Rush to Institution, from 1865 to 1920* (Evanston, IL: Northwestern University Press, 1990); Victor Rosewater, *History of Cooperative Newsgathering in the United States* (New York: Appleton, 1930); and Walter R. Mears, "A Brief History of AP," in *Breaking News: How the Associated Press Covered War, Peace, and Everything Else* (New York: Princeton Architectural Press, 2007), 403–13.

28. Silberstein-Loeb, *International Distribution*, 46.

29. For more on the AP-UPA scandal, see Schwarzlose, *Nation's Newsbrokers*, 109–79.

30. Rosewater, *Cooperative Newsgathering*, 340–61.

31. Mears, "Brief History," 409.

32. In 1958 INS merged with UP to form the United Press International agency.

33. Mears, "Brief History," 406–7.

34. Eric Sevareid, *Not So Wild a Dream* (New York: Knopf, 1969), 106.

35. Fernsler to Byron Price, November 3, 1932 and Kennedy to Cooper, October 9, 1933, both EKP, Box 1, Folder 2, APCA.

36. Cooper to Price, August 13, 1935, Price to Cooper, August 15, 1935, and Cooper to J. R. Youatt, August 23, 1935, all EKP, Box 1, Folder 2, APCA.

37. *Ed Kennedy's War*, 9.

38. Lloyd to Kent Cooper, May 12, 1937, EKP, Box 1, Folder 2, APCA.

39. *Ed Kennedy's War*, 39, 43.

40. Sulzberger, *Long Row of Candles: Memoirs and Diaries, 1934–1954* (New York: Macmillan, 1969), 92–93.

41. Kennedy to John Evans, June 16, 1940, EKP, Box 1, Folder 4, APCA.

42. *Ed Kennedy's War*, 61.

43. War Diary, April–December 1940, Public Relations Branch, General Headquarters for the Middle East, WO169/43, The National Archives of the UK, Kew (London), England (henceforth TNA).

44. AP (NY) to Kennedy, November 15, 1940; Cooper to Kennedy, December 16, 1940, both EKP, Box 1, Folder 4, APCA; *Ed Kennedy's War*, 64.

45. Edward Kennedy, "Italians Give Up to U.S. Reporters," *New York Times*, January 24, 1941.

46. *Ed Kennedy's War*, 74.

47. Edward Kennedy, "Greek King Abandons Athens," April 23, 1941; "War Correspondents Hides in Ditch with Soldiers to Escape Bullets," April 21, 1941, and "Reporter Tells How Anzacs Left Greece," May 1, 1941, AP Clipping File, *Associated Press, Stories and Newsfeatures, 1937–1985* (Provo, UT: Ancestry.com Operations, 2013), https://www.ancestry.com/collections/50017/.

48. Kennedy to Ralph Ingersoll, September 30, 1941, EKP, Box 1, Folder 5, APCA.

49. Cooper to Kennedy, January 29, 1942, Kennedy to Cooper, March 29, 1942, and Evans to Cooper, May 2, 1942, all EKP, Box 1, Folder 6, APCA.

50. Surles to Maxwell, July 10, 1945, RG 165, Entry 499, Box 6, NARA.

51. AP wire story, July 6, 1942 and JMR to John Evans, July 8, 1942, both EKP, Box 1, Folder 6, APCA.

52. Maxwell to Surles, July 12, 1942, RG 165, Entry 499, Box 6, NARA.

53. Surles to Maxwell, July 13, 1942, RG 165, Entry 499, Box 5, NARA.

54. Edward Kennedy, "Eyewitness at Axis Port's Bombing," October 3, 1942, AP Clipping File, *Associated Press, Stories and Newsfeatures, 1937–1985*; Gould to Cooper, October 7, 1942, EKP, Box 1, Folder 6, APCA.

55. John B. Romeiser, ed., *Combat Reporter: Don Whitehead's World War II Diary and Memoirs* (New York: Fordham University Press, 2006), 44–45.

56. Romeiser, *Combat Reporter*, 112–13.

57. Cooper to Kennedy (via Robert Bunnelle in London), February 24, 1943, and Gould to Hackler, March 30, 1943, both EKP, Box 1, Folder 7, APCA.

58. Forward Headquarters PRO to Surles, September 11, 1943, RG 165, Entry 499, Box 16, NARA.

59. Cooper to Bunnelle, Grover, O'Sullivan, McDaniel, Gallagher, and Kennedy, March 1, 1943 and Kennedy to Cooper, February 28, 1944, both AP02A.3 Subject File, Box 63, APCA.

60. *Ed Kennedy's War*, 120.

61. Feder's comments quoted in Gould to Cooper, May 16, 1944, and copied an excerpt from Morin to Glenn Babb, June 12, 1944, both EKP, Box 1, Folder 9, APCA.

62. *Ed Kennedy's War*, 123.

63. Dupuy, "Behind the Elephants," 196–97.

64. Boyd Lewis, *Not Always a Spectator: A Newsman's Story* (Vienna, VA: Wolf's Head Press, 1981), 94.

65. Tupper to Chief, INC, AFHQ, September 19, 1944, RG 331, Entry 240P, Box 38, NARA; Tupper to Chief, INC, AFHQ, September 16, 1944, and McChrystal to Burnham, September 17, 1944, both WO204/5426, TNA.

66. At least one historian contends that military authorities attempted to deny Kennedy the Paris post because of his previous conflicts with them, but I could find no evidence of this. Kennedy's problems in getting accredited to SHAEF and traveling to France appear more likely the result of normal wartime bureaucratic delays. See Casey, *The War Beat, Europe*, 295.

67. *Ed Kennedy's War*, 145; and *Press Censorship in the European Theater of Operations, 1942–1945* (Paramus, NJ: 201st Field Press Censorship Detachment, 1953), 45.

68. UP dateline, "Decision West of Rhine Implied," *New York Times*, November 21, 1944; AP New York to AP Paris, November 21, 1944 and Kennedy to Babb, November 22, 1944, AP02A.2 Foreign Bureau Files, Box 5 (Paris), APCA.

69. Lewis, *Not Always a Spectator*, 136. One wonders if such gallantry served Lewis well in the Darwinian world of agency reporting.

70. "Roosevelt Expected to Visit Italy; Rosenman Flies There from Paris," *New York Times*, February 15, 1945; Kennedy to AP New York, February 15, 1945, AP02A.2 Foreign Bureau Correspondence, Box 5 (Paris), APCA; and "'Scandal,'" Editorial, *Washington Post*, February 15, 1945.

71. Hilldring (War Department) to McSherry (SHAEF), February 16, 1945, RG 165, Entry 499, Box 61, NARA; Allen to Hilldring, February 21, 1945, RG 331, Entry 56, Box 129, NARA.

72. Major Harold Leyshon, Memo re Kennedy and Smith, April 12, 1945 and Capt. Henry Andrews, Memo re Kennedy and Smith, April 12, 1945, both Thor Smith Papers, Box 6, EL.

2. The Military's Approach to the Press

1. Porch, "'No Bad Stories,'" 87; Moskos and Ricks, *Reporting War When There Is No War*, 15.

2. See Arthur Lubow, *The Reporter Who Would Be King: A Biography of Richard Harding Davis* (New York: Scribner, 1992). Davis died in 1916 when only fifty-one.

3. Michael S. Sweeney and Natascha Toft Roelsgaard, *Journalism and the Russo-Japanese War: The End of the Golden Age of Combat Correspondence* (Lanham, MD: Lexington Books, 2019).

4. Joseph T. Mathews, *Reporting the Wars* (Minneapolis: University of Minnesota Press, 1957), 159 and Mary S. Mander, *Pen and Sword: American War Correspondents, 1898–1975* (Urbana: University of Illinois Press, 2010), 41–42.

5. C. E. Montague quoted in Mathews, *Reporting the Wars*, 168.

6. Michael S. Sweeney, *The Military and the Press: An Uneasy Truce* (Evanston, IL: Northwestern University Press, 206), 39.

7. Mathews, *Reporting the Wars*, 164; William G. Shepherd, *Confessions of a War Correspondent* (New York: Harper, 1917), 113–14.

8. Sweeney, *Military and the Press*, 40.

9. Daniel Hallin, "Media and War," in *International Media Research: A Critical Survey*, ed. John Corner, Philip Schlesinger, and Roget Silverstone (New York: Routledge, 1997), 208.

10. Sir Philip Gibbs, *Adventures in Journalism* (New York: Harper and Brothers, 1923), 237.

11. Mander, *Pen and Sword*, 40.

12. Sweeney, *Military and the Press*, 44, 52.

13. Mander, *Pen and Sword*, 49; Mathews, *Reporting the* Wars, 169–70.

14. Sweeney, *Military and the Press*, 55.

15. Mander, *Pen and Sword*, 48; Sweeney, *Military and the Press*, 58–59.

16. Knightley, *First Casualty*, 126.

17. For more on the spectatorial attitudes of US writers, see Malcolm Cowley, *Exile's Return* (New York: Viking Press, 1951), 42–44.

18. Allan M. Winkler, *The Politics of Propaganda: The Office of War Information, 1942–1945* (New Haven: Yale University Press, 1978), 3. John Maxwell Hamilton's recent *Manipulating the Masses: Woodrow Wilson and the Birth of American Propaganda* (Baton Rouge: Louisiana State University Press, 2020) is a most canny assessment of the Creel Committee and its impact.

19. Mathews, *Reporting the Wars*, 155.

20. Price notebook, August 24, 1942, Byron Price Papers, Box 3, Folder 5, WHS.

21. The Roosevelt administration variously created or reconfigured the Office of Facts and Figures, the Office of Governmental Reports, the Office of Civilian Defense, and the Office of the Coordinator of Information, among other entities with overlapping and often conflicting briefs.

22. "Memorandum Approved Jointly by the State, War, and Navy Departments, and the Office of Censorship," May 20, 1942, RG 165, Entry 499, Box 18, NARA.

23. The best account of the Office of Censorship is Sweeney, *Secrets of Victory*.

24. For more on the OWI, see Winkler, *Politics of Propaganda*.

25. Dupuy, "Behind the Elephants," 10.

26. The best account of the press in the Pacific theater is Steven Casey's superb *The War Beat, Pacific: The American Media at War against Japan* (New York: Oxford University Press, 2021). For more about the Johnston episode, see Elliot Carlson, *Stanley Johnston's Blunder* (Annapolis, MD: Naval Institute Press, 2017).

27. "History of AFHQ Part I (August–December 1942)": 71, RG 498, Entry 579, Box 3782, NARA.

28. For AFHQ planning process, see "Public Relations Policies re Torch," October 9, 1942, RG331, Entry 3A, Box 67, NARA.

29. John D'Arcy-Dawson, *Tunisian Battle* (London: Macdonald, 1943), 28.

30. Casey, *War Beat, Europe*, 70. Casey cites a Wes Gallagher column from the time as his source for the US implementation of this system.

31. Milton Eisenhower, *The President Is Calling* (Garden City, NY: Doubleday, 1974), 138.

32. Alan Moorehead, *End in Africa* (New York: Harper and Brothers, 1943), 97; McClure to Maj. Gen. Frederick Lawson, January 19, 1943, WO204/5426, TNA.

33. For negotiations with the French in the run-up to TORCH, see Arthur Layton Funk, *The Politics of TORCH: The Allied Landings and the Algiers Putsch, 1942* (Lawrence: University of Kansas Press, 1974) and Robert D. Murphy, *Diplomat among Warriors* (Garden City, NY: Doubleday, 1964). For assessments of Darlan, see Funk, *Politics of TORCH*, 22–23; William L. Langer, *Our Vichy Gamble* (Hamden, CT: Archon Books, 1965), 164–65; and for a revealing French perspective, Albert Kammerer, *De débarquement africain au meurtre de Darlan* (Paris: Flammarion, 1949), 542–55.

34. John MacVane, *Journey into War* (New York: D. Appleton-Century, 1943), 91.

35. Broadcast script, December 25, 1942, Cecil Brown Papers, Box 1, Folder 9, WHS.

36. A. J. Liebling, *The Road Back to Paris* (Garden City, NY: Doubleday, Doran, 1944), 231, 235.

37. Ernie Pyle, "Snakes in Our Midst," in *Ernie's War*, ed. David Nichols (New York: Simon & Schuster, 1986), 64–65. How this story passed the censor is something of a mystery. Pyle's biographer, James Tobin suspects a simple bureaucratic mistake, a story placed on the wrong spike. It is also possible, though, that the story was intentionally passed by a censor who was opposed to the US policy of expediency and that it was, in essence, leaked to the public. Tobin, *Ernie Pyle's War* (New York: Free Press, 1997), 70–71.

38. Richard Fine, "'Snakes in Our Midst': The Media, the Military and American Policy toward Vichy North Africa," *Journalism History* 27, no. 4 (2010): 59–82.

39. Dwight D. Eisenhower, *Crusade in Europe* (Garden City, NY: Doubleday, 1948; repr., New York: Avon, 1968), 139. Citation refers to the Avon edition.

40. Of the many accounts of the episode in Patton's biographies and other sources, perhaps the most comprehensive and well-documented is Carlo D'Este, *Patton: A Genius for War* (New York: HarperCollins, 1995), 533–46. Mentions of the press's role in the episode are also found in Sweeney, *The Military and the Press*, 104–6; Robert W. Desmond, *Tides of War: World News Reporting, 1940–1945* (Iowa City: University of Iowa Press, 1984), 314; Mathews, *Reporting the Wars*, 215–16; Knightley, *First Casualty*, 320–21; and Frederick Voss, *Reporting the War: The Journalistic Coverage of World War II* (Washington, DC: Smithsonian Institution Press, 1994), 173.

41. Col. Donald E. Currier to Col. Richard T. Arnest, August 12, 1943, Dwight D. Eisenhower Pre-Presidential Papers (henceforth DDEPP), Box 91, EL.

42. Lt. Col. Perrin Long to The Surgeon, NATOUSA, August 16, 1943, DDEPP, Box 91, EL.

43. Eisenhower to Patton, August 17, 1943, Alfred Chandler, ed., *Papers of Dwight D. Eisenhower: The War Years* (Baltimore: Johns Hopkins University Press, 1970), 3:1340.

44. Harry C. Butcher, *My Three Years with Eisenhower* (New York: Simon & Schuster, 1946), 388, 393; Demaree Bess, "Report of an Investigation," August 19, 1943, DDEPP, Box 91, EL.

45. Eisenhower, *Crusade in Europe*, 199; Col. Donald Currier to Inspector General, NATOUSA, September 7, 1943, "Statement of Lt. Col. Wasden, 15th Evacuation Hospital," and Patton to Eisenhower, August 29, 1943, all DDEPP, Box 91, EL.

46. Kennedy to Babb, December 11, 1943, AP02A.3 Subject Files, Box 61, Patton, APCA; Butcher, *My Three Years*, 403.

47. "L'Affair Patton: Charge," *New York Daily News*, December 14, 1943, Clipping, AP02A.3 Subject Files, Box 61, Patton, APCA; C. P. Trussell, "Report on Patton Asked of Stimson," *New York Times*, November 25, 1943.

48. "Headquarters Denies Reprimanding Patton," *New York Times*, November 23, 1943; *Ed Kennedy's War*, 111; Butcher, *My Three Years*, 450.

49. "Drew Pearson's Story about Patton Is Confirmed after a False Denial," *Mobile Register*, November 24, 1943; Ward E. Duffy to Cooper, November 30, 1943, both AP02A.3 Subject Files, Box 61, Patton, APCA.

50. Morton to Gould, December 7, 1943, AP02A.3 Subject Files, Box 61, Patton, APCA. A "confidential note to desk" was the same as a service message—that is, a business telegram sent via the Army between reporters in the field to their home offices.

51. Kennedy to Babb, December 11, 1943, AP02A.3 Subject Files, Box 61, Patton, APCA.

52. Gould to Chandler, December 2, 1943, AP02A.3 Subject Files, Box 61, Patton, APCA.

53. Jock Lawrence, "Some Personal Memoirs," 29, Justus "Jock" Lawrence Papers, Box 2, EL; Dupuy, "Overseas with SHAEF" Diary, March 18, 1944, August 7, 1944, September 13, 1944, September 20, 1944, and September 21, 1944, Dupuy Papers, Reel 1, WHS. There are more than a dozen references to the "Headless Horseman" throughout the diary. General McClure was successful in opposing the creation of the Advisory Council. See McClure to Chief of Staff, March 16, 1944, RG 331, Entry 1, Box 46, NARA.

54. Liebling, "The A.P. Surrender," 60.

55. Charles McGrath, "So That Happened," *New Yorker*, November 12, 2018, 86.

56. Jack Redding, "History of SHAEF PRD," 3, Ernest Dupuy Papers, Reel 2, WHS.

57. Dupuy, "Overseas with SHAEF" diary, September 20, 1944, April 12, 1944, Ernest Dupuy Papers, Reel 1, WHS.

58. A raft of such complaints reached the Secretary of War's desk. See RG 107, Entry 102, Box 1, NARA. See also minutes of the meetings between SHAEF officials and press representatives, the Representative Press Working Committee, INF1/974, TNA.

59. For British complaints about the transmitter in the US sector, see Dupuy to David Sarnoff, July 7, 1944, RG 331, Entry 1, Box 3, NARA. For complaints throughout the war about British favoritism toward the BBC, see, for example, John Redding, "AFHQ Publicity and Psychological Warfare in the Mediterranean," March 14, 1944, RG 331, Entry 82, Box 2.

60. Eisenhower to Surles, September 6, 1944, W.B. Smith Papers, Box 27, EL

61. Harry Butcher to Ruth Butcher, September 8, 1944, Harry Butcher Papers, Box 3, EL; Butcher diary, August 26, 1944, Butcher Papers, Box 6, EL.

62. Eisenhower to Allen, September 12, 1944, W.B. Smith Papers, Box 27, EL.

63. See "Invasion of Europe: Representative Press Working Committee" files, INF1/974, TNA, and "Correspondents Committee," Folder 334-1, RG 331, Entry 82, Box 11, NARA.

64. A. J. Liebling, *Normandy Revisited* (New York: Simon & Schuster, 1958), 74–75.

65. Colonel Barney Oldfield, *Never a Shot in Anger* (New York: Dell, Sloan and Pearce, 1956), 139–41.

66. James T. Quirk to Elizabeth Quirk, March 29 and April 18, 1945, James T. Quirk Papers, Box 1, TL.

67. George Hicks to Anne Hicks, February 25, 27, and 28, 1945, all George Hicks Papers, Box 1, Folder 3, WHS.

68. Robert J. Casey, *This Is Where I Came In* (New York: Bobbs-Merrill, 1945), 228.

69. Ball to Gould, March 23, 1945, AP02A.03A Subject Files, 1900–1950, Box 65, SHAEF, APCA.

70. John Steinbeck, *Once There Was a War* (New York: Viking, 1958), xii; Fletcher Pratt, "How the Censors Rigged the News," *Harper's* 192 (February 1946): 98.

3. Reims

1. Forrest C. Pogue, *The Supreme Command* (Washington, DC: U.S. Army Center for Military History, 1954), 475–77; Marshall to Eisenhower, May 2, 1945, and SHAEF Forward to War Department, May 2, 1945, both Walter Bedell Smith Papers, Box 37, EL.

2. Patricia Beard, *Newsmaker: Roy W. Howard* (Guildford, CT: Lyons Press, 2016), 75.

3. "United Press Admits Peace Report Is False," *New York Times*, November 9, 1918.

4. Beard, *Newsmaker*, 78.

5. "United Press Admits Peace Report Is False," *New York Times*, November 9, 1918.

6. Surles to Eisenhower and Butcher to Surles, both September 7, 1944, RG 331, Entry 1, Box 3, NARA; Cooper, "Confidential Note to Editors," April 14, 1945, Robert McLean Papers, Box 24, APCA.

7. Sidney Shalett, "Surrender Offers by Nazis Reported," *New York Times*, April 28, 1945. The sequence of events leading up to Bell's report was reconstructed by the *New York Times*'s editor Edwin James in a cable to the publisher Arthur H. Sulzberger sent on May 8, 1945, and included in a letter Sulzberger sent to Robert McLean on May 10, 1945, EKP, Box 1, Folder 10, APCA.

8. A full account of the false surrender story is contained in clipping of James T. Howard, "How the Nation Got Its False Peace Report," *PM*, April 30, 1945, and Purcell to Cooper, April 29, 1945, both in Robert McLean Papers, Box 24, Folder 343, APCA.

9. Dupuy to Laura Dupuy, April 29, 1945, Dupuy Papers, Reel 1, WHS.

10. Eisenhower to Military Mission in Moscow (Archer and Deane), April 24, 1945, RG 331, Entry 82, Box 4, NARA.

11. Allen to Surles, May 1, 1945, RG 331, Entry 56, Box 129, NARA; Anne R. Kenney, "'She Got to Berlin': Virginia Irwin, *St. Louis Post-Dispatch* War Correspondent," *Missouri Historical Review* 79, no. 4 (July 1985): 462–66. Irwin had taken a leave of absence from the paper in 1941 to serve in England as a Red Cross volunteer before being accredited as a war correspondent when the *Post-Dispatch* committed to placing its own reporter in the SHAEF press corps rather than rely on agency and syndicate coverage. For more on Irwin's career as a war correspondent and on women war correspondents generally, see Nancy Caldwell Sorel, *The Women Who Wrote the War* (New York: Arcade, 1999) and Lilya Wagner, *Women War Correspondents of World War II* (Westport, CT: Greenwood Press, 1989).

12. Another intrepid woman war correspondent, the UP's Ann Stringer, actually broke the link-up story. She had cajoled friends in the army to lend her a small plane to take her to Torgau. After being rowed across the river to meet the Russian troops on the other side, she then hitched a ride back to Paris on a C-47, beating her competitors who had been taken back to the nearest press camp overland by jeep. ("Ann Stringer, 71, Dies; A War Correspondent," *New York Times*, January 12, 1990.)

13. Allen to Military Mission to Moscow, May 1, 1945, RG 331, Entry 56, Box 129, NARA. Both Tully's and Irwin's uncensored stories were included in this cable.

14. Allen to Military Mission to Moscow, May 1, 1945, RG331.

15. Kenney, "'She Got to Berlin,'" 473.

16. Kenney, "'She Got to Berlin,'" 474; Allen to Surles, May 1, 1945, RG 331, Entry 56, Box 129, NARA.

17. Dupuy, "Overseas with SHAEF" diary, April 30, 1945, Ernest Dupuy Papers, Reel 1, WHS; Dupuy, "Behind the Elephants," 377.

18. PRD War Diary, May 6, 1945, RG 331, Entry 58, Box 71, NARA; Kenney, "'She Got to Berlin,'" 475.

19. PRD War Diary, May 6, 1945, RG 331, Entry 58, Box 71, NARA.

20. Allen to Archer and Deane, May 3, 1945, RG 331, Entry 82, Box 4, NARA.

21. Dupuy, "Behind the Elephants," 373; Dupuy, "Overseas with SHAEF" diary, May 4, 1945, Ernest Dupuy Papers, Reel 1, WHS.

22. Pogue, *Supreme Command*, 419, 487.

23. Walter Bedell Smith, *Eisenhower's Six Great Decisions* (New York: Longmans, Green, 1956), 200; Butcher, *My Three Years*, 818.

24. Alan Moorehead, *Eclipse* (1945; New York: Harper and Row, 1968), 281; Alexander to Combined Chiefs of Staff, May 2, 1945, and Eisenhower to Alexander, May 2, 1945, both Walter Bedell Smith Papers (WWII Documents), Box 37, EL; AGWAR to Eisenhower, May 2, 1945, RG 331, Entry 56, Box 130, NARA; Joint Chiefs of Staff to Eisenhower, May 3, 1945, RG 331, Entry 1, Box 3, NARA.

25. Pogue, *Supreme Command*, 478–79.

26. Moorehead, *Eclipse*, 282–83; 21st Army Group to SHAEF Forward, May 3, 1945, Cable Log In, Walter Bedell Smith Papers (WWII Documents), Box 25, EL.

27. Moorehead, *Eclipse*, 284.

28. Michael Jones, *After Hitler* (New York: New American Library, 2015), 124; Moorehead, *Eclipse*, 286; SHAEF PRD, "Negotiations for the Surrender," May 7, 1945, Harry Butcher Papers, Box 4, EL; Moorehead, *Eclipse*, 288.

29. Dupuy, "Behind the Elephants," 382; Butcher, *Three Years*, 821.

30. Dupuy, "Behind the Elephants," 382.

31. Smith, "Surrender Snafu," unpublished manuscript, [1948], Thor Smith Papers, Box 7, EL.

32. Bunnelle to Kennedy, May 4, 1945, EKP, Box 5, Folder 40, APCA.

33. AP New York to Kennedy, May 4, 1945, EKP, Box 5, Folder 40, APCA.

34. J. C. Oestreicher, *The World Is Their Beat* (New York: Duell, Sloan and Pearce, 1945), 8.

35. Butcher, *Three Years*, 361.

36. Pogue, *Supreme Command*, 485.

37. *Papers of Dwight David Eisenhower: War Years*, 4:2685; Dupuy, "Overseas with SHAEF" diary, May 4, 1945, Ernest Dupuy Papers, Reel 1, WHS.

38. Dupuy, "Behind the Elephants," 390.

39. Dupuy, "Behind the Elephants," 390–91.

40. *Ed Kennedy's War*, 153–54; Dupuy, "Behind the Elephants," 391; Butcher, *Three Years*, 823.

41. Charles Christian Wertenbaker, "Surrender in Reims," *Life* 18, no. 21 (May 21, 1945): 27; SHAEF PRD, "Negotiations for the Surrender."

42. Dupuy, "Behind the Elephants," 391.

43. Original Butcher diary, May 5, 1945, Butcher Papers, Box 6, EL; Butcher, *Three Years*, 823.

44. Butcher divorced his first wife and married Mollie Ford in 1946. Ford was among the small coterie that formed Eisenhower's "family" after he was appointed Supreme Commander and with whom he would relax in the evenings and on weekends. Others included Butcher, Kay Summersby, and Bedell Smith's secretary Ruth Briggs. Eisenhower's relationship with Summersby was subject to intense scrutiny. Summersby herself later wrote that many senior SHAEF staff had mistresses during the war (believable given the times and wartime stress). Butcher's relationship with Ford lends credence to this. In a long letter to her mother, Ford would provide a revealing first-hand report of events in Reims on May 7. An unvarnished account of Eisenhower's relationship with Summersby, as well as the romantic entanglements of others in his senior staff, is found in Jean Edward Smith, *Eisenhower in War and Peace* (New York: Random House, 2013).

45. Butcher, *Three Years*, 823.

46. Original Butcher diary, May 5, 1945, Harry Butcher Papers, Box 6, EL; Pogue, *Supreme Command*, 486.

47. SHAEF PRD, "Negotiations for the Surrender."

48. Butcher, *Three Years*, 824; SHAEF PRD, "Negotiations for the Surrender."
49. Butcher, *Three Years*, 824.
50. Pogue, *Supreme Command*, 484; Butcher, *Three Years*, 824.
51. Dupuy, "Behind the Elephants," 391–92.
52. *Ed Kennedy's War*, 154. Matthews apparently told Kennedy about the incident later.
53. Original Butcher diary, May 5, 1945, Butcher Papers, Box 6, EL. This incident is not included in Butcher's diary published as *My Three Years with Eisenhower*.
54. Butcher, *Three Years*, 824–25.
55. Butcher, *Three Years*, 825.
56. SHAEF PRD, "Negotiations for the Surrender"; Pogue, *Supreme Command*, 486.
57. SHAEF PRD, "Negotiations for the Surrender"; Pogue, *Supreme Command*, 486.
58. Butcher, *Three Years*, 826–27.
59. SHAEF PRD, "Negotiations for the Surrender"; Butcher, *Three Years*, 827.
60. Original Butcher diary, May 5, 1945, Harry Butcher Papers, Box 6, EL.
61. *Ed Kennedy's War*, 154. Burroughs Matthews was one of the few PRD officers that Kennedy liked and respected.
62. *Ed Kennedy's War*, 154–55.
63. Butcher, *Three Years*, 827; Mollie Ford to mother, May 10, [1945], Butcher Papers, Box 4, EL; SHAEF PRD, "Negotiations for the Surrender."
64. SHAEF Forward to Military Mission in Moscow, May 6, 1945, Walter Bedell Smith Papers, Box 27, EL.
65. Pogue, *Supreme Command*, 486.
66. SHAEF PRD, "Negotiations for Surrender."
67. Dupuy, "Behind the Elephants," 392; Butcher, *My Three Years*, 829.
68. Dupuy, "Behind the Elephants," 396.
69. Smith to Dupuy, March 15, 1946, Thor Smith Papers, Box 3, EL.
70. SHAEF PRD, "Operation JACKPLANE," April 30, 1945, Thor Smith Papers, Box 6, EL.
71. Dupuy, "Behind the Elephants," 392, 396; *Ed Kennedy's War*, 155.
72. *Ed Kennedy's War*, 155; SHAEF PRD, "Official Press Party May 6, 1945," Thor Smith Papers, Box 6, EL; Gerald Clark, *No Mud on the Back Seat: Memoirs of a Reporter* (Montreal: Robert Davies Publishing, 1995), 13; Osmar White, *Conquerors' Road* (New York: Cambridge University Press, 2003), 110–11. Although not published for decades, White's account of the last months of the war was written in 1945.
73. Dupuy, "Behind the Elephants," 404; Butcher, *My Three Years*, 828.
74. Butcher, *My Three Years*, 828.
75. Ford to mother, May 10, [1945], Butcher Papers; Butcher, *My Three Years*, 828–29.
76. SHAEF PRD, "Negotiations for the Surrender."
77. Original Butcher diary, May 6, 1945, Harry Butcher Papers, Box 6, EL. Thor Smith recollects this authorization differently.
78. Dupuy, "Behind the Elephants," 393; Smith to Dupuy, March 15, 1946, Thor Smith Papers, Box 3, EL.
79. Dupuy, "Behind the Elephants," 397–98; Raymond Daniell, "Fiasco at SHAEF Is Bared," *New York Times*, May 9, 1945.
80. Thor Smith to Mary Smith, May 10, 1945 and Thor Smith to Dupuy, March 15, 1946, Thor Smith Papers, Box 3, EL; Dupuy, "Behind the Elephants," 400.
81. Allen to Chief of Staff (Bedell Smith), May 8, 1945, RG 331, Entry 6, Box 10, NARA; Boyd Lewis, "V-E Day: Just the Beginning," *Overseas Press Bulletin* 20, no. 18 (May 1, 1965): 4; and Daniell, "Fiasco by SHAEF." The only other person on the plane to publish an account of the pledge was Gerald Clark, in a memoir written fifty years later. His wording was

exactly the same as Allen's, suggesting it came not from memory but from Allen's subsequent written account. Much of Clark's description of the surrender also seems to have come from the SHAEF PRD "Negotiations for Surrender" briefing paper which he presumably kept.

82. Dwight Bentel, "Kennedy Details Incidents Before His Flash Surrender," *Editor & Publisher*, June 9, 1945, 7; Kennedy, *Ed Kennedy's War*, 156.

83. *Ed Kennedy's War*, 157.

84. Dupuy, "Overseas with SHAEF" diary," May 7, 1945, Reel 1, Ernest Dupuy Papers, WHS; Dupuy, "Behind the Elephants," 403.

85. White, *Conquerors' Road*, 111; Dupuy, "Overseas with SHAEF" diary," May 7, 1945; Dupuy, "Behind the Elephants," 402.

86. Original Butcher diary, May 6, 1945, Harry Butcher Papers, Box 6, EL; SHAEF PRD, "Negotiations for Surrender."

87. D.K.R. Crosswell, *Beetle: The Life of General Walter Bedell Smith* (Lexington: University of Kentucky Press, 2010), 920.

88. Eisenhower to Combined Chiefs of Staff (SCAF 354), May 6, 1945, Walter Bedell Smith Papers, Box 27, EL; Pogue, *Supreme Commander*, 487.

89. *Ed Kennedy's War*, 157–59; Smith to Dupuy, March 15, 1946, Thor Smith Papers, Box 3, EL; Boyd Lewis, "V-E Day," 4. Smith thought they had simply followed their reporters' instincts to the story; however, it is more likely that they had been alerted by Wertenbaker when he returned to Paris from Reims the day before. This, in any case, is what Kennedy suspected.

90. Dupuy, "Behind the Elephants," 403; Raymond Daniell, "Fiasco by SHAEF."

91. Ford to mother, May 10, [1945], Butcher Papers.

92. Original Butcher diary, May 6, 1945, Butcher Papers.

93. Ford to mother, May 10, [1945], Butcher Papers.

94. Pogue, *Supreme Command*, 487.

95. Ford to mother, May 10, [1945], Butcher Papers.

96. Butcher, *My Three Years*, 832.

97. Thor Smith to Mary Smith, May 10, 1945, Thor Smith Papers, Box 3, EL.

98. Smith to Dupuy, [April 1946], Thor Smith Papers, Box 3, EL.

99. SHAEF PRD, "Negotiations for the Surrender"; Gerald Clark, *No Mud*, 97–98; Boyd Lewis, "V-E Day," 5.

100. Kennedy, "I'd Do It Again," 38; Clark, *No Mud*, 99; SHAEF PRD, "Negotiations for the Surrender."

101. Clark, *No Mud*, 98, 100; SHAEF PRD, "Negotiations for the Surrender"; Kennedy, "I'd Do It Again," 38; White, *Conquerors' Road*, 113–14.

102. Pogue, *Supreme Command*, 488.

103. Clark, *No Mud*, 100.

104. Clark, *No Mud*, 100; SHAEF PRD, "Negotiations for the Surrender"; Kennedy, "I'd Do It Again," 38; Boyd Lewis, "V-E Day," 5.

105. Daniell, "Fiasco by SHAEF."

106. Lewis, "V-E Day," 5; Kennedy, "I'd Do It Again," 38; Thor Smith to Mary Smith, May 18, 1945, Thor Smith Papers, Box 3; and Mary Smith to Thor Smith, May 11, 1945, Thor Smith Papers, Box 5, both EL.

107. Ford to mother, May 10, [1945], Butcher Papers.

108. Smith to Dupuy, [April 1946], Thor Smith Papers, Box 3, EL; *Ed Kennedy's War*, 160; Boyd Lewis, "Sortie to Reims: The Inside Story of a Controversial 'Scoop,'" *Army* (June 1975): 34.

109. Ford to mother, May 10, [1945], Butcher Papers; Kennedy, *Ed Kennedy's War*, 160.

110. Lewis, "Sortie to Reims," 34.

111. *Ed Kennedy's War*, 161.

112. Butcher, *My Three Years*, 833–34; SHAEF PRD, "Negotiations for Surrender"; SHAEF Forward to War Department (SCAF 355), May 7, 1945, in *The Papers of DDE*, 4:2696.

113. *Papers of Dwight David Eisenhower: Occupation, 1945*, ed. Alfred E. Chandler, Jr. and Louis Galambos (Baltimore: Johns Hopkins University Press, 1978), 6:1; Butcher, *My Three Years*, 834.

114. *Papers of Dwight David Eisenhower: Occupation, 1945*, 6:2–3; SHAEF Forward to War Department (SCAF 359), Outgoing Cable Log, Walter Bedell Smith Papers, Box 27, EL; Mollie Ford to mother, May 10, [1945].

115. Archer and Deane (Military Mission in Moscow) to SHAEF Forward, May 7, 1945, Incoming Cable Log; Eisenhower to Military Mission in Moscow (SCAF 361), Outgoing Cable Log; Eisenhower to Combined Chiefs of Staff (SCAF 360), Outgoing Cable Log, all Walter Bedell Smith Papers, Box 25, EL. In the event, Eisenhower did not go to Berlin, sending Air Marshal Tedder in his place. Winston Churchill and his staff together convinced Eisenhower that he would be just window dressing for the Russians (Butcher, *My Three Years*, 835).

4. "Unmention Use Phone"

1. Lewis, "Sortie to Reims," 35; Kennedy, "I'd Do It Again," 38. See also Dwight Bentel, "Kennedy Details Incidents Before His Surrender Flash," *Editor & Publisher*, June 9, 1945, 7.

2. Oldfield, *Never a Shot*, 249.

3. Lewis, "Sortie to Reims," 35.

4. Oldfield, *Never a Shot*, 249–50. Oldfield directly quotes Kennedy on this issue, but I could not find any other published or unpublished source for such. Oldfield contends that even if the flashes went out simultaneously, Kennedy's longer story would likely have been beaten by the other agencies.

5. Thor Smith to Mary Smith, May 10, 1945, Thor Smith Papers, Box 3, EL; Dupuy, "Behind the Elephants," 406; Kennedy, "I'd Do It Again," 38; Dupuy, "Behind the Elephants," 407.

6. Smith to Dupuy, [April 1946], Thor Smith Papers, Box 3, EL; Dupuy, "Behind the Elephants," 399.

7. Kennedy, "I'd Do It Again," 39; Morton P. Gudebrod statement to Col. Ralph, May 12, 1945, RG 331, Entry 6, Box 10, NARA.

8. Bentel, "Kennedy Details Incidents," 62.

9. Appendix I (Cable Log) to Cooper to AP Board of Directors, June 7, 1945, New York Times Company Records, Arthur Hays Sulzberger Papers (henceforth AHS Papers), Box 274, Manuscripts and Archives Division, NYPL.

10. Kennedy, "I'd Do It Again," 39; *Ed Kennedy's War*, 162.

11. Bentel, "Kennedy Details Incidents," 62.

12. Russell Shepherd to FCC Chairman Porter, September 24, 1945, Harry Butcher Papers, Box 16, EL; Kennedy, "I'd Do It Again," 39; *Ed Kennedy's War*, 163; Appendix I (Cable Log) to Cooper to AP Board of Directors, June 7, 1945, AHS Papers.

13. Kennedy, "I'd Do It Again," 39.

14. Oldfield quotes Kennedy on this in *Never a Shot in Anger*, 251. Kennedy made essentially the same point in *Ed Kennedy's War*, 164.

15. Merrick to Col. Warden, May 7, 1945, RG 331 Entry 6, Box 10, NARA.

16. Thor Smith to Mary Smith, May 10, 1945 and Thor Smith to Dupuy, March 15, 1946, Thor Smith Papers, Box 3, EL.

17. "Ex-Censor, Attorney Here Now, Verifies Kennedy's War Story," clipping, [1945], Richard Merrick Papers, Box 1, Army History and Education Center, Carlisle, PA; Lewis, "Sortie to Reims," 36.

18. *Ed Kennedy's War*, 164; Kennedy, "I'd Do It Again," 39.

19. G. J. Tolhurst (SHAEF Rear) to Thor Smith (SHAEF Main), May 8, 1945, Thor Smith Papers, Box 6, EL. Tolhurst's cable contained the text of a covertly intercepted service message from AP London to AP New York.

20. Dwight Bentel, "Scene in AP Office When Story Arrived," *Editor & Publisher*, May 12, 1945, 60, 62, emphasis added; Alan Gould, "Scoop & Woe," *Cleartime: The AP Alumni Newsletter* 92 (April 1980), 9.

21. Morton P. Gudebrod, statement to Col. Ralph, May 12, 1945, RG 331, Entry 6, Box 10, NARA.

22. Robert Bunnelle, "The Scoop Brought Down the House and Closed the War," *Overseas Press Bulletin*, May 1, 1965, 3.

23. Kennedy to AP (London), May 7, 1945, EKP, Box 5, Folder 40, APCA.

24. Tolhurst (SHAEF Rear) to Smith (SHAEF Main), May 8, 1945, Thor Smith Papers, Box 6, EL.

25. AP London (Bunnelle) to AP Paris, May 7, 1945, EKP, Box 5, APCA.

26. Appendix I (Cable Log) to Cooper to AP Board of Directors, June 7, 1945, AHS Papers.

27. Babb to AP (London), May 7, 1945, EKP, Box 2, Folder 18, APCA; Appendix I (Cable Log) to Cooper to AP Board of Directors, June 7, 1945, AHS Papers; Bunnelle to Babb, May 7, 1945, EKP, Box 2, Folder 18, APCA.

28. AP (New York) to AP (Paris), May 7, 1945, EKP, Box 5, Folder 40, APCA; AP (New York) to AP (London), May 7, 1945 and Bunnelle to AP (NY), May 7, 1945, both EKP, Box 2, Folder 18, APCA; Appendix I (Cable Log) to Cooper to AP Board of Directors, June 7, 1945, AHS Papers.

29. Smith to Dupuy, [April 1946], Thor Smith Papers. Box 3, EL; Lewis, "Sortie to Reims," 36; Dupuy, "Behind the Elephants," 408a; "SHAEF Announcement," AP Wire Story, May 7, 1945, EKP, Box 3 Folder 21, APCA.

30. Captain Raymond Kuhn to Allen, May 8, 1945, Capt. Erford Bedient to Allen, May 8, 1945, and Lt. Col. Burroughs Matthews to Allen, 8 May 1945, all RG 331, Entry 6, Box 10, NARA; Bentel, "Kennedy Details Incidents," 62.

31. Bentel, "Kennedy Details Incidents," 62; Matthews to Allen, May 8, 1945, RG 331, Entry 6, Box 10, NARA. This implies Kennedy had already had an encounter with Warden about how he got the story out, or that he simply misremembered and confused Warden with his colleague Richard Merrick.

32. *Ed Kennedy's War*, 166; Smith, "Surrender Snafu," typescript, [1948], Thor Smith Papers, Box 7, EL.

33. "Brief of Telephone Conversation between Admiral Leahy and Mr. Churchill," May 7, 1945, RG 165, Entry 491, Box 2, NARA.

34. Frank S. Adams, "Wild Crowds Greet News in City While Others Pray," and Sidney Shalett, "President 'Expects' to Give Broadcast," both *New York Times*, May 8, 1945; and "County Swept with Premature Rumor of Peace," Chester (PA) *Times*, May 7, 1945, Philadelphia *Evening Bulletin* Scrapbooks, Box 12, APCA.

35. "Celebrating the Victory," *Times* (London), May 8, 1945.

36. "Teletype Conference between Col. McCarthy and Lt. Col. Scott," May 7, 1945, RG 165, Entry 491, Box 2, NARA.

37. "Teletype Conference between Col. McCarthy and Lt. Col. Scott," May 7, 1945, RG 165.

38. "Telephone Conversation between Col. McCarthy and Mr. Churchill," May 7, 1945, RG 165, Entry 491, Box 2, NARA.

39. "Teletype Conferences between Col. McCarthy and Lt. Col. Scott," and "Teletype Conference between Col. McCarthy and General Deane," both May 7, 1945, RG 165.

40. AP (NY) to Kennedy, May 7, 1945, EKP, Box 2, Folder 18, APCA.

41. AP (NY) to AP (London), May 7, 1945, EKP, Box 2, Folder 18, APCA; Appendix I (Cable Log) to Cooper to AP Board of Directors, June 7, 1945, AHS Papers; Bunnelle to AP (New York), May 7, 1945, and Bunnelle to Babb, May 7, 1945, both EKP, Box 2, Folder 18, APCA.

42. Appendix I (Cable Log) to Cooper to AP Board of Directors, June 7, 1945, AHS Papers.

43. Bunnelle to AP (NY), May 7, 1945, EKP, Box 2 Folder 18, APCA.

44. Cooper to Eisenhower, May 7, 1945, and Cooper to Stimson, May 7, 1945, both EKP, Box 2, Folder 18, APCA.

45. Cooper to Truman, Cooper to AP members, and Cooper to Early, all May 7, 1945, EKP, Box 2, Folder 18, APCA.

46. Bunnelle to AP (NY), May 7, 1945, EKP, Box 2 Folder 18, APCA.

47. Don Doane, "Don Doane and His Dastardly Act," *Cleartime* 94 (June 1980): 4.

48. Teleprinter transcript, May 7, 1945, Thor Smith Papers, Box 6, EL.

49. Major Allan Paris to Thor Smith, 8 May 1945, RG 331 Entry 6, Box 10, NARA.

50. Bunnelle to Cooper, May 7, 1945, and Bunnelle to Cooper, second cable, May 7, 1945, both EKP, Box 2, Folder 18, APCA.

51. Morin to Cooper, May 7, 1945, EKP, Box 2 Folder 18, APCA; Morin to Cooper (second cable) and Morin to Bunnelle, both May 7, 1945, Thor Smith Papers, Box 6, EL.

52. AP (NY) to Bunnelle, May 7, 1945, EKP, Box 2, Folder 18, APCA; Cooper to Bunnelle, 7 May 45, EKP, Box 2, Folder 19, APCA; Cooper to AP (London), May 7, 1945, EKP, Box 2 Folder 18, APCA; and Gould, "Scoop & Woe," 9.

53. Major Schwartz to Col. Ralph, May 8, 1945, RG 331, Entry 6, Box 10, NARA.

54. "Conference between Col. Hill and General Allen," transcript, May 7, 1945, RG 165, Entry 499, Box 58, NARA.

55. Morin to AP New York, May 7, 1945, Thor Smith Papers, Box 6, EL.

56. Appendix I (Cable Log) to Cooper to AP Board of Directors, June 7, 1945, AHS Papers; Roy Howard to Associated Press, May 7, 1945, EKP, Box 4, Folder 34, APCA.

57. "Suspension Reaction," AP Wire Story, May 7, 1945, EKP, Box 4, Folder 34, APCA.

58. Dana Adams Schmidt, "Londoners Dance in Packed Streets," *New York Times*, May 8, 1945.

59. "Outburst of Joy in America," *Times* (London), May 8, 1945; Adams, "Wild Crowds," *New York Times*, May 8, 1945.

60. "Overseas with SHAEF" Diary, May 7, 1945, Ernest Dupuy Papers, Reel 1, WHS; Thor Smith to Mary Smith, May 8, 1945, Thor Smith Papers, Box 3, EL; and *My Three Years*, 836. Tarfu = totally and royally fucked up; Fumtu = fucked up more than usual.

61. *Ed Kennedy's War*, 166.

62. Bunnelle to Kennedy, May 7, 1945, EKP, Box 4, Folder 40, APCA.

63. AP Bulletin from Paris, May 7, 1945, EKP, Box 4, Folder 34, APCA.

64. AP Wire Story, May 7, 1945, EKP, Box 4, Folder 34, APCA.

5. At the Hotel Scribe

1. Cooper to Kennedy, May 7, 1945, EKP, Box 2, Folder 18, ACPA.

2. Relman Morin, AP Wire Story, May 8, 1945, Thor Smith Papers, Box 5, EL.

3. "Suspension Reaction," AP Wire Story, [May 8, 1945], EKP, Box 6, Folder 50, APCA.

4. "Suspension Reaction," [May 8, 1945], EKP.

5. "First Add—Suspension Reaction," [May 8, 1945], EKP, Box 4, Folder 28; "Pulitzer for Kennedy," *Paterson News*, [May 8, 1945], EKP, Box 8, Scrapbook 1, both APCA.

6. Cooper to Kennedy, and Cooper to Surles, both May 8, 1945, EKP, Box 2 Folder 18, APCA.

7. Eisenhower to Marshall, May 8, 1945, Walter Bedell Smith Papers, Box 28, EL; emphasis added.

8. The account of the meeting, unless otherwise noted, is taken from "Transcript of Correspondents' Meeting," May 8, 1945, RG 331, Entry 82, Box 11, NARA.

9. Correspondents letter to General Eisenhower, May 8, 1945, RG 331 Entry 85A, Box 44, NARA.

10. Long to AP (NY), May 8, 1945, EKP, Box 5, Folder 42, APCA.

11. Watson's comment was noted by one of the AP's observers in the meeting and was not part of the official transcript. "Complete Text of SHAEF Official Transcript," May 8, 1945, EKP, Box 3, Folder 23, APCA.

12. Long to AP (NY), May 8, 1945.

13. "Complete Text of SHAEF Official Transcript," May 8, 1945, EKP.

14. Long to AP (NY), May 8, 1945, EKP.

15. Daniell, "Fiasco By SHAEF At Reims Is Bared," *New York Times*, May 9, 1945; quotation from story heading in *Reno Evening Gazette*, May 9, 1946, Thor Smith Papers, Box 6, Folder 6, EL; Kennedy, "I'd Do It Again," 40.

16. Allen to Surles, May 8, 1945, RG 331, Entry 56, Box 130, NARA; Clifton Daniel, "Final Surrender Signed in Berlin Ruins, Soviet Joins in Proclaiming Triumph," *New York Times*, May 9, 1945.

17. De Luce to AP (NY), AP (NY) to AP (Paris), and AP (London) to AP (Paris), all May 8, 1945, EKP, Box 5, Folder 41, APCA.

18. Allen to Surles for Cooper, May 8, 1945, RG 331 Entry 56, Box 130, NARA.

19. AP (NY) to AP (Paris), May 8, 1945, EKP, Box 2, Folder 19, APCA.

20. Morin to AP (NY), May 8, 1945, Cooper to Kennedy, May 7, 1945, and Cooper to Eisenhower, May 7, 1945, all EKP, Box 2, Folder 19, APCA; AP Wire Story, "Precede Paris—Kennedy Suspension," [May 8, 1945], Thor Smith Papers, Box 6, EL.

21. Cooper to AP (Paris) and De Luce to AP (NY), both May 8, 1945, EKP, Box 5, Folder 41, APCA; "Add—Kennedy: How Jodl Gave In," clipping [May 1945], EKP, Box 8 Scrapbook 1, APCA.

22. "Investigation of Associated Press Transmission of News Stories on German Surrender before Release," May 1945, Thor Smith Papers, Box 6, EL.

23. Barney Oldfield, *Never a Shot*, 251.

24. Lewis, "Sortie to Reims," 36.

25. Casey, *The War Beat*, 338–39.

26. Surles to Allen, May 12, 1945, RG 165, Entry 499, Box 58, NARA.

27. Gould, "Scoop & Woe," 1.

28. Bunnelle, "The Scoop Brought Down the House," 3; see also Dupuy, "Behind the Elephants," 407.

29. Brock to Kennedy, May 8, 1945, EKP, Box 5, Folder 41, APCA.

30. Lait to Kennedy, May 8, 1945, EKP, Box 5, Folder 41, APCA.

31. Graham Hovey, "Kennedy," AP Wire Story Copy, May 7, 1945, EKP, Box 3, Folder 22, ACPA.

32. Marshall to Eisenhower, May 8, 1945, RG 331, Entry 1, Box 4, NARA.

33. Hill (BPR) to SHAEF PRD, May 8, 1945, Thor Smith Papers, Box 6, EL.

34. Mary Smith to Thor Smith, May 7 and 8, 1945, Thor Smith Papers, Box 5, EL.

35. Thor Smith to Mary Smith, May 8, 1945, Thor Smith Papers, Box 3, EL.

36. Butcher, *Three Years*, 835.

37. Allen to SHAEF G-3, April 11, 1945, RG 331, Entry 82, Box 4, NARA.

38. Deane to Eisenhower, April 29, 1945, RG 331, Entry 82, Box 4, NARA.

39. Butcher, *Three Years*, 837.

40. Butcher provides a full account in *Three Years*, 836–49; Dupuy wrote a six-page letter to his wife on returning from Berlin.

41. Butcher, *Three Years*, 837.

42. Butcher, *Three Years*, 843.

43. Ernest Dupuy to Laura Dupuy, May 9, 1945, Ernest Dupuy Papers, Reel 1, WHS.

44. Ernest Dupuy to Laura Dupuy, May 9, 1945, Dupuy Papers.

45. Thor Smith to Mary Smith, May 14, 1945, Thor Smith Papers, Box 3, EL.

46. Raymond Daniell, "Fiasco By SHAEF."

47. Boyd D. Lewis, "Breach of Faith Laid to A.P. Man," *Philadelphia Inquirer*, May 9, 1945, *Evening Bulletin* Scrapbooks, Series II, Box 12, Folder 17, APCA; Clinton B. Conger to Boyd Lewis, May 9, 1945, Thor Smith Papers, Box 6, EL; and Kingsbury-Smith to Eisenhower, May 9, 1945, RG 331, Entry 6, Box 10, NARA.

48. AP Wire Story, Dateline London May 9, [1945], RG 216 Office of Censorship, Entry 1A, Box 541, NARA; Bunnelle to Cooper, May 9, 1945, EKP, Box 2, Folder 18, APCA.

49. Cooper to Morin, May 9, 1945, EKP, Box 2, Folder 19, APCA.

50. Morin to Cooper, May 9, 1945, EKP, Box 2, Folder 18, APCA.

51. Morin to Cooper, message #2, May 9, 1945, EKP, Box 2, Folder 18, APCA. It seems as if this second message may have been received by the AP before the first, which was received at least twelve hours after Morin filed it in Paris. It is unclear whether SHAEF held up the transmission.

52. "Master Mind Folly," *Daily Mirror* (NY), May 9, 1945, EKP, Box 8, Scrapbook 1, APCA.

53. John Pennekamp, "Behind the Front Page: In Our Business We Doff Our Hats To a Man With a Scoop," *Miami Herald*; "Left at the Post," *Parsons (KS) Sun and Republican*, both May 9, 1945, EKP, Box 8, Scrapbook 1, APCA.

54. "Scripps Papers Lash A.P. Surrender 'Scoop,'" *Philadelphia Inquirer*, May 9, 1945, in *Evening Bulletin* Scrapbooks, Box 12, Folder 17, APCA; "The Journalistic Double Cross," Kansas City (KS) *Kansan* and "A Pledge Is Still a Pledge," *Seattle Star*, both May 9, 1945, RG 216 Entry 1A, Box 541, NARA.

55. "How the AP Handled the German Surrender Story," *San Antonio Express*, May 9, 1945, EKP, Box 8, Scrapbook 1, APCA.

56. Surles to Allen, May 9, 1945, RG 331, Entry 56, Box 130, NARA.

57. "Text of Statement of Brig. Gen. Frank A. Allen, Jr.," May 9, 1945, EKP, Box 2, Folder 19, APCA; emphasis added.

58. Thor Smith to Mary Smith, May 14, 1945, Thor Smith Papers, Box 3, EL; Pinkley to Eisenhower, May 10, 1945, RG 331 Entry 6, Box 10, NARA.

59. Gladwyn Hill, "Peace Jeopardized By AP, SHAEF Says," *New York Times*, May 10, 1945.

60. "Text of Statement of Edward Kennedy in Reply to Brig. Gen. Frank A. Allen, Jr.," May 9, 1945, EKP, Box 2, Folder 19, APCA.

61. Cooper to Gallagher, May 9, 1945, EKP, Box 2, Folder 18, APCA.

62. Reid to Cooper, May 8, 1945, AP02A.01 U.S. Bureaus/Members Correspondence, Box 63a, Correspondence with Directors folder, APCA; Cooper to Reid, May 9, 1945, EKP,

Box 2, Folder 18, APCA; Cooper's response to Reid was sent out on the AP wire as a brief story (RG 216, Entry 1A, Box 541, NARA).

63. Dupuy to Allen, May 10, 1945, RG 331, Entry 82, Box 4, NARA.

64. Gallagher to Cooper, May 10, 1945, EKP, Box 2, Folder 19, APCA.

65. Cooper to Kennedy, May 19, 1945, EKP, Box 2, Folder 19, APCA.

66. Wilson to Cooper, May 10, 1945, EKP, Box 2, Folder 19, APCA. Because of his suspension, Kennedy's response had to be relayed through another AP staffer.

67. Bunnelle to AP New York, May 10, 1945, EKP Box 2, Folder 18, APCA.

68. Cooper, *Right to Know: An Exposition on the Evils of News Suppression and Propaganda* (New York: Farrar, Straus and Cudahy, 1956), 228–29. Kennedy returned the $1,000 check.

69. AP Wire Story, Dateline Philadelphia, May 10, [1945], RG 216, Entry 1A, Box 541, NARA.

70. Cooper to Gallagher, May 10, 1945, EKP, Box 1, Folder 10, APCA.

71. Cooper, *Right to Know*, 230.

72. "Expression of Regret," *Washington Star*, May 11, 1945; Butcher to Early, May 11, 1945, Harry Butcher Papers, Box 4, EL.

73. Gladwyn Hill, "Army Sends 2 Home for Trip to Berlin," *New York Times*, May 11, 1945.

74. Cooper to Kennedy, May 11, 1945, EKP, Box 1 Folder 10, APCA.

75. Cooper to Gallagher, May 11, 1945, EKP, Box 1, Folder 10, APCA.

76. Bunnelle to Babb, May 11, 1945, EKP, Box 2, Folder 18, APCA.

77. AP (Paris) to Babb and Hawkins, May 11, 1945, EKP, Box 2, Folder 18, APCA.

78. "SHAEF Censorship Code," *New York Times*, May 12, 1945.

79. "New Censor Rules Provoke Dispute," *New York Times*, May 12, 1945.

80. See Dwight Bentel, "SHAEF Turmoil Goes On," *Editor & Publisher*, May 19, 1945, 8.

81. The letters of correspondents and servicemen alike are replete with touching and, at times, desperate anguish that they had not heard from their families for weeks or even months.

82. Mary Smith to Thor Smith, May 11, 1945, Thor Smith Papers, Box 5, EL.

83. Thor Smith to Mary Smith, May 14, 1945, Thor Smith Papers, Box 3, EL.

84. "Statement by Morton P. Gudebrod," May 12, 1945, RG 331, Entry 6, Box 10, NARA.

85. "Statement by Edward Kennedy," May 12, 1945, RG 331, Entry 6, Box 10, NARA.

86. Thor Smith, "Surrender Snafu," Draft, [1947], Thor Smith Papers, Box 7, EL.

87. Allen to Chief of Staff, May 12, 1945, RG 331, Entry 6, Box 10, NARA.

88. Allen to Surles, May 14, 1945, and Allen to Kennedy and Allen to Gudebrod, May 14, 1945, both RG 331, Entry 6, Box 10, NARA; "Correspondents," AP Wire Story, May 14, 1945, RG 216, Entry 1A, Box 541, NARA.

89. AP Wire Story, May 15, 1945, EKP, Box 2, Folder 19, APCA; Cooper, "Private Note to Members," May 14, 1945, RG 216, Entry 1A, Box 541, NARA; and AP (New York), "Note to Members," May 15, 1945, EKP, Box 2, Folder 19, APCA.

90. Thor Smith to Mary Smith, May 14, 1945, Thor Smith Papers, Box 3, EL.

6. The Debate

1. "Allies in Germany Bar Foreign Press," *New York Times*, May 11, 1945.

2. Dupuy, "Behind the Elephants," 431–33.

3. Thor Smith to Mary Smith, May 17, 1945, Thor Smith Papers, Box 3, EL.

4. Thor Smith to Mary Smith, May 18, 1945, Thor Smith Papers, Box 3, EL.

5. Mary Smith to Thor Smith, May 18, 1945, Thor Smith Papers, Box 5, EL.

6. Thor Smith to Mary Smith, May 22, 1945, Thor Smith Papers, Box 3, EL.

7. Cooper to AP Cable Desk Staff, May 15, 1945, Robert McLean Papers, Box 24, APCA.

8. McLean to Cooper, May 19, 1945, EKP, Box 1, Folder 10, APCA.

9. Cooper to McLean, May 21, 1945, EKP, Box 1, Folder 10, APCA.

10. McLean to Cooper, May 22, 1945, EKP, Box 1, Folder 10, APCA.

11. Cooper to McLean, May 23, 1945, EKP, Box 1, Folder 10, APCA.

12. Guy to Cooper, May 21, 1945, EKP, Box 1, Folder 12, APCA.

13. McLean to Guy, May 24, 1945, EKP, Box 1, Folder 12, APCA.

14. Guy to McLean, May 28, 1945, EKP, Box 1, Folder 12, APCA.

15. McLean to Guy, June 2, 1945, EKP, Box 1, Folder 12, APCA.

16. Whiteleather to McLean, May 18, 1945, EKP, Box 1, Folder 10, APCA.

17. Cooper to McLean, [May 1945]; Cooper to Bunnelle, May 23, 1945; Bunnelle to Cooper, May 24, 1945, all EKP, Box 1, Folder 10, APCA.

18. "Benjamin M. McKelway, Ex-Editor in Washington," *New York Times*, September 1, 1976.

19. McKelway to Cooper, May 22, 1945, EKP, Box 1, Folder 11, APCA.

20. Cooper to McKelway, May 25, 1945, EKP, Box 1, Folder 11, APCA.

21. Sulzberger to Marshall, May 10, 1945, AHS Papers, Box 274, NYPL.

22. Marshall to Sulzberger, May 19, 1945, AHS Papers, Box 274, NYPL. In addition to the *New York Times*, the *New York Herald Tribune*, the *Chicago Tribune*, and the *Chicago Daily News* also syndicated their foreign reporting.

23. James to Sulzberger, May 8, 1945, EKP, Box 1, Folder 11, APCA.

24. "Disservice to the Press," *New York Times*, May 10, 1945.

25. Arthur Hays Sulzberger, [May 1945] AHS Papers, Box 274, NYPL. The memo is undated but certainly written at this time.

26. Kluckhohn to Sulzberger, two telegrams, May 10, 1945, AHS Papers, Box 274, NYPL.

27. Poynter to McLean, May 11, 1945, EKP, Box 1, Folder 10, APCA.

28. McLean to Sulzberger, May 11, 1945, Sulzberger to McLean, May 16, 1945, and McLean to Sulzberger, May 18, 1945, all AHS Papers, Box 274, NYPL.

29. Cooper to Sulzberger, May 25, 1945, AHS Papers, Box 274, NYPL.

30. Sulzberger to Cooper, May 28, 1945, AHS Papers, Box 274, NYPL.

31. Sulzberger complained to McLean that the *Times* had published Allen's statement under a three-column head, but was upset that it had not received Kennedy's statement from the AP in time to run it in fairness as well. Cooper explained that the *Times* had already gone to press when Kennedy's statement had arrived.

32. Cooper to Sulzberger, May 28, 1945, EKP, Box 1, Folder 12, APCA.

33. A.J. Liebling, "The A.P. Surrender," *New Yorker*, May 19, 1945, 57–62.

34. Janet Flanner to William Shawn, May 21, 1945, *New Yorker* Records, Box 418, NYPL.

35. *Ed Kennedy's War*, 172–73.

36. AP Wire Story, May 30, 1945, EKP, Box 3, Folder 25, APCA.

37. Thor Smith to Mary Smith, June 2, 1945, Thor Smith Papers, Box 3, EL.

38. Thor Smith, "Surrender Snafu—First Draft," [1948?], Thor Smith Papers, Box 7, EL.

39. *Ed Kennedy's War*, 173–74.

40. Surles to Eisenhower, May 19, 1945, Eisenhower Pre-Presidential Papers, Box 134A, EL.

41. Kennedy "I'd Do It Again," 41.

42. By far the largest archive was that compiled by the Associated Press, which kept a careful state-by-state scrapbook of such clippings, mostly drawn from AP member papers. If the sample is at all skewed it may underrepresent Scripps-Howard or United Press papers which were more likely to be critical of the AP and Kennedy.

43. "Adventure in Journalism," *Brownsville (TX) Herald*, May 10, 1945, EKP, Box 13, APCA; "Who Is This Man Kennedy?," *Meadville (PA) Tribune-Republican*, May 10, 1945, Philadelphia *Evening Bulletin* Scrapbooks, Box 12, APCA; "All Honor to Him," *Coffeyville (KS) Daily Journal*, [May 1945] and "Political Censorship," *Winfield (KS) Courier*, May 9, 1945, both EKP, Box 13, APCA. Box 13 of the EKP contains the scrapbook of editorial clippings, organized by state, that were collected by the Associated Press, not by Kennedy.

44. "The News 'Gets Through,'" *Hagerstown (IN) Exponent*, and "Your Right to the News," Rochester (NY) *Times Union*, both May 10, 1945, EKP, Box 13, APCA; "News Is When You Find It," May 11, 1945, RG 216, Entry 1A, Box 541, NARA; "Edward Kennedy's Triumph," Arkansas City (KS) *Daily Traveler*, [May 1945], EKP, Box 13, APCA.

45. "Freedom Must Entail Responsibility," Louisville *Courier-Journal*, May 10, 1945, EKP, Box 13, APCA.

46. "The Sack for This Man," *Charlotte News*, May 11, 1945; "A Smear of the Press from Within," *Honolulu Advertiser*, [May 1945]; "Disgrace to His Profession," Macon (GA) *Telegraph*, May 12, 1945; and "The War's Greatest Blunder," Lansing (MI) *State Journal*, May 13, 1945, all EKP, Box 13, APCA.

47. "AP's McLean Regrets," *Chicago Times*, May 11, 1945, EKP, Box 13; "The Emotion Is Real," *New York Herald Tribune*, May 8, 1945, Philadelphia *Evening Bulletin* Scrapbooks, Box 12; "The Brass Hats and Mr. Kennedy's Scoop," *Norfolk Virginian-Pilot*, May 9, 1945, EKP, Box 13, all APCA.

48. "Censorship Stupidity," *Cheyenne (WY) Tribune*, May 10, 1945.

49. "Messy Situation," *Greensboro (NC) Daily News*, May 10, 1945; and "Censors and the News," *Augusta (GA) Chronicle*, May 13, 1945, all EKP, Box 13, APCA.

50. "Victory Is Our Business!," *Cleveland News*, May 11, 1945, EKP, Box 13, APCA.

51. "He Violated Code," *Marshfield (WI) News-Herald*, May 11, 1945, EKP, Box 1, APCA; "The Case of Mr. Kennedy," *Abilene (TX) Reporter-News*, May 17, 1945, RG 216, Entry 1A, Box 541, NARA; and "Too Much Attention Is Concentrated on Kennedy, Not Enough on Big Shots," *Knoxville Journal*, May 12, 1945, EKP, Box 13, APCA.

52. "Post-Surrender News," *Hartford Courant*, May 12, 1945; "Kennedy Did His Job," *Hillsdale (MI) Daily News*, May 12, 1945; and "That AP Surrender Scoop," *Fort Wayne Journal-Gazette*, May 10, 1945, all EKP, Box 13, APCA.

53. "Too Much Off the Record," *Texarkana Gazette*, and "The Paris Censorship," *Alabama Journal*, May 10, 1945, both EKP, Box 13, APCA.

54. "For a New Yalta," Philadelphia *Evening Bulletin*, 17 May 1945, AHS Papers, Box 274, NYPL.

55. "Dangerous Inroads," *Columbus (OH) Dispatch*, [May 1945], EKP, Box 13, APCA.

56. See Betty Houchin Winfield, *FDR and the News Media* (Urbana: University of Illinois Press, 1990).

57. Tom O'Reilly, "Kennedy Got American Scoop on Brits," *PM*, May 10, 1945; and Charles Van Devander and William O. Player Jr., "Washington Memo: Kennedy May Be in SHAEF Doghouse but He's a Hero to His Colleagues," *New York Post*, May 8, 1945, both EKP, Box 8, Scrapbook 1, APCA.

58. "Surrender Secret," *Kennebec Journal*, May 10, 1945, EKP, Box 13, APCA.

59. "The Brass Hats and Mr. Kennedy's Scoop," *Norfolk Virginian-Pilot*, May 9, 1945, EKP, Box 8, Scrapbook 1, APCA; and Austin V. Wood, "Thinking It Over: Deceiving Americans Should Cease," *Wheeling (WV) News-Register*, May 13, 1945, EKP, Box 13, APCA.

60. "This Right Was Ours!" *Altoona (PA) Tribune*, May 11, 1945; "We Applaud Kennedy's Decision," *Clovis (NM) News Journal*, May 9, 1945; and "Petition of the Fifty-Four," Portland *Oregonian*, May 11, 1945, all EKP, Box 13, APCA.

7. The Aftermath

1. Sophie Smoliar, "Ed Kennedy Back; 'Did My Duty,'" *PM*, June 5, 1945, Philadelphia *Evening Bulletin* Scrapbooks, Box 12, Folder 18, APCA; "Night Lead Kennedy," AP Wire Story, June 4, 1945, EKP, Box 3, APCA; *Ed Kennedy's War*, 175.

2. *Ed Kennedy's War*, 175.

3. Dwight Bentel, "Kennedy Details Incidents Before His Surrender Flash," *Editor & Publisher*, June 9, 1945, 7.

4. Cooper to AP Board of Directors, June 7, 1945, EKP, Box 1, Folder 13, APCA.

5. Cooper to AP Board of Directors, appendix II, June 7, 1945, EKP, Box 1, Folder 13, APCA.

6. Cooper to AP Board of Directors, June 7, 1945, EKP; emphasis added.

7. Noyes to Cooper, June 9, 1945; McLean to Cooper, June 14, 1945; Stuart Perry to Cooper, June 18, 1945; and J.R. Knowland to Cooper, July 9, 1945, all EKP, Box 1, Folder 14, APCA.

8. Paul Bellamy to Cooper, June 11, 1945, EKP, Box 1, Folder 14, APCA.

9. Roberts to Cooper, June 14, 1945, EKP, Box 1 Folder 14, APCA.

10. Harte to Cooper, June 16, 1945, and Booth to Cooper, June 18, 1945, both EKP, Box 1, Folder 134, APCA.

11. Cooper to Roberts, June 26, 1945, EKP, Box 1, Folder 14, APCA.

12. *Ed Kennedy's War*, 179.

13. *Ed Kennedy's War*, 180.

14. Paul Miller to Claude Jagger, May 21, 1945, EKP, Box 1, Folder 10, APCA.

15. *Ed Kennedy's War*, 181.

16. *Ed Kennedy's War*, 182.

17. *Ed Kennedy's War*, 182; Minutes, AP Board of Directors Meeting, October 5, 1945, McLean Papers, Box 2, APCA; and Draft Minutes, Board of Directors Meeting, Board of Directors Files, Box 2, APCA. Cooper's intervention, mentioned in draft minutes, was deleted before the minutes were printed in the AP's annual report.

18. Kent Cooper, Personnel Change Memo, October 19, 1945, EKP, Box 1, Folder 12, APCA; Robert Booth to Kennedy, November 9, 1945, EKP, Box 6, Folder 18, APCA. Kennedy's resignation letter exists in Kennedy's papers, with a note saying it had been handed back to him.

19. Clipping, *Detroit News*, November 5, 1945 and Danton Walker, clipping, *New York Daily News*, [1945], both EKP, Box 8, Scrapbook 1, APCA; "How and Why Ed Kennedy, the Famous A.P. Correspondent, Scooped the World on the War's Greatest Story," *Picture News* (February 1946), 10–14, EKP, Box 7, Folder 65, APCA; and Ruth Ridings, "Gavreau Edits News Book Done In Comic Style," *Editor & Publisher*, January 26, 1946, 32.

20. *Ed Kennedy's War*, 182; Shepherd to Porter, September 24, 1945, Harry Butcher Papers, Box 16, EL.

21. Kennedy to McCrary, January 8, 1946, EKP, Box 6, Folder 58, APCA; Bedell Smith to Lt. Col. Root, March 14, 1946, EKP, Box 6, Folder 60, APCA.

22. New Hampshire Senator Styles Bridges, for one, had offered to raise the issue in the Military Affairs Committee when Kennedy had returned in the summer, but at the time Kennedy demurred.

23. "AP Man Restored as Army Writer," *New York Times*, July 22, 1946.

24. 79 Cong. Rec. S9611-13 (1946) (Statement of Sen. Downey).

25. "The Strange Case of Ed Kennedy," *Newsweek*, August 5, 1946, 64–65; Herb Graffis, "Kennedy's Case," *Chicago Times* [July 1946], AP Subject File, Box 79, APCA.

26. Jack Harris (*Hutchinson News-Herald*) to Cooper, July 23, 1946, and Cooper to Harris, July 26, 1946, both AP Subject Files, Box 79, APCA; Cooper to McLean, July 14, 1947, Robert McLean Papers, Box 22, APCA.

27. Cooper to Storke, September 13, 1946, and Storke to Cooper, September 16, 1946, both EKP Box 2, Folder 15. APCA.

28. "Biographical Note," Lyn Crost Papers, Ms. 2005.46, Brown University Library, Providence, RI, https://www.riamco.org/render?eadid=US-RPB-ms2005.46&view=biography.

29. "Talk by Edward Kennedy to the Texas Press Association" typescript, June 20, 1947, EKP, Box 7, Folder 67, APCA.

30. King to Cooper, June 23, 1947, AP Subject Files, Box 79, Kennedy Folder, APCA.

31. 80 Cong. Rec. S4279 (1948) (Statement of Sen. Capper).

32. Statement of Sen. Capper, 4279.

33. "Capper Resolutions Reopen Kennedy Case," *Editor & Publisher*, April 17, 1948, 25, 137.

34. "Kennedy Asks for Hearing on Medal Bill," *Editor & Publisher*, May 15, 1948, 38.

35. Charles W. Morton, excerpt from "*Atlantic Monthly* Bulletin," July 1948, Thor Smith Papers, Box 7, EL.

36. Kennedy, "I'd Do It Again," 36–41.

37. Smith to Morton, July 2, 1948, Thor Smith Papers, Box 7, EL.

38. Smith to Matthews, and Smith to Pawley, both July 12, 1948, Thor Smith Papers, Box 7, EL.

39. Pawley to Smith, July 5, 1948, Thor Smith Papers, Box 7, EL.

40. Smith, "Surrender Snafu," [July 1948], and Morton to Smith, July 29, 1948, both Thor Smith Papers, Box 7, EL.

41. Frank Starzel (AP General Manager) to McLean, February 7, 1952, EKP, Box 2, Folder 16, APCA.

42. Kent Cooper, *The Right to Know*, 211–36; "Statement from A.P. Correspondent on Censor-Banned Surrender Story," North American Alliance, April 10, 1956, EKP, Box 3, Folder 26, APCA.

43. Kennedy to Cooper, May 11, 1956, EKP, Box 2, Folder 16, APCA.

44. Kennedy, "Truth in News," *Monterey Peninsula Herald*, [May 1959], Thor Smith Papers, Box 7, EL.

45. Smith to Lewis, June 8, 1959, Thor Smith Papers, Box 7, EL.

46. Lewis to Smith, June 10, 1959, Thor Smith Papers, Box 7, EL; Boyd Lewis, "V-E Day: Just the Beginning" and "Sortie to Reims: The Inside Story of a Controversial 'Scoop,'" *Army* (Jun 1975): 28–31, 34–37.

8. Media-Military Relations in the Good War

1. Frank Luther Mott, *American Journalism, A History: 1690–1960*, 3rd ed. (New York: Macmillan, 1962), 757.

2. Julia Kennedy Cochran, "Epilogue," in *Ed Kennedy's War*, 196.

3. Paul Bellamy to Cooper, May 14, 1945, AP 02A.01 U.S. Bureaus, Member Correspondence, Box 63a, APCA.

4. Virgil Pinkley, "Eisenhower on Censorship," *Editor & Publisher*, April 21, 1945, McLean Papers, Box 19, Folder 255, APCA.

5. Kennedy to Cooper, September 22, 1937, and Kennedy to Evans, September 24, 1937, both EKP, Box 1, Folder 2, APCA; *Ed Kennedy's War*, 20–21.

6. Kennedy to Ralph Ingersoll, September 30, 1941, EKP, Box 1, Folder 5, APCA.

7. "Minutes of Meeting . . . to Hear Grievances Against the Censorship," [1941], EKP, Box 6, Folder 59, APCA.

8. Roy Hoopes, *Ralph Ingersoll* (New York: Atheneum, 1985), 251–52.

9. Kennedy to Ingersoll, September 30, 1941, EKP.

10. Surles to AFHQ and Cairo, October 22, 1943, RG 165, Entry 499, Box 16, NARA.

11. Kennedy to Cooper, April 2, 1944, EKP, Box 1, Folder 9, APCA.

12. Phillips to Surles, December 21, 1943, RG 165, Entry 499, Box 35, NARA.

13. Kennedy to Glenn Babb, January 26, 1944, and Paul Miller to Paul Mickelson, January 29, 1944, both AP02A.2 Foreign Bureau Correspondence 1944–46, Box 5, Africa file, APCA.

14. Kennedy to Cooper, May 3, 1944, RG 165, Entry 499, Box 35, NARA; *Ed Kennedy's War*, 117.

15. Cooper to Wilson, May 4, 1944, AP02A.2 Foreign Bureau Correspondence, Box 5, Africa file, APCA; Tupper to Surles, May 4, 1944, RG 165, Entry 499, Box 35, NARA.

16. Surles to Tupper, May 5, 1944, and Surles to Devers, May 12, 1944, both RG 165, Entry 499, Box 35, NARA.

17. Hull to Algiers, May 13, 1944, and AFHQ Caserta to War Department and AFHQ Algiers, May 13, 1944, both RG 165, Entry 499, Box 35, NARA.

18. Scott-Bailey to McChrystal, May 15, 1944, Tupper to Surles, May 21, 1944, and Surles to Tupper, May 31, 1944, all RG 165, Entry 499, Box 35, NARA.

19. McKelway to Cooper, May 22, 1945, EKP, Box 1, APCA.

20. Murphy, *Diplomat among Warriors*, 241.

21. Crosswell, *Beetle*, 916–17.

22. "Code of Ethics," Society of Professional Journalists, https://www.spj.org/ethics code.asp.

23. "WWII Correspondent, Fired for Big Scoop on Surrender, Gets Posthumous Apology from the AP, "*Washington Post*, May 7, 2012.

24. Allen to Surles for Cooper, May 8, 1945, RG331, Entry 56, Box 130, NARA.

25. *Ed Kennedy's War*, 165; Liebling, "The A.P. Surrender," 57; and Maureen McKernan to Cooper, May 14, 1945, U.S. Bureaus/Member Correspondence, Box 63a, New York folder, APCA.

26. Fulton Lewis to Cooper, May 9, 1945, U.S. Bureaus/Member Correspondence, Box 63a, District of Columbia folder, APCA. It would be useful to know just how widespread such combination reporting was and in what circumstances it was used.

27. Andy Rooney, interview with author, September 22, 2008, New York, NY.

28. *Senate Committee on Governmental Affairs, Pentagon Rules on Media Access to the Persian Gulf War,* 102nd Cong., 21 (1991) (statement of Walter Cronkite).

29. Studs Terkel, *The Good War: An Oral History of World War Two* (New York: Pantheon, 1984); Michael Adams, *The Best War Ever: America and World War II* (Baltimore: Johns Hopkins University Press, 1994), xiii; and Kenneth Rose, *Myth and the Greatest Generation: A Social History of Americans in World War II* (New York: Routledge, 2008), 6. Other useful assessments of US cultural memory of the war are John Bodnar, *The "Good War" in*

American Memory (Baltimore: Johns Hopkins University Press, 2010, and most important Paul Fussell, *Wartime: Understanding and Behavior in the Second World War* (New York: Oxford University Press, 1989).

30. Neil Hickey, "Access Denied: Pentagon's War Reporting Rules Are Toughest Ever," *Columbia Journalism Review* 40, no. 5 (January/February 2002): 31; Frank Aukofer and William P. Lawrence, *America's Team: The Odd Couple, A Report on the Relationship between the Media and the Military* (Nashville, TN: Freedom Forum First Amendment Center, 1995), 38, 63; Sweeney, *The Military and the Press,* 6; and Knightley, *The First Casualty*, 344–54.

31. Liebling, "The A.P. Surrender," 60; Sevareid, *Not So Wild a Dream*, 379–80.

32. Oldfield, *Never a Shot*, 40; for one example, see James Quirk to Elizabeth Quirk, November 9, 1944, Quirk Papers, Box 1, TL; and Dupuy, "Overseas with SHAEF," October 16, 1944, January 25, 1945, February 11, 1945, Dupuy Papers, Reel 1, WHS.

33. Thor Smith to Mary Smith, July 23, 1944 and August 28, 1944, both Thor Smith Papers, Box 3, EL.

34. A few other historians have presented a more nuanced narrative of Second World War reporting, most notably Casey in *The War Beat, Europe* and *The War Beat, Pacific*. See also Nicholas Evan Sarantakes, "Warriors of the Word and Sword: The Battle of Okinawa, Media Coverage, and Truman's Reevaluation of Strategy in the Pacific," *Journal of American-East Asian Relations* 23 (2016): 334–67.

35. Siân Nicholas, "*War Report* (BBC 1944–45) and the Birth of the BBC War Correspondent," in *War and the Media: Reportage and Propaganda, 1900–2013*, ed. Marc Connelly and David Welch (New York: I. B. Tauris, 2005), 156.

36. Mathews, *Reporting the Wars*, 176.

37. Allan M Winkler, *The Politics of Propaganda: The Office of War Information, 1942–45* (New Haven: Yale University Press, 1978), 12–13.

38. R. H. Lockhart, *Comes the Reckoning* (New York: Arno Press, 1972); see also Gordon Wright, *The Ordeal of Total War, 1939–1945* (New York: Harper and Row, 1968), 74.

39. Sweeney, *Secrets of Victory*, 31–36.

40. George P. Thomson, *Blue Pencil Admiral: The Inside Story of Press Censorship* (London: Samson Low and Marston, 1947), 6, 33.

41. Thomson, *Blue Pencil Admiral*, 155.

42. Murphy to Combined Chiefs of Staff, January 23, 1943, RG 165, Entry 499, Box 29, NARA.

43. Transcript of Eisenhower Press Conference, May 22, 1944, Thor Smith Papers, Box 6, EL.

44. Moskos and Ricks, *Reporting War When There Is No War*, 8; Porch, "No Bad Stories," 85.

45. Brianna Buljung, "From the Foxhole: American Newsmen and the Reporting of World War II," *International Social Science Review* 86, no. 1&2 (2011): 58.

46. See Daniel Hallin, *The "Uncensored War": The Media and Vietnam* (New York: Oxford University Press, 1986) and Michael Arlen, *Living-Room War* (New York: Viking Press, 1969); Porch, "No Bad Stories," 91, 92.

47. Philip M. Taylor, *War and the Media: Propaganda and Persuasion in the Gulf War* (Manchester, UK: Manchester University Press, 1998), 2–4; Nan Levinson, "Snazzy Visuals, Hard Facts and Obscured Issues," *Index on Censorship* 4&5 (1991): 27; and Porch, "No Bad Stories," 94–95.

48. Jason DeParle, "After the War: Long Series of Military Decisions Led to Gulf War News Censorship," *New York Times*, May 5, 1991. DeParle may not have been aware of the

tour system that the military employed in the First World War let alone the press controls imposed during the Russo-Japanese War earlier in the century.

49. Taylor, *War and the Media*, xviii; DeParle, "After the War"; and Hallin, "Media and War," 214.

50. DeParle, "After the War"; Hallin "Media and War," 215.

51. See Pascale Combelles-Siegel, *The Troubled Path to the Pentagon's Rules on Media Access to the Battlefield: Grenada to Today* (Carlisle Barracks, PA: Strategic Studies Institute, 1995).

52. John Briscoe, "The Kennedy Affair" (master's thesis, University of Missouri, 1949), 4, 124.

53. Julia Kennedy Cochran, "Epilogue," in *Ed Kennedy's War*, 201.

54. *Ed Kennedy's War*, 187.

55. Kennedy to Cooper, August 30, 1944, EKP, Box 1, Folder 9, APCA.

SOURCES

Archives and Collections

Army Heritage and Education Center, Carlisle, PA (AHEC)

Russell L. Maxwell Papers
Robert A. McClure Papers
Richard H. Merrick Papers

Associated Press Corporate Archives, New York, NY (APCA)

AP 02A.3 Associated Press Subject Files
AP 01.01 Board of Directors Files
AP01.4B Robert McLean Papers
AP 02.1 Records of General Manager Kent Cooper
AP 02A.01 U.S. Bureaus, Member Correspondence
AP 02A.02 Foreign Bureau Correspondence, 1944–46
AP 21.39 Edward Kennedy Papers (EKP)
AP 39.7 Philadelphia *Evening Bulletin* Scrapbooks

Cornell University Library, Division of Rare and Manuscript Collections, Ithaca, NY

A. J. Liebling Collection

Dwight D. Eisenhower Presidential Library, Abilene, KS (EL)

Harry C. Butcher Papers
Thomas Jefferson Davis Papers
Dwight David Eisenhower Pre-Presidential Papers
Justus Baldwin (Jock) Lawrence Papers
Thor M. Smith Papers
Walter Bedell Smith Papers

Hoover Institute, Stanford University Palo Alto, CA

Robert Murphy Papers

National Archives and Records Administration College Park, MD (NARA)

Records Groups:
107 Office of the Secretary of War
165 War Department General and Special Staffs
208 Office of War Information (OWI)
216 Office of Censorship
218 U.S. Joint Chiefs of Staff (JCS)
313 Naval Operating Forces
331 Allied Operational and Occupation Headquarters, World War II (SHAEF)
407 Adjutant General's Office, 1917–
497 Africa-Middle East Theater of Operations (WWII Army)
498 Headquarters, European Theater of Operations, United States Army
(World War II)

The National Archives (United Kingdom), Kew, England (TNO)

Records of the Foreign Office (FO)
Records of the Ministry of Information (MOI)
Records of the Prime Minister (PREM)
Records of the War Office (WO)

Manuscripts and Archives Division, New York Public Library, Astor, Lenox, and Tilden Foundation, New York, NY (NYPL)

New Yorker Archive
New York Times Company Records, Arthur Hays Sulzberger Papers (AHS)

Harry S. Truman Presidential Library, Independence, MO (TL)

James T. Quirk Papers
John M. Redding Papers

Wisconsin Historical Society, Madison, WI (WHS)

Homer Bigart Papers
Harold Boyle Papers
Cecil Brown Papers
Charles Collingwood Papers
R. Ernest Dupuy Papers
John MacVane Papers
Merrill Mueller Papers
Byron Price Papers

Books

Adams, Michael C. C. *The Best War Ever: America and World War II*. Baltimore: Johns Hopkins University Press, 1994.

Allan, Stuart, and Barbie Zelizer, eds. *Reporting War: Journalism in Wartime*. New York: Routledge, 2004.

Allen, Craig. *Eisenhower and the Mass Media*. Chapel Hill: University of North Carolina Press, 1993.

Arlen, Michael. *Living-Room War*. New York: Viking Press, 1969.

Atkinson, Rick. *An Army at Dawn: The War in North Africa, 1942–1943*. New York: Henry Holt, 2002.

Aukofer, Frank and William P. Lawrence. *America's Team: The Odd Couple- A Report on the Relationship between the Media and the Military*. Nashville, TN: Freedom Forum First Amendment Center, 1995.

Beard, Patricia. *Newsmaker: Roy W. Howard*. Guilford, CT: Lyons Press, 2016.

Bedell Smith, Walter. *Eisenhower's Six Great Decisions* New York: Longmans, Green, 1956.

Bodnar, John. *The "Good War" in American Memory*. Baltimore: Johns Hopkins University Press, 2010.

Butcher, Harry C. *My Three Years with Eisenhower*. New York: Simon & Schuster, 1946.

Carlson, Elliot. *Stanley Johnston's Blunder: The Reporter Who Spilled the Secret behind the U.S. Navy's Victory at Midway*. Annapolis, MD: Naval Institute Press, 2017.

Casey, Robert J. *This Is Where I Came In*. New York: Bobbs-Merrill, 1945.

Casey, Steven. *The War Beat, Europe: The American Media at War against Nazi Germany*. New York: Oxford University Press, 2017.

——. *The War Beat, Pacific: The American Media at War against Japan*. New York: Oxford University Press, 2021.

Clark, Gerald. *No Mud on the Backseat: Memoirs of a Reporter*. Montreal: Robert Davies Publishing, 1995.

Clark, Mark W. *Calculated Risk*. New York: Harper and Brothers, 1950.

Cloud, Stanley, and Lynne Olson. *The Murrow Boys: Pioneers on the Front Lines of Broadcast Journalism*. Boston: Houghton-Mifflin, 1996.

Collier, Richard. *Fighting Words: The War Correspondents of World War II*. New York: St. Martin's Press, 1989.

Cooke, John Byrne. *Reporting the War: Freedom of the Press from the American Revolution to the War on Terrorism*. New York: Palgrave Macmillan, 2007.

Cooper, Kent. *Kent Cooper and the Associated Press: An Autobiography*. New York: Random House, 1959.

——. *The Right to Know: An Exposition of the Evils of News Suppression and Propaganda*. New York: Farrar, Straus and Cudahy, 1956.

Cowley, Malcolm. *Exile's Return: A Literary Odyssey of the 1920s*. New York: Viking Press, 1951.

Crosswell, D. K. R. *Beetle: The Life of General Walter Bedell Smith*. Lexington: University of Kentucky Press, 2010.

D'Arcy-Dawson, John. *Tunisian Battle*. London: Macdonald & Co., 1943.

Desmond, Robert W. *Tides of War: World News Reporting, 1940–1945*. Iowa City: University of Iowa Press, 1984.

Davis, Kenneth S. *Soldier of Democracy: A Biography of Dwight Eisenhower*. Garden City, NY: Doubleday, Doran, 1945.

D'Este, Carlo. *Patton: A Genius for War*. New York: HarperCollins, 1995.

Edelman, Murray. *Constructing the Political Spectacle*. Chicago: University of Chicago Press, 1988.

Eisenhower, Dwight D. *Crusade in Europe*. New York: Doubleday & Co., 1948.

——. *Papers of Dwight David Eisenhower: Occupation, 1945*, vol 6. Edited by Alfred E. Chandler Jr. and Louis Galambos. Baltimore: Johns Hopkins University Press, 1978.

——. *Papers of Dwight David Eisenhower: The War Years*, 4 vols. Edited by Alfred E. Chandler Jr. Baltimore: Johns Hopkins Press, 1970.

Eisenhower, Milton S. *The President Is Calling*. Garden City, NY: Doubleday, 1974.

Funk, Arthur Layton. *The Politics of TORCH: The Allied Landings and the Algiers Putsch, 1942*. Lawrence: University of Kansas Press, 1974.

Fussell, Paul. *Wartime: Understanding and Behavior in the Second World War.* New York: Oxford University Press, 1989.

Gibbs, Sir Philip. *Adventures in Journalism.* New York: Harper, 1923.

Hallin, Daniel. *The "Uncensored War": The Media and Vietnam.* New York: Oxford University Press, 1986.

Hamilton, John Maxwell. *Manipulating the Masses: Woodrow Wilson and the Birth of American Propaganda.* Baton Rouge: Louisiana State University Press, 2020.

Hoopes, Roy. *Ralph Ingersoll.* New York: Atheneum, 1985.

Howe, George F. *Northwest Africa: Seizing the Initiative in the West.* Washington, DC: Office of the Chief of Military History, Department of the Army, 1957.

Huebner, Andrew J. *The Warrior Image: Soldiers in American Culture from the Second World War to the Vietnam Era.* Chapel Hill: University of North Carolina Press, 2008.

Hull, Cordell. *Memoirs of Cordell Hull.* 2 vols. New York: Macmillan, 1948.

Ingersoll, Ralph. *Action on All Fronts: A Personal Account of This War.* New York: Harper and Brothers, 1942.

Jones, Michael. *After Hitler.* New York: New American Library, 2015.

Kammerer, Albert. *Du débarquement Africain au meurtre de Darlan* [From the African invasion to the death of Darlan]. Paris: Flammarion, 1949.

Kennedy, Edward. *Ed Kennedy's War: V-E Day, Censorship, & the Associated Press.* Edited by Julia Kennedy Cochran. Baton Rouge: Louisiana State University Press, 2012.

Knightley, Phillip. *The First Casualty.* New York: Harcourt Brace Jovanovich, 1975.

Langer, William L. *Our Vichy Gamble.* 1947. Reprint, Hamden, CT: Archon Books, 1965.

Lewis, Boyd. *Not Always a Spectator: A Newsman's Story.* Vienna, VA: Wolf's Head Press, 1981.

Liebling, A. J. *The Road Back to Paris.* Garden City, NY: Doubleday, Doran, 1944.

Lockhart, R. H. *Comes the Reckoning.* 1947. Reprint, New York: Arno Press, 1972.

McCreedy, Maj. Kenneth C. *Planning the Peace: Operation Eclipse and the Occupation of Germany.* Fort Leavenworth, KS: School of Advanced Military Studies, 1994–95.

MacVane, John. *Journey into War.* New York: Appleton-Century, 1943.

———. *On the Air in World War II.* New York: William Morrow, 1979.

Mander, Mary S. *Pen and Sword: American War Correspondents, 1898–1975.* Urbana: University of Illinois Press, 2010.

Mathews, Joseph T. *Reporting the Wars.* Minneapolis: University of Minnesota Press, 1957.

Middleton, Drew. *Our Share of Night: A Personal Narrative of the War Years.* New York: Viking Press, 1946.

———. *Where Has Last July Gone?: Memoirs.* New York: Quadrangle/New York Times Books, 1973.

Moorehead, Alan. *Eclipse.* 1945. Reprint, New York: Harper and Row, 1968.

———. *End in Africa*. New York: Harper and Brothers, 1943.

Moseley, Ray. *Reporting War: How Foreign Correspondents Risked Capture, Torture and Death to Cover World War II*. New Haven: Yale University Press, 2017.

Moskos, Charles C., and Thomas E. Ricks. *Reporting War When There Is No War: The Media and Military in Peace and Humanitarian Operations*. Chicago: Robert R. McCormick Tribune Foundation, 1996.

Mott, Frank Luther. *American Journalism, A History: 1690–1960*. 3rd ed. New York: Macmillan, 1962.

Murphy, Robert. *Diplomat among Warriors*. Garden City, NY: Doubleday, 1964.

Oestreicher, J. C. *The World Is Their Beat*. New York: Duell, Sloan and Pearce, 1945.

Oldfield, Barney. *Never a Shot in Anger*. New York: Dell, Sloan and Pearce, 1956.

Pendar, Kenneth Whittemore. *Adventure in Diplomacy: Our French Dilemma*. New York: Dodd & Mead, 1945.

Pogue, Forest C. *The Supreme Command*. Washington, DC: Army Center for Military History, 1954.

Press Censorship in the European Theatre of Operations 1942–1945. Paramus, NJ: 201st Field Press Censorship Organization, 1945–49.

Pyle, Ernie. *Ernie's War: The Best of Ernie Pyle's World War II Dispatches*. Edited by David Nichols. New York: Simon & Schuster, 1986.

Rame, David. *Road to Tunis*. New York: Macmillan, 1944.

Romeiser, John B., ed. *Combat Reporter: Don Whitehead's World War II Diary and Memoirs*. New York: Fordham University Press, 2006.

Rooney, Andy. *My War*. New York: Times Books/Random House, 1995.

Rose, Kenneth D. *Myth and the Greatest Generation: A Social History of Americans in World War II*. New York: Routledge, 2008.

Rosewater, Victor. *History of Cooperative Newsgathering in the United States*. Evanston, IL: Northwestern University Press, 1990.

Schwarzlose, Richard A. *The Nation's Newsbrokers*. Vol. 2, *The Rush to Institution, from 1865 to 1920*. Evanston, IL: Northwestern University Press, 1990.

Sevareid, Eric. *Not So Wild a Dream*. 1946. Reprint, New York: Knopf, 1969.

Shepherd, William G. *Confessions of a War Correspondent*. New York: Harper, 1917.

Silberstein-Loeb, Jonathan. *The International Distribution of News: The Associated Press, Press Association, and Reuters, 1848–1947*. New York: Cambridge University Press, 2014.

Smith, Jean Edward. *Eisenhower in War and Peace*. New York, Random House, 2013.

Sorel, Nancy Caldwell. *The Women Who Wrote the War*. New York: Arcade Publishing, 1999.

Sperber, A. M. *Murrow: His Life and Times*. New York: Freundlich Books, 1986.

Steinbeck, John. *Once There Was a War*. 1958. Reprint, New York: Penguin, 1977.

Sulzberger, Cyrus. *A Long Row of Candles: Memoirs and Diaries, 1934–1954*. New York: Macmillan, 1969.

Sweeney, Michael S. *The Military and the Press: An Uneasy Truce*. Evanston, IL: Northwestern University Press, 2006.

———. *Secrets of Victory: The Office of Censorship and the American Press and Radio in World War II*. Chapel Hill: University of North Carolina Press, 2001.

Sweeney, Michael S., and Natasha Loft Roelsgaard. *Journalism and the Russo-Japanese War: The End of the Golden Age of Combat Correspondence*. Lanham, MD: Lexington Books, 2019.

Taylor, Philip M. *War and the Media: Propaganda and Persuasion in the Gulf War*. Manchester, UK: Manchester University Press, 1998.

Terkel, Studs. *The Good War: An Oral History of World War Two*. New York: Pantheon, 1984.

Thomson, George P. *Blue Pencil Admiral: The Inside Story of the Press Censorship*. London: Sampson, Low, Marston & Co., 1947.

Tobin, James. *Ernie Pyle's War: American Eyewitness to World War II*. New York: Free Press, 1997.

Voss, Frederick. *Reporting the War: The Journalistic Coverage of World War II*. Washington, DC: Smithsonian Institution Press, 1994.

Wagner, Lilya. *Women War Correspondents of World War II*. Westport, CT: Greenwood Press, 1989.

Weber, Ronald. *Dateline—Liberated Paris: The Hotel Scribe and the Invasion of the Press*. Lanham, MD: Rowman & Littlefield, 2019.

White, Osmar. *Conquerors' Road*. New York: Cambridge University Press, 2003.

Whitehead, Don. *"Beachhead Don" Reporting the War from the European Theater, 1942–1945*. Edited by John B. Romeiser. New York: Fordham University Press, 2004.

Wiant, Susan E. *Between the Bylines: A Father's Legacy*. New York: Fordham University Press, 2011.

Winfield, Betty Houchin. *FDR and the News Media*. Urbana: University of Illinois Press, 1990.

Winkler, Allan M. *The Politics of Propaganda: The Office of War Information, 1942–1945*. New Haven: Yale University Press, 1978.

Wright, Gordon. *The Ordeal of Total War, 1939–1945*. New York: Harper and Row, 1968.

Young, Peter, and Peter Jesser. *The Media and the Military: From the Crimea to Desert Strike*. New York: St. Martin's Press, 1997.

Articles and Chapters

Bennett, W. Lance. "Toward a Theory of Press-State Relations in the United States." *Journal of Communication* 40, no. 2 (Spring 1990): 103–25.

Buljung, Brianna. "From the Foxhole: American Newsmen and the Reporting of World War II." *International Social Science Review* 86, no. 1 & 2 (2011): 44–64.

Bunnelle, Robert. "The Scoop That Brought Down the House and Closed the War." *Overseas Press Bulletin* 20, no. 18 (May 1, 1965): 3.

Combelles-Siegel, Pascale. "The Troubled Path to the Pentagon's Rules on Media Access to the Battlefield: Grenada to Today." Carlisle Barracks, PA: Strategic Studies Institute, 1995.

Cronkite, Walter. Testimony. Senate Committee on Governmental Affairs, *Pentagon Rules on Media Access to the Persian Gulf War*, 102nd Cong., 1st sess., February 20, 1991, 2.

DeParle, Jason. "After the War: Long Series of Military Decisions Led to Gulf War News Censorship." *New York Times*, May 5, 1991.

Doane, Don. "Don Doane and His Dastardly Act." *Cleartime: THE AP Alumni Newsletter* 94 (June 1980): 4.

Fine, Richard. "The Development of the 'Pyle Style' of War Reporting: French North Africa, 1942–43." *Media History* 23, no. 3–4 (2017): 1–15.

——. "Edward Kennedy's Long Road to Reims: The Media and the Military in World War II." *American Journalism* 33, no. 3 (2016): 317–39.

——. "'Snakes in Our Midst': The Media, the Military and American Policy Toward Vichy North Africa." *Journalism History* 27, no. 4 (2010): 59–82.

Gottschalk, Jack A. "'Consistent with Security': A History of American Military Press Censorship." *Communications and the Law* 35 (Summer 1983): 35–52.

Gould, Alan. "Scoop & Woe." *Cleartime: The AP Alumni Newsletter* 92 (April 1980): 1, 9.

Hallin, Daniel, "Media and War." In *International Media Research: A Critical Survey*, edited by John Corner, Philip Schlesinger, and Roger Silverstone, 206–31. New York: Routledge, 1997.

Hickey, Neil. "Access Denied: Pentagon's War Reporting Rules Are Toughest Ever." *Columbia Journalism Review* 40, no. 5 (January/February 2002): 26–31.

Kaplan, Richard L. "American Journalism Goes to War, 1898–2001: A Manifesto on Media and Empire." *Media History* 9 (2003): 209–19.

Kennedy, Edward. "I'd Do It Again." *Atlantic Monthly* 182, no. 2 (August 1948): 36–41.

Kenney, Anne R. "'She Got to Berlin': Virginia Irwin, *St. Louis Post-Dispatch* War Correspondent." *Missouri Historical Review* 79, no. 4 (July 1985): 456–79.

Levinson, Nan. "Snazzy Visuals, Hard Facts and Obscured Issues." *Index on Censorship* 4 & 5 (1991): 27–29.

Lewis, Boyd. "Sortie to Reims: The Inside Story of the Controversial 'Scoop.'" *Army* (June 1975): 28–31, 34–37.

——. "V-E Day: Just the Beginning." *Overseas Press Bulletin* 20, no. 18 (May 1, 1965): 1, 4.

Liebling, A. J. "The A.P. Surrender." *New Yorker*, May 19, 1945, 57–62.

——. "Letter from Paris." *New Yorker*, September 9, 1944, 44–50.

Mears, Walter R. "A Brief History of AP." In *Breaking News: How the Associated Press Covered War, Peace, and Everything Else*, 403–13. New York: Princeton Architectural Press, 2007.

Nicholas, Siân. "*War Report* (BBC 1944–45) and the Birth of the BBC War Correspondent." In *War and the Media: Reportage and Propaganda, 1900–2013*, ed. Marc Connelly and David Welch, 139–61. New York: I. B. Tauris, 2005.

Porch, Douglas. "'No Bad Stories': The American Media-Military Relationship." *Naval War College Review* 50, no. 1 (Winter 2002): 85–107.

Pratt, Fletcher. "How the Censors Rigged the News." *Harper's* 192 (February 1946): 97–105.

Rid, Thomas. *War and Media Operations the U.S. Military and the Press from Vietnam to Iraq*. New York: Routledge Net Library, 2007.

Sarantakes, Nicholas Evan. "Warriors of the Word and Sword: The Battle of Okinawa, Media Coverage, and Truman's Reevaluation of Strategy in the Pacific." *Journal of American-East Asian Relations* 23 (2016): 334–67.

Wertenbaker, Charles Christian. "Surrender in Reims." *Life* 18, no. 21 (May 21,1945): 27–31.

Magazines and Newspapers

Chicago Tribune
Editor & Publisher
New York Herald Tribune
New York Times
New Yorker
Newsweek
Richmond Times-Dispatch
Time
Washington Post
World's Press News (UK)

Other Sources

AP Clipping File. *Associated Press, Stories and Newsfeatures, 1937–1985*. Provo, UT: Ancestry.Com Operations, 2013. https://www.ancestry.com/collections/50017/.

Briscoe, John. "The Kennedy Affair." Master's thesis, University of Missouri, 1949.

Dupuy, R. Ernest. "Behind the Elephants: SHAEF Public Relation from the Pentagon to Berlin." Unpublished manuscript in R. Ernest Dupuy Papers, Wisconsin Historical Society.

Rooney, Andy. Interview with author. September 28, 2008. New York, NY.

Society of Professional Journalists. "Code of Ethics." www.spj.org/ethicscode.asp.

INDEX

Page numbers in italics refer to figures.